Domnica Radulescu is an American writer of Romanian origin living in the United States, where she arrived in 1983 as a political refugee. She settled in Chicago, where she obtained a Ph.D. in Romance Languages from the University of Chicago.

She is the author of three critically acclaimed novels, *Train to Trieste, Black Sea Twilight,* and *Country of Red Azaleas,* and of award-winning plays. *Train to Trieste* has been published in thirteen languages and is the winner of the 2009 Library of Virginia Best Fiction Award. Radulescu received the 2011 Outstanding Faculty Award from the State Council of Higher Education for Virginia and is twice a Fulbright scholar. She is a distinguished service professor of comparative literature in Virginia.

For Zoila and Mireya Valdivieso, without whom, my dreams might have never made it out of their suitcase.

For Henry, who supports all my dreams.

To the memory of my father, who taught me to pursue all my dreams.

Mottos

"Strangely, or rather quite logically, it is at moments like this when I find myself between two languages, that I believe I can see and feel more intensely than ever." *Andrei Makine*

"Exile is the un-healable rift between a human being and a native place, between the self and its true home. Its essential sadness can never be surmounted." *Edward Said*

Domnica Radulescu

DREAM IN A SUITCASE

The Story of an Immigrant Life

AUSTIN MACAULEY PUBLISHERS™

LONDON * CAMBRIDGE * NEW YORK * SHARJAH

Ordering Information
Quantity sales: Special discounts are available on quantity purchases by corporations, associations, and others. For details, contact the publisher at the address below.

Publisher's Cataloging-in-Publication data
Radulescu, Domnica
Dream in a Suitcase

ISBN 9781649795397 (Paperback)
ISBN 9781649795403 (Hardback)
ISBN 9781649795410 (ePub e-book)

Library of Congress Control Number: 2021947230

www.austinmacauley.com/us

First Published 2022
Austin Macauley Publishers LLC
40 Wall Street, 33rd Floor, Suite 3302
New York, NY 10005
USA

mail-usa@austinmacauley.com
+1 (646) 5125767

Acknowledgments

I wish to thank my parents, Stella and Gheorghe, for the immeasurable love, encouragement, and joy of life they unfalteringly gifted me throughout my life's journey. I want to thank my sons, Alexander and Nicholas, for the beauty, light, and laughter they have brought into my life. I thank Paul Friedrich for his many valuable lessons and insights into life and art and his unshaken belief in my work.

I owe a significant debt of gratitude to Washington and Lee University, for the Lenfest sabbatical leave support and summer grants that have afforded me the time to complete this book.

Profound gratitude is extended to Roxana Cazan, for her impeccable editorial work on my manuscript and her many valuable insights.

I am deeply grateful to my partner, Henry, for always standing by me in happy and difficult times alike and for the laughter and joy he brings every day into my life.

Praise for *Dream in a Suitcase*

"A smart, insightful story of escape, survival, and emotional triumph. From Radulescu's girlhood years during the suffocating oppression of the Ceausescu dictatorship, through her crazy student days in Chicago to her current life in a small, sleepy, and sometime stultifying southern town in the US, Radulescu found ways to maintain her joie de vivre—through whirlwinds of lovers, travel adventures, and especially artistic creation. *Dream in a Suitcase* is sometimes excruciatingly dark, sometimes rollickingly funny, but always entertaining and provocative." Bárbara Mujica, award-winning author of *Frida*, *Sister Teresa*, and *I Am Venus*.

"As in a fairy tale, the dream locked in the small suitcase that the young Romanian woman takes away from a country where she cannot live freely, will take the reader on a zigzag adventure on the roller coaster back and forth between country of birth and country of adoption, in a frenzied odyssey where Ulysses is a woman in search of an Ithaca who regularly offers herself and hides herself. An extraordinary story of our time, surfing the geography of exile to make it the place where one is at home everywhere and told in the feminine, in a language that is translatable in all the others." Michèle Sarde, award winning author of *Colette, Free and Fettered*, *History of Eurydice during the Ascent*, and *Returning from Silence*, finalist for the Goncourt Prize for literature.

Table of Contents

The Escape

Bucharest, the spring of 1983. The lines for food are interminable, the secret police omnipresent, the potholes in the sidewalks as deep as graves. Only the forsythias break the grayness with splashes of dazzling yellows. At street corners, the Gypsies sell posies of *ghiocei*, snowdrops, the first flowers that bloom, creeping out of the snow, white on white, bell-shaped beauties that grow in the wooded regions around the capital city.

During the day, I attend my courses in English Literature at the University of Bucharest. I hop on crowded slow buses that seem to have forgotten their destination, and I move through the tired Bucharest masses of people grinding my teeth and staring at the pavement covered in slush from the recent snow.

At night, I go to the theater: *The Master and Margarita*, *Iphigenia*, *The Tempest*, *Caligula*, or just a good old Romanian comedy of mistaken identities and purloined letters. After the theater, I go to another theater. I go to the theater held in the attic of the Headquarters of the Communist Youth. This theater is called the Attic.

On the first floor of the headquarters, the halls are studded with large portraits of the Communist 'Gods': Marx, Engels, Lenin, and the Romanian Dictator with his touched-up lips that make him look like a dreamy pig. I rush up the stairs all the way to the top of the building and open the door to the Attic. There aren't any portraits of any of the 'Gods' here.

The brooding theater director and my theater comrades are practicing their different parts in the hallway or inside. I realize that once I enter this space, I start breathing at a steady pace. I change into my practice clothes, which are also our costumes for everything.

At first, I did not like the gray and black costumes, the gray canvas stools that serve as a set for every show depending on how we set them up or stack them up or line them up. The modern theory of theater has reached us too despite our ferocious dictatorship. I thought, *Hell, isn't everything gray enough in this stupid country? Aren't our clothes drab enough? Isn't our food lousy enough?*

The director had decreed that we needed to create something out of nothing; that was the great secret of that theater practice. But it was in the acting, in the mind-body wholeness, the breathing, the authentic gesture, the truthful voice that the colors emerged. That made sense to me, particularly since we had plenty of nothing in our country, so we might as well make it into something.

Once during a show inspired by an old Romanian ballad, my arms lifted like wings of their own will, guided from a point in the center of my being, just as he had taught us. The theory worked. I was an eager bird ready for takeoff. That was when the colors emerged too. I was mauve and vermilion, the colors of my favorite candy sold at the corner shop when I was a little girl. I became all candy. I wanted to eat myself. Now I love the gray of our costumes and furniture, because there is gray and there is something worse than gray. The gray in The Attic turns into myriads of colors and makes you fly. The gray of the outside brings you down into a pile of shit.

Some of the women actors and I are working on a surprise show: Samuel Beckett's play, *Happy Days*, about a woman trapped to her waist in a mound of earth from where she is still carrying on her life as if it was no big deal, reciting bits of poetry, recalling broken bits of her past, and even putting on makeup and going on about her daily routines, as much as her precarious position allows.

We understand the feeling of being trapped, imprisoned, unable to do this or that, so we take on the part of the brave woman buried alive with a vengeance. We divide Winnie's monologue into four parts that represent her different sides and voices. We free her from her suffocating mound of earth that traps her to her waist and then to her neck. We take liberties; we can do whatever we want in this gray Attic space.

Here in this theater, we live in a free country. I am the poetic Winnie, the one who burns love letters and fantasizes about going up in flames herself one day in a spontaneous combustion. I mutter my lines all throughout the day: on the crowded smelly trolley buses, in line for our monthly ration of bread, or on my way home as the steps of the secret police agent who has been following me for a few months now clap on the pavement like a bad omen a few feet behind me.

When I get home late after rehearsals, my father is waiting for me in his trench coat smoking one cigarette after another, ready to call the police, thinking I've been kidnapped by the Securitate, secret police, cut to pieces by a serial killer, run over by a car, or taken advantage of by an evil boy. I tell him, "Dad, I've just been at the theater! We are practicing a women's show."

"There must be boys in this play, too," he says.

"No, there aren't any, it's just girls."

After we all calm down, my parents and I plan for my escape to Italy. If and when I can finally receive the passport I had applied for, I must buy my plane ticket right away, "because the bastards might change their mind and take your documents away, and then you'll never leave, and you'll be stuck in this hell hole forever," says my father.

He is the optimist in our family, while my mother, an artist, writes poetry about death and the meaninglessness of life. If and when my passport arrives, I have to get my plane ticket right away, meet with such and such person as soon as I get to Rome, and in case I can't find her, call this other such and such person. Go to such and such organization for political refugees and ask for asylum. I'm not really listening.

Winnie has taken possession of me and is combusting in mauve and vermilion. Why am I planning my escape just now when I got this fabulous role and the show will premiere in a couple of months? The theater director will be blown away by our modernist women's show, and next thing I know, I'll be playing Gertrude in *Hamlet*. Maybe things will get better in our country by the time I'll play in *Hamlet*, and a brave person will also poison the dictator, having learned something useful from the evil Claudius.

We work on the show of *Happy Days* through the beginning of summer when Bucharest is flooded with the heavy dizzying fragrance of the lindens in bloom. It's not like any other fragrance, but it seeps into your psyche like a drug and makes you feel better about everything, as if the vicious shortages, the secret police, the demagoguery of the news, the shameless claims of the Party that we live in a socialist paradise, were only a temporary fluke and everything will get better tomorrow.

Even the secret police guy in his suit and tie following me from morning until night seems almost benevolent, almost like a mistake that awaits to be corrected. I become emboldened by my Winnie persona and the linden fragrance euphoria and I turn around and smile at him a few times, then start running and get on a random bus, which he misses, and I have a good laugh when I see his frustrated face as he remains on the sidewalk.

It's not even clear why he has been following me all this time, other than the fact that I applied for the passport and visa to Italy and that I take part in the non-communist activities of the theater in the attic housed in the Communist Youth Headquarters. The secret police agents are getting bored, I think. They have nothing better to do with their time but to follow me around as I walk from my classes home, from home to the theater, from the theater back home again.

It's not just for being involved in anti-communist activities that people are being followed these days, but simply for the obstinacy of not displaying communist attitudes and enthusiasm. I might as well do something delinquent, start a secret organization, or write anti-communist manifestos the way some university students had done a few years before until they were caught, beaten up, and placed on the blacklist of the Securitate. Some of those students ran away, crawling across the border into Yugoslavia, and nobody ever heard of them again.

Miracle of all miracles, my passport arrives in mid-August, when the linden flowers and their perfume are all gone. A torrid dusty heat settles over Bucharest, and the most persistent smell is that of melting tar. We make more plans late at night with the curtains drawn, whispering to each other in case the Securitate has tapped our apartment. I get the passport. I pack my suitcase. I go to rehearsals.

Winnie is all over the city uttering her happy sad vermilion lines, opening her umbrella on a sunny day, putting on makeup before going to sleep, forcing her breath into regular rhythms. And sometimes, she sings just for the sheer joy of singing.

I don't tell any of my theater friends that I plan on leaving the country. If I tell, I'd never know what could happen to me. One of them might turn me in, and then I'll never leave. The opening night comes and goes, and two more performances also pass, and I am ready to leave. Forever.

The performances gather a full house. I'm burning the stage with Winnie's burning lines and am floating above the ground like a mythological bird. Now I understand the Phoenix; that's what I want to be, a bird that puts herself on fire and molds herself back to life out of her goddamn ashes. I know I want to do this for the rest of my life.

The suitcase chosen for my big escape is waiting to be packed. My mother and I pack at night, with the curtains drawn, "because you never know whether or not they might be watching us." We live in the "you never know" universe.

I choose a few clothes for all kinds of weather, the volume of short stories I wrote, a volume of Romanian poetry, two black and white pictures from the opening night of *Happy Days*, a handful of family pictures, my grandmother's silk kimono with the multicolored peacock on the back that was my Winnie costume, and a pretty paisley dress in case I go to the theater, out there, in the unknown where I'm about to plunge.

"Yes, Mama, I'm sure there will be a Shakespeare play in the refugee camp in Rome."

"You never know," my mother says as she nods, carefully folding the dress. "And hopefully, you won't have to stay in the camp but with my friend."

The awaited day arrives. I suddenly don't want to leave any more. It's too hard, too scary, too permanent. My mother won't hear of it, as she says, "You must go, it's your chance to leave now or never!"

How about never, I think. I am terrified and say, "It's not so bad here after all, Mama!"

As she laughs and cries at the same time, my mother reminds me that it is just that bad in this country, that here I cannot even use my university degree. "Nothing will become of you here. Your dreams of being a writer will go nowhere in this country," she says.

"The secret police will eat us all," my father agrees, "goddamn the secret police, and may they all turn to dust one day and get what they deserve."

"I'll be an actress," I say. "I'll teach English in high school."

"If you're lucky," my mother says, "you'll teach the alphabet to some country kids in the boonies."

"And swim through the mud to class every day," adds my father.

"What actress can you be in this country?" my mother asks mockingly. "You'll have to recite poetry for the Party and prostitute yourself for some no-good part in a second-rate show by a second-rate playwright."

"If we're lucky, we'll obtain our passports too, and we'll all meet," my father says, but I see his eyes welling up. He is "the patriot" in the family who still loves this "poor miserable country", as he calls it, "because it's ours and not theirs."

19

I'm something of a patriot myself because I'm holding on to the "poor miserable country" for dear life now that I have to leave it and stare into the abyss of an endless unknown somewhere among strangers. Suddenly, Rome with its majestic art and history doesn't interest me anymore. Suddenly, Chicago in America, where I'm supposed to eventually arrive if it all goes according to plan, looms scary and unwelcoming.

"You've made your decision, now stick to it," yells my mother as I'm wiping my tears and washing my face, cupping my palms under the anemic trickle of water from the faucet. Then my father recounts again the story of the famine he suffered during the war, my mother recounts the terror of the Stalinist years, my father picks it up with the list of family and friends who had served heavy years in high security political prisons where they were thrown by the bloody communists and their Securitate.

If not for myself alone, I owe it to an entire family line and some family friends on top of that. I must go through with my defection plan and rip my heart right out of my chest forever so that they can all be vindicated by my glorious escape and the glorious career I'm supposed to achieve once "over there".

I gather the last typed pages of my short story collection and put them in my suitcase, folded between summer and winter clothes, even though I know it's dangerous to take manuscripts across the border. We take a taxi to the airport and crowd in the backseat, pretending we are all happy and excited about my impending trip.

I have a tourist visa, and plan to stay beyond its limits. Taxi drivers too can be informers, as can priests, teachers, sales assistants, doctors, cobblers, pharmacists, theater staff, and every single member of our society, tempted by the promise of a few extra kilos of meat or coffee added to their monthly ratios, or out of fear, or simply because it's easier to obey those in power than to defy them.

No, Mr. Secret Police Officer, I won't tell on my work colleague, on my neighbor, on my best friend, or on my own mother and father. You can keep your meat and coffee and stick them up your ass. I had told my special Securitate follower something similar to this when he asked me to help with a bit of telling here, a bit of telling there, "then we'll arrange a nice job for you after you get your degree."

I said, "No, no, leave me alone please, I don't want a nice job," and ran away without stopping for ten blocks. But still, this hazy sunny late summer day in Bucharest, as it all speeds by me from the backseat of the taxi car, has its charm and beauty and carries in it all my life up to this moment. When you leave like that, you never come back. I know it because we never got to hear about acquaintances who managed to escape, as if they had perished. They had defected, 'good for them', and were gone as if they had never existed, 'betrayers' to the "evil West," the unfathomable, blissful West.

Bucharest blooms into a magnificent city as we pass through it on the way to the airport; the elegant Atheneum where I had attended so many classical concerts, the chestnut studded boulevards, the old Cismigiu park with the hundred-year-old trees, its rare flowers and its pond with swans. My father had taken me many times to visit Cismigiu park on late summer days like this one.

We pass my old school building with its nineteenth century style architecture and inner courtyard where Queen Maria used to take her walks when she was a student there before the Great War, before the communists, before Romanians were running out of their country in every direction, every way they could. And we pass the Headquarters of the Communist Party with the Attic theater hidden under its roof where they are playing *Happy Days* tonight, in a few hours, and from where I will be absent.

All these beloved places swish by me as the taxi driver rushes us to the airport. I am praying for an accident, a delay, a speeding ticket, anything so that I miss my plane. My mother holds my hand tightly, as if afraid I'll spring out of the car at the traffic lights. I know she fears this might be the last time we get to hold hands, and maybe we never will again.

I can't understand what "forever" means at this moment in time although it already seems encrusted in my heart and flesh. "Forever", "never", "ever"— all useless yet heavy words. All I know is that what I'm about to do today will never be undone.

At the airport, I speed through all the check points, except when the border policewoman interviews me, and that seems to take forever. She checks my luggage and asks questions about each single item in the carefully packed suitcase, "What are you doing with a winter coat in the summer?"

"I'm going on a trip in the Alps." In my mind, I'm yelling at my mother who minutes before us leaving the apartment insisted that I take the winter coat. I said it was a bad idea since I was supposed to be traveling for two weeks in torrid heat and the coat might raise suspicions. She won that fight at home, and now I might lose this one.

"What are these typed pages doing here?"

"They are schoolwork for when I come back."

"Where are you going to stay while abroad?"

"At youth hostels."

"Are you carrying any foreign currency?"

"Only the allowed sum of 50 dollars." I have planned it all and anticipated all the questions. This is my hardest exam ever. Only I have not anticipated the knot of fear in my chest and my mind racing, *What if she stops me, what if she just stops me, and I'll never leave again?*

Then I think to myself, *So what if she stops me, what the fuck, I'll just go back to the theater. They'll be happy to see me back.* The knot of grief in my chest is choking me as I see my mother and father wait behind the line that separates them from the ticketed travelers. My mind is racing, *For the last time, for the last time, for the last time.*

The Customs officer searches through all my belongings, clothes for summer, clothes for winter, the volume of poetry. While she does so, she scoffs and turns everything on all sides. As I watch her smug face and her blunt fingers rummaging shamelessly through my suitcase, I remember again why I am doing this. I know it's a matter of life and death that I pass this obscene inspection and get on that plane to Italy and then somehow to Chicago in America, far away from the likes of this woman and her colleague and the millions like them who inspect, inform, denounce, following prescribed orders from a psychopathic dictator.

And just now when I want to leave more than ever, it seems I might be stopped on a technicality, a sweater, a winter coat, a short story I wrote on a sleepless night. If I'm stopped, I'll never be able to leave again. I'll rot in this country of informers and drown in the muds in the boonies teaching the alphabet to six-year-olds with a useless diploma in English literature, just like my mother predicted. I'll be followed by three, not one, secret police agents and die of an illegal abortion if God forbid, I might get an unplanned pregnancy, as I would probably be married to a blasé teacher or country doctor in the same village in the boonies of the most rural of rural Romania.

Images of communist doom and of a future in black erupt in my conscience at a nauseating speed as I am standing in front of the Customs officers with my suitcase wide open like an obscene show of violated privacy. The Customs woman looks at me, talks to the other Customs officers, looks at me again and says, "Go!"

I stand and stare at her. My mother hears her from behind the line where she stands to see me off. With oceans of tears in her eyes, she says, "Go!" But I just stand there. I gather all my energy to start moving and once I move, I feel free. I walk towards the plane at a steady pace without looking back at my suitcase or at my parents, not knowing if my luggage will even make it on board the plane. I don't care about the suitcase. I am my one and only suitcase.

Beginnings

I wanted to fly like the boy with the red balloon. That's why I almost fell out the window and died. Huge white and pink roses looked at me from the garden of the little church across the street. A cat meowed loudly, and a big communist parade crossed our street all at the same time. I live in a tiny apartment in the city of Bucharest with my parents.

"It's a matchbox apartment", that's what my mother always says when she complains about how small and suffocating our living quarters are. She likes the location near the city center and thinks we are lucky to own our apartment with its private bathroom and minuscule kitchen. It's 23 August 1968, two days after the Russians invaded Czechoslovakia, a neighboring communist country but not as bad as ours.

I turned seven in June. I was born a month after my grandmother died of a stroke in the middle of the street. My parents were so poor that they lived in one rented room and shared the bathroom with several other families so that sometimes my mother had to pee in the flowerpots she kept on the small balcony of the rented room. My father struggled for years to obtain the right to rent an apartment. He had to bribe many communist housing directors to obtain this 'matchbox' apartment. "At least it's private, and we don't have to share any part of it," he always says.

Today is the official Romanian national holiday, when we are supposed to celebrate the "liberation" of 1944, the year when the Soviets reclaimed Romania from the fascist occupation. My father refers to it as the "so-called" liberation and says it was the "most calamitous event in Romanian history since the invasion of the Ottoman Empire".

When my father uses the word "calamitous", it's like thunder, like the Russian tanks are rolling down our street. "The Turks just wanted our land, but the Russians wanted to possess our minds and souls," he says. This is also the summer when the young daughter of my parents' friends who are both actors fell out of their apartment's balcony to her death. Her body was crushed on the asphalt, and she died on the spot. Her mother lost her mind. And a neighbor's child down the street died locked inside his family's refrigerator. He wanted to play a trick on his parents and hid inside the refrigerator, but he got stuck inside, and when they opened the door to the fridge to look for something to eat, they found him frozen like a block of ice.

Many children died the same way. I keep wondering why his parents didn't open the refrigerator earlier, why they didn't worry about him being quiet for so long in their equally small matchbox apartment. My father always says that when a child is too quiet for too long, it means that some mischief is going on. A lot of bad things happen in silence, like people disappearing. We live with bad things we can't talk about.

The summer I turn seven years old is a bad summer because children die everywhere in stupid accidents. Because my mother is nervous all the time, and she picked up smoking cigarettes like my father. My parents and all their friends talk in whispers about the invasion of Czechoslovakia and say that Russian tanks will drive into Bucharest any minute now just like they did into Prague.

They also say that even though he is an illiterate idiot and an imbecile, our president was brave to stand up to Russia and speak in a public address held in the Palace Square about how terrible the Russians were. I don't care about his speeches. I care about the tanks and the children who fall out of balconies or freeze to death in their refrigerators.

I sit for hours at the window. I am bored and wish I had a sister or a brother to play with. My mother doesn't want another child because we can't live four people in our matchbox apartment. Everything is lonely this afternoon and it smells like petunia flowers and garbage from the outside. The parade in celebration of the national holiday is going to pass on the main boulevard near our building any moment, and I am ready to watch it. Right now, everything is so quiet that you could clearly hear the cuckoo bird, and the calls of a Gypsy woman asking for empty bottles that she could collect and then resell. Some cats in the back yard meowed so loudly under our windows that I had to look out and see what was happening.

Curiosity pushes me to bend so much out the window that half of my body is now outside the window and I am losing my balance. I take a hold of the window frame. The communist parade finally arrives with trumpets blaring

25

and people chanting slogans that praise our president and his wife. I feel that everything is turning upside down, as if I am going to fly. I will fly like the boy with the red balloon.

Perhaps I let out a scream, I don't know, because the next second my father grabs me and pulls me back inside the house and spanks me for the first time in my life. For a while, I think that maybe I already fell out the window and that was why I am being spanked. But it is so that I never ever do that again. I don't cry at all at the spanking.

My parents keep saying, "You almost died; you almost fell out the window." And I don't get it why they must repeat that instead of being happy that I *didn't* fall out the window. I feel brave, as if I had an adventure and I risked my life. I think if the Russians come with their tanks into our city, maybe people should fly out the windows of their homes.

My father talks about the invasion again. This is all he talks about. My mother doesn't care so much about it and yells at my father, "Stop talking politics for a while, can you? This girl almost fell out the window and you go on and on with the damn invasion. It's not going to happen here, I'm telling you."

That's all I needed to hear, that "it's not going to happen here". My mother is always right. When she said that my father was going to lose his job because he taught some books he wasn't supposed to in his classes, he lost his job. He smoked so much until he couldn't breathe, and we had to call the doctor who didn't want to consult him when he saw my father smoking.

The doctor said, "Stop smoking, then you'll breathe again." When she said he was going to find another job at the other university, he did. And he'd better not teach those books again, or he'll lose this job too and then "how are we going to live on my salary alone? We'll have to move in with Mimi again."

Mimi is my aunt, my father's sister, and she works where they make animation films like the ones I see on TV. She is very funny with all the faces she makes. It would be nice to move in with her. She doesn't live in a 'matchbox' apartment, but she shares the bathroom and kitchen with other people in their building, which my mother hates. My mother says, "Better live privately in a box than live in a big room and share a bathroom with a whole bunch of uneducated neighbors." I don't know why all of Aunt Mimi's neighbors are uneducated.

23 August 1968 is a messy scary day I hope never happens again. It's the day when I could have almost fallen out of the window, the day I could have died. But I didn't, so, in the end, it's a good day because my father saved my life and my mother thinks the Russians won't invade Romania with their tanks. It's a good day because my mother is going to read to me from the book with the boy flying above the city of Paris hanging on to a red balloon. Or maybe this is another day in the same summer with the frozen child in the refrigerator and the occupation of Prague. I can't keep track of the days in this summer after my almost falling out the window of my 'matchbox' apartment.

On another day, my mother makes me take swimming lessons in the lake next to the park with the Ferris wheel, with a whole bunch of other children and a teacher who yells at us and throws us into the water. I practice the "pluta" or floating on my back like a wooden plank with my teacher many times. Eventually, he lets go of me, and I see that the water is holding me on top of it.

I am floating on the water without a tube to help me float and then I learn the swimming moves in no time. The teacher says I have a talent for swimming, but then I swim too far. I lose my breath and almost drown. I imagine that drowning isn't as bad as scraping my knee on the pavement, but then I swallow a lot of water and I start frantically flailing my arms and legs as I try to keep my head out of the water.

I manage to grab the rope separating our swimming area from the rest of the lake just in time not to drown. I am shaking with fear and the cold water. I almost die twice this summer. I don't tell anyone about the second time.

The same day when I almost drown, my mother brings the news that her uncle who was in prison for many years because of the communists, is so sick that he is almost dying. "For sure being in prison for seven years gave him the cancer," my father says.

Our family from Brasov comes to stay with us because they want to visit with the dying uncle and our apartment is ready to explode with so many people. We borrow a folding bed from my mother's friend, turn the sofa into another bed and our whole apartment becomes one big bedroom, and we can barely breathe from the heat and my father's smoking. The boy in the red balloon is flying above the city of Paris.

The morning star turned prince in the famous Romanian poem with 99 stanzas that my father knows by heart is also flying in the sky, stopping only to visit a beautiful girl at night. Another boy in a French book my mother reads to me befriends the deer and other kind animals in a magic forest. There are no books about people who live like us in a 'matchbox' apartment and with family members who went to prison and are dying of pancreas cancer, who all crowd in one big bed and lose their jobs and smoke all the time.

When I grow up, I will write a book about our family and I will give it a happy ending, like the story about the poor girl who saved the fish dying in the sand by throwing it back into the water. The fish was a fairy, and to thank the girl, she made her and her parents rich forever and gave them a beautiful castle in the mountains. In my book, the kitten I saved from the street and brought inside our building turns into a fairy who gives us a palace at the seaside and kills all the bad communists who take away my father's job and put our family in prison where they die of cancer.

My mother's uncle dies, and everybody goes to the funeral. My parents leave me with friends of my father who live in an apartment that is bigger than ours, with a dark hallway. They also share a bathroom and a kitchen with other uneducated neighbors. The man who is my father's friend also was in prison before because he recited a poem he wasn't supposed to at a party. A poem about God, and we are not supposed to talk about God.

The wife's name is Lutza, which sounds funny, and she cooks all day in the shared kitchen. They have more food than we do, and many jars of cherry and rose petal preserves. I eat the preserves until I get sick. I want to know what the husband ate in prison, but I'm too shy to ask, and he has a very sad look; maybe it's from the prison days; maybe he'll die of cancer too.

This is the worst summer of my life with so many people dying and my parents leaving me with their friends all the time and the terrible heat. Then when everybody leaves our apartment, my parents decide we are going on a vacation to the seaside because my mother is tired of everything and my father made enough money this summer from his tutoring students in preparation for the university exam, that we can afford it.

The students are so desperate to pass the exam that their parents do anything for them. They bring us whole fish from the Danube river and whole hens and pheasants from their country homes because my father will make them all go to the university. And my father curses the communists because of how hard it is to go to the university with their "evil system". Everything in our lives is bad because of the communists.

The sea is my favorite place; it smells salty, and there are many kinds of blue everywhere in the water and the sky. There is violet, red, and blue when the sun sets and yellow blue and purple blue when the sun rises. Sometimes my mother takes me to the beach very early in the morning. She wraps me up in a big white sheet on the beach and we watch the colors appear in the sky and on the sea like the watercolors in art class.

My father comes with us to protect us, and he walks up and down the boardwalk smoking. The food has many colors too, the Turkish candy, the sesame honey candy, the peach nectar, the corn on the cob that only the Gypsy girl in the corner sells and all the colors of the cotton candy. Since there is more food here than in Bucharest, I don't get it why we don't live here. We would be so much healthier.

When the seagulls fly to the sea at sunset to get their dinner fish, my mother lets me run on the beach, touch the water one more time before bed, and say goodnight to it and to the waves and the fish. Then when the moon comes up, my mother shows me the golden bridge that the moonlight makes on the sea from our hotel window and tells me how she swam on that bridge of the moon when she was young. My father says she is still young and kisses her on the mouth.

My parents even let me go on the carousel with the happy music in the city center, the wooden horses going up and down. I get dizzy and see colored moons flying everywhere. The moon makes a huge bridge over everything like a golden dust. The salty air makes me dizzy and hungry both. I eat the funnel cake and corn on the cob. I wonder why the communists don't take away all the food at the seaside, the way they do in Bucharest. It would be so much better to live here close to the sea, but my father says, "Wait till winter comes and tourist season is over, and the beach is all deserted and the locals are starving."

Bucharest is still better because it's the same all year round with little food but not completely starving.

More people in our family die this year and next year. My grandmother who survived famine and the war, when the Russians came in with their huge tanks, had a heart attack. My grandfather who walked six kilometers through the forest to go to work every day during the war when the Americans were bombing everything, died of a paralysis disease. My parents cry so much. They take turns crying. One cries Monday, the other Wednesday and still they must go to work even when their parents die.

"Goddam the communists and their rotten party and the secret police"—everybody curses the communists for everything. Maybe in the country of the boy with the red balloon, people don't die so much because they don't have the communists. The fear and nerves during the war and after the war, also killed my other grandmother who died of a stroke in the street a month before I was born.

Again, my parents leave me with friends but this time in the same building where Aunt Mimi lives, and they are more fun than the friends in the big dark apartment because they are artist painters. They make huge paintings of abstract drawings with circles and splashes of oil paints that look like the mistakes I make in art class when the water drips everywhere and the colors bleed.

The communists allow them to exhibit their abstract paintings in the art gallery in the city center. It is easier if you are an artist of abstract paintings because the communists are stupid and don't understand it. You can hide things you hate about the communists inside the abstract paintings, and the police can't catch you because they can't find the bad thing anywhere in the painting. This is how dumb they are.

This year with all the dying people is also my first school year. I don't like any of my classes, except for the drawing one. The reading and the calligraphy classes are stupid because I already learned how to read and write in the French classes that my mother took me to on Mondays before I started school. My French teacher was a white-haired lady I loved. I called her 'Madame'.

The music class is awful because I don't have a good voice and can't keep a tune, and the math class is just so and so. I only like the multiplication problems because they are all about animals in the State cooperatives. Now that I'm in school, we must go to the parades in the street to greet the stupid president when he passes through the city center. I can only say he's stupid at home; otherwise, my parents will go to prison.

An important thing happens when I'm in second grade. My mother's best friend disappears because she ran away to another country with no communists. I think she ran away to France where the boy with the red balloon lives. My father says, "Good for her, good for her! I wish I could do that."

My mother is sad because she'll never see her friend again. She was my mother's most beautiful friend, with green eyes and long black hair that my father said made men go crazy about her. She brought me chewy colored candy like I never saw before and had the best laugh in the world. In this country, if someone escapes to another country with no communists they can never come back again.

"Smart woman, how did she do it?" my parents' friends ask. "She had courage. Kudos to her."

When my father goes on a bus trip to Istanbul with other people in a group, I'm terrified he will never come back just like my mother's friend. I will die if that happens. My mother and I see my father to the bus near the Palace Square where the president made the speech about Russia invading Czechoslovakia. My father picks me up in his arms as he always does when he goes somewhere, kisses me, and tells me he will bring me special shoes, nice smelling erasers, and a Turkish toy.

I don't care about any of that. I tell him please don't stay in Istanbul and not come back like Mama's best friend. My parents look at each other with a grin and tell me I am talking stupidly; of course, he's not going to stay and he'll come back to me.

"Turkey is not that far," he says. "Before you know it, I'll be back." He waves at me from the bus. I want to cry for a long time. I have no idea why my father has to go to Turkey, which was once the Ottoman Empire. My mother pulls me from the bus station, and we walk home in the late summer's heat.

Some trees have already begun to shed their leaves and I know it's not too long before I am to return to school. Maybe second grade will be better than first grade. I miss my father already and I hope he comes back from Turkey with special Turkish shoes and a lot of Turkish candy.

The Arrival of Zoila Valdivieso

There are no clear paths that I can follow backwards through my childhood and teenage years trying to make sense of them. Between eight and fourteen, in the minuscule apartment where I lived with my parents in Bucharest, a shroud of sleepy indolence, boredom, and anxiety seems to have spread over that span. The shroud is peppered with torn holes through which you can grasp blotches of color and movement, intervals of passion, excitement, or catastrophe as if peeping through keyholes. It's as if looking through a keyhole and watching my own life unfolding in fractured episodes on the other side of time and space. On the other side of the world.

More people we knew died of natural or unnatural causes, and nobody we knew had any babies. The school days passed in a drudgery of subjects taught by stern and tired teachers in classrooms with wobbly wooden desks, under the "benevolent" gaze of the leader, the "beloved father of the nation", whose picture hung at the front of the room, larger than life.

Some days were sprinkled with a few joyful moments such as the volleyball matches during recess, or mischievous times of skipping class and crossing the street to the park with swings, wooden benches, and lush chestnut and linden trees. A constant secrecy enveloped everything we did. Everybody seemed to play a part, live beneath a veil of fear, talk in whispers, and always check back over their shoulder to assure themselves they were not followed, spied on.

This paranoia became habit. Because the adults all did it, the children began taking after them. "Don't say that out loud", "be careful what you say", "don't tell the teacher that…", "nobody knows that…", "You can't say that". So much was about speaking, as if saying things was the same as doing things. And because people would lose their jobs or go to prison or simply disappear on account of things they said or didn't say, then indeed saying something was the same as doing something.

So then, we did things we weren't supposed to do in silence, and most of the things we said out loud were vacuous. Only the things we said in whispers were true, heavy, and dangerous. Because of that, the whispers behind closed doors, in a back alley, in an empty park gave us a sense of excitement and heroism.

My father's two-week trip to Istanbul gave us rich subjects of conversation for a full year. The Turkish bazaars became for a while my father's favorite conversation topic: piles and mounds of 24-karat gold jewelry from where apparently his bus travel companions stole with impunity and stuffed their pockets with filigree gold and precious stones, while others had unscrewed the bus ashtrays and hid illegal amounts of dollars they had gotten from foreign students with which they bought Turkish leather jackets and jewelry.

Upon their return to Romania, they sold their spoils on the black market for thousands of *leis*. Some of the people that left with my father never returned. They took advantage of moments of inattention on the part of the secret police assigned to the group and got lost in the crowds of the bazaars, becoming one with the mounds of rubies and 24-karat gold filigree earrings.

At times, my father regretted not having done the same. He would have asked for political asylum, and then brought my mother and me over. I was terrified of hearing such discussions and wondered what we would have done in Turkey, other than wander about the luscious bazaars all day. My mother seemed to echo my thoughts, and she cautioned that it was unlikely she and I would have gotten permission to join him in Turkey, were he to have taken such a step.

Then what? She asked, were we going to spend years and years of our lives applying for the emigration visas and standing in line for days at the police headquarters only to have our requests denied a million times, like such and such friends who hadn't been able to be reunited with the rest of their family in Austria or West Germany or Denmark?

"Is that what you want, for us to spend years separate from one another, waiting for visas we'll never get? Do you want me to lose my job, maybe even lose our apartment? How will I be able to raise our daughter?" Either way you looked at it, calamity lurched at every corner and was ready to pounce on us, to destroy our family with a merciless blow and endless food lines.

My father's Turkish adventure emboldened my parents to undertake more extensive travels abroad, to the countries in Eastern Europe that the Party allowed them to visit. Then followed the years when they started traveling to Western countries where only rarely one could go. They left me behind in the care of my aunt and uncle in Brasov, the mythic city cradled in the lap of indomitable Carpathians and featuring the Black Church built by the Teutonic Knights twelve hundred years ago.

They went by train, because that was the only way they could afford it. First it was Western Germany. The next summer they went to France and Italy, staying with immigrant friends, sleeping in railway stations, or the cheapest motels near the railway stations, carrying canned foods and dry salami for a full month in their suitcases and illegally stuffing hidden compartments of their duffle bags with Romanian *leis* they were going to exchange for francs or liras once they crossed into the free world.

That was how most Romanians traveled, risking being caught at the border and thrown in prison, surviving on canned foods for weeks once they managed to cross the border without incidents. If they returned at all, which my parents always did, having left me as gage in the country, they would pine for the rest of the year for the freedom and the abundance they had seen in the West, regretting their return home.

My parents always booked seats in the train with sleeper cars, the train that left Bucharest for Vienna. The train made a five-minute stop in Brasov. My aunt and uncle took me late at night to the train station so I can wave to my parents for a few minutes as they arrived by train from Bucharest on their way to their great adventure abroad. It always felt heartbreaking to see them leave, a foreboding of many separations to come, of final partings and hopeless longings.

A vague memory of a momentous encounter in that same station a few years earlier always fluttered in my mind in addition to the heavy anxieties I was filled with on account of my parents' leaving the country for a full month, risking the fate of our family. It was the time when my grandfather met his brother who returned from the Soviet Union after having been considered lost and gone since the war and whom he was able to find with the help of the Red Cross.

The whole family went to meet Great Uncle Petea at the station, and a big commotion of tears, embraces, and snippets of wartime stories were exchanged on that same platform where we were now waiting to meet my parents if only for a few minutes on their way to glamorous France. Great Uncle Petea went back to Russia never to be heard of again. *He had become too Russian*, said my grandfather, and then he never mentioned his brother again.

My parents walked onto the steps of their train car, not daring to step all the way onto the platform for fear of being left there as the train stationed only for a moment. My mother wore a worried look as if she regretted her decision to embark on that trip, while my father smiled mischievously, excited about their impending adventure. My uncle lifted me up to them, so my parents could hug and kiss me goodbye, then the train rolled slowly out of the station with my parents still waving goodbye standing on the steps, then climbing in, closing the train door, and settling at a window from where they could still see us.

The sharp whistle of the locomotive sounded like an ominous foreboding of death and catastrophes. Only after the train was almost out of sight wrapped in curls of smoke, did I sob like mad in my uncle's arms, wanting to run after the train, yelling that I was going to eat poisoned leaves from their garden should my parents never come back. Travelers on the platform stared at us suspiciously, disgusted by such a melodramatic tantrum thrown by an unruly child.

In my parents' absence and in the backyards of the neighborhood where my aunt and uncle lived near the train station, I climbed all the trees in sight with my two cousins and the neighborhood children, ate green plums and grapes, picked and ate all the varieties of flowers, leaves, and poisonous berries, until one evening when I almost died from it.

I hollered squeaky renditions of American pop songs I had heard on the radio at the top of my lungs perched on a picnic table, disturbing the neighbors' siestas, and caught dragonflies and beetles for my insect collection. The insects roamed freely inside the apartment to my aunt's horror, until my parents' arrival and my departure back to the capital were anxiously awaited by relatives and neighbors alike.

All the boredom accumulated in our 'matchbox' Bucharest apartment turned into inexhaustible energy and wildness on the chilly mountain summer nights with fireflies and smell of fresh pines under an orange and maniacally full moon. Communism, the Russians, the secret police, and all the terrifying dramas of our Bucharest life dissipated under the magic aura of the forests and peaks of the Carpathians, the strong fresh air, and the provincial summer laziness of the neighborhood.

Then with the summer of 1975, a clarity entered my life as if I had suddenly become aware of where and how we lived. With the clarity came a new kind of pain. It was the summer of my encounter with the American lady from Chicago at the Mangalia beach. We often saw foreigners from France, Italy, or Germany who came to our beaches for the special mud treatments and because the beaches were cheap, endless and in their view, "exotic."

There were special stores where one could shop using foreign currency; they carried all the things we craved for and which ordinary Romanians could only get on the black market for a third of their monthly salaries, like Toblerone chocolate, Rexona soap, deodorant, pantyhose, or jeans.

We watched the foreign tourists both with envy and with the superiority of the oppressed. "Oh, you have communist ideas, don't you? Let's see you live here in our place for a month, standing in lines for food and having the secret police watch your every move, and let's see what you think of communism then!" Because apparently. most westerners who graced our country with their visit and their foreign currencies had socialist or communist ideas, which to us was one and the same thing.

My father said they were sick and tired of the capitalist abundance in their own countries and wanted to experience if only for one summer the miserable poverty of our bloody dictatorship while shopping in the special stores for foreigners. At least that was our idea of their ideas.

However, the American woman we met that summer was different from any of those foreigners, and she changed our lives. My father's friend from the university who worked in the English department had been asked by a Romanian émigré in Chicago to act as tour guide for this single American woman of Cuban origin who had the fancy to spend her summer vacation of 1975 at the Black Sea where we also happened to spend part of our summer vacation.

My father's friend asked us to help him out and spend some time with the American visitor as well, since he also had to spend time with his girlfriend. My parents were ready to oblige, though neither of them knew a word of English, and they were in fact relying on my knowledge of English acquired through private lessons and many hours of school instruction.

We all went to meet this woman at the tiny train station in the resort town of Mangalia on a torrid July afternoon. Her apparition was cinematic. In a second, seeing her on the steps of the shabby train, wearing a pair of white

36

pants, a polka dot navy blue silk blouse, a red scarf tied around her black hair, and a glorious smile lighting her round face gave me a tremor of joy and sadness at the same time. I had a double sense of being out of place yet rooted in the arid ground of that poor country.

A thirst for adventure and an irreparable longing suddenly entered my life at the sight of the Cuban American woman called Zoila Valdivieso, who descended on that July afternoon on the dusty, drab platform in Mangalia's train station, at a time when communist shortages and people's despair peaked.

The woman with a glamorous name dragged after her a multitude of suitcases and duffel bags, which several young men who had apparently travelled with her from Bucharest and befriended her on the way, were more than eager to help carry down the train steps. She exuded joy and something else that we couldn't quite figure out at first. She was adorable beyond anything else we had ever encountered, as she wore her haute couture with such nonchalance.

Every morning at the beach, my parents and I waited for her arrival, as she descended from her fancy hotel reserved only for foreign tourists, curious about what new beach robe or headband she was going to wear; was she going to sport the bright yellow robe with the navy hair band, the bright green shirt with the white loose pants, or was she going to surprise us with a completely new outfit pulled out of one of her bottomless suitcases?

She accompanied us everywhere; she ate lunch and dinner with us at the same bed and breakfast where we stayed summer after summer, causing a sensation among the hosts and patrons every time she showed up. She generously gave away her scarves, blouses, or jewelry to anyone who complemented her on how beautiful such or such an item was. We stopped complimenting her because every time we admired an item, she would gift it to us, and that started to feel embarrassing.

By the end of our stay in Mangalia that summer, not only my family, but also the girlfriend of my father's friend from the English department together with an entire group of Romanian tourists and their bed and breakfast hostesses were clad in glamorous dresses, pants, scarves that we proudly exhibited on our evening promenade on the boardwalk or in the morning on our way to the beach. Hearing our complaints and experiencing the food shortages in Romanian stores made Zoila cry with pity.

On some afternoons while everybody was taking their siesta, she would invite me to her room in the fancy Siemens hotel that closed the line of beach hotels mostly available to party members and secret police 'celebrities', to keep her company. Those were my 'travel abroad' afternoons, as I sat in her room, amidst her multicolored American clothes, cosmetics, books, and mesmerizing fragrance that enveloped her everywhere she went.

She asked me about my life and that of my parents. *It was hard, wasn't it,* did we think of *maybe one day coming to America*? I shushed her and explained through signs that the room was probably tapped, that the secret police were listening to all the foreigners in their rooms, and that I shouldn't have even been there with her in the first place. She laughed copiously at my sign language and whispered commentaries about our lives and her feelings about it.

"I love you and your parents, I understand how hard it is, I left Cuba when Castro came, then I brought my family to America. I want to help you too, now you are also my family." I turned on the TV to cover her declarations and plans for our future, which brought on more giggles and laughter. On TV, Nicolae Ceausescu was visiting a wheel bearing factory in the north of the country while in the Siemens hotel room, Zoila Valdivieso was offering me and my family her unconditional empathy and was welcoming me to her home and life in Chicago.

Zoila complimented my English and urged me to perfect it, and I thought I was in the best and yet unwritten episode of an American soap opera, the one about the American Cuban woman from Chicago who saves the poor Romanian family from communist misery. Better than any of the Dallas episodes about the bored and neurotic Sue Ellen, the devious JR, or the sultry Pamela.

"Your country is very beautiful," she also added and went on to compliment the kindness of the people.

"Some people are not so kind, some are secret police," I whispered, which for some reason brought on more peals of laughter from her as she listened carefully to every accented English word I uttered in heavy whispers.

The last afternoon at the seaside, when I visited her again in the hotel room, she seemed sad and said to me, "If you ever want to come to America when you grow up, I'll help you, all right?" I knew she meant for good and not just for a visit; if I wanted to come to America like my mother's best friend or other friends and acquaintances who were gone forever.

The truth was I did not want to be any of those people. I did not want to leave for good. I loved our vacations at the Black Sea even though the produce was lousy and the best hotels were monopolized by the Party or foreign tourists from Western countries. I loved our vacations in my aunt's house in Brasov with the view of the Carpathians and the fresh and cool summer mornings and evenings, the pine smells, the hikes in the forest, the fun games with my cousins, whom I considered my sisters from another mother.

I looked forward to walking with my father in the Bucharest parks, listening to his tales about the history of the old city. A confusing and heavy kind of longing entered me during those afternoons in Zoila's hotel room, a restlessness about my future. It was the first time I even seriously thought about my future. The communists seemed to rule forever. America was a mirage I only knew from movies occasionally broadcast on national television.

Zoila Valdivieso was a fairy godmother that had miraculously appeared in my life with lots of temptations and unexpected generosity. My country was still the place I knew and loved, and the thought of leaving it forever, hard as things were, produced in me a sharp agony of longing and pain as if I had already left it and was on a plane to America, crying my heart out for everything I had lost. The proverbial 'dor', the untranslatable Romanian word that signifies an inexplicable longing and yearning for everything you lost or might have lost, or might have had but never got, with its haunting echoes and images of melancholy tunes spread over rolling hills with mythic shepherds and their picturesque sheep, gripped my entire being in its hold and tied me to my native land tighter than ever.

dor

I was at the crossroads of opposing desires; to stay and hold on to my sea, my mountains, my childhood, my family for dear life, or to leave, to fly, to see the world, to do and say whatever the hell I wanted without fearing prison, persecution, or untimely death. It would have been better if America came to Romania, just like that good hearted Zoila had come and brought color and excitement to our lives for the summer of 1975. But that had also been touched with danger.

There had been a good chance we might have all been punished by the Securitate for having had such close relations with a foreigner from the ultimate capitalist country, home of drugs, gangsters, and overall depravation as our daily communist propaganda told us. Zoila wasn't taking any drugs though and seemed anything but depraved. And despite her flamboyant clothing, she was more prudish than many Romanian women I knew.

The family and friends that she talked to us about using their first names as if we had all known them for a lifetime, didn't sound like gangsters or depraved people either. Pablo was married to Nancy, and they both worked in a bank; Paco was an accountant; Mireya was an artist; Martha a schoolteacher, as were her friends Mimi, Gladys, and Jack. They all sounded like the characters in one of my English textbooks.

Theirs was a different America than that of the soap opera series and movies we saw on TV, and this America emerged in my life that summer through the encounter with the vivacious and kind-hearted Zoila from Chicago. A smiling and benevolent America, where poor refugees from communist Cuba could become anything they wanted and lived in pretty houses in Florida. And if they felt like it, they could move to Chicago like Zoila had done.

She had offered me delicious glimpses of that America in her hotel room, scattered with piles of bright colors, silks, perfumes, unrestrained giggles, and animated hand gestures. Everything was in movement and color, a kaleidoscope that kept me entranced and breathless.

On the last day of our seaside vacation, my mother had a brilliant idea that was going to seal our relationship with Zoila forever. Not wanting to part with her just yet and filled with gratitude for all her generosity, my mother invited her to accompany us to our next vacation spot in Brasov, where my mother's sister lived, my other summer paradise. She accepted without a moment's hesitation and made plans to join us in a week after she finished her mud treatments at the hotel spa.

She accompanied us to the tiny train station in Mangalia from where we were traveling to the city of Brasov, and this time she lingered on the platform while we waved at her from the train as if she were the local and we were the tourists. She felt like family indeed as if remote roots sprawling under miles and miles of earth and ocean somehow connected us from Cuba to Romania via the formidable United States of America.

The entire family waited for her a week later at the train station in Brasov with flowers and unrestrained excitement. She descended from the train with one less suitcase for, as we learned later, she had left it for the masseuse at the spa with an entire set of outfits which must have thrilled the entire female staff at the Siemens hotel. My aunt and uncle put her up in their best of the two rooms in their small apartment, apologizing for the anemic trickle of water in the shower, the cramped space of their living quarters, the limited food choices, and really in an unspoken manner, for the indignity of living under a communist regime.

Zoila showed no sign of aggravation or surprise as if she had lived in those conditions her entire life. She devoured the food that my uncle managed to obtain with massive efforts from his relatives in the countryside, with unabashed appetite. She sprinkled salt on the watermelon, crossed one of her legs under her when she sat at the table, and laughed wholeheartedly at my uncle's attempts to communicate with her via large gestures and loud Romanian words.

Her entire being and personality were to us a novelty and an additional proof of the freedom of expression she carried in her person from America, as we became more acutely aware of the embarrassing and oppressive misery we lived under and our desperate but useless efforts to hide it. Plus, we knew that the local Securitate must have been in communist heaven to have such rich material to spy on: an American citizen living for a full week with us and most likely corrupting us and the entire neighborhood with oodles of capitalist miasmas and high-quality clothing.

Zoila's departure from Brasov and her return to America a week later were for us as sad as a funeral. Neighbors came out on the staircase teary eyed wearing the gifts she had given away during the week. They all offered her their own gifts: jars of walnut or plum preserves and bottles of sour cherry brandy, which she stuffed in her two remaining suitcases.

My aunt packed a lunch for her train ride and remained behind on the balcony to not be seen crying. My father hugged Zoila warmly and patted her on her head as if she were his own daughter. My uncle kissed her hand innumerable times, while my mother and I held her hands in our hands for long minutes and promised to never forget her.

The train station, the neighborhood, the entire city felt empty and irreparably gray after her departure. The apartment wore the air of a funeral home where we returned with sad faces and started picking up little objects that she had left behind as if they were sacred relics: a golden barrette, a red headband, one of her coral lipsticks. My aunt placed them all in a special drawer with precious objects in the mahogany dresser in the main room, the one Zoila had slept in.

That day, I hung out with the neighborhood children till late in the evening, talked and joked more than usual. I even let neighborhood boys chase me in the fragrant coolness of the mountain air, emboldened by the knowledge I now held a priceless secret: a tiny corner of America.

My America Now

I now live in a house with bay windows, a red front door, green chimneys, and an orchard in the back. I am the first in my family to own a house in America, to dislocate my Romanian family line and thrust it into the red clay earth of a small town in the Shenandoah valley, in a southern state of the old confederacy. Not New York, not Chicago, not Los Angeles, not Cleveland, or Philadelphia where most Romanian Americans, and indeed most immigrants, live.

American small towns are mostly inhabited by American-born people. *It's the urban areas that are famous 'melting pots',* I thought when I was living in Chicago, working on my university degrees one after another, managing several jobs at the same time: from drugstore cashier and media equipment operator to French teacher for kindergarten, from English as a second language instructor to refugees from Cambodia and Laos to French lecturer at the university.

In the end, all those degrees and my collection of jobs earned me a teaching position at a university in a town the size of three Chicago blocks. The French call this kind of town 'l'Amérique profonde', or 'deep America', the kind that no French tourists or any other foreign tourist is interested in visiting, the one where everyone, from the auto mechanic with a deep southern accent to the cashier at the local organic foods store or the colleague in the computer programming department, comment on my accent and ask me about Romania, despite my having lived here a couple of decades too many.

I had never heard of the Shenandoah valley before I moved to the area, but I must have had intimations that such a place existed in America while growing up in the capital city of Bucharest, also called the little Paris of the Balkans. I must have known that beyond enormous ranches portrayed in the *Dallas* soap opera, beyond the gangster-ridden neighborhoods in movies about Chicago, New York, or San Francisco, and beyond the canyons traversed by John Wayne or Clint Eastwood in their famous Westerns, there was also an in between space, mellow and misty, a place that looked more like the valleys and peaks of my native Carpathians.

Otherwise, it wouldn't make sense why I'm still holding on to the house with bay windows, a red door, and green chimneys that had belonged to a famous local sheriff before I bought it. It wouldn't make sense that I didn't run at a hundred miles an hour towards the first large urban area peppered with theaters and art galleries after the first month spent in this "deep America".

I was the eighth owner of the house in one hundred and fifty years and the only woman owner ever, referred to as "femme sole" in the title to the house. Black people were not allowed to buy property on my street until the nineteen thirties. And even today, the real estate agents only show the newcomers to the town the houses in my neighborhood and the adjoining ones, not any of the houses where the small Black communities live, beyond an invisible but a very real dividing line.

The sheriff's son who sold me the house, a large man with a white beard coming down to his chest who hunted deer and bear, recounted in great detail the story of the house; how the children used to slide down the banister, how they gathered around one of the eight fireplaces in the winter because the parents could not afford to heat the "whole damn house", how he used to sleep in the tiniest room downstairs although he was six foot four and his head touched one wall while his feet touched the opposite wall.

After the war, they had built a family farm in the enormous back yard. They raised cattle and chickens, and even hosted a carnival and a state fair, complete with a Ferris wheel. One of his sisters died of a mysterious death in one of the upstairs bedrooms, a southern Faulknerian bona fide melodrama. I bought a house with a heavy history, two staircases, and with the memory of a Ferris wheel in its backyard.

For some reason, it felt like the closest thing to the house my father grew up in before the war at the other end of the world. A house I only knew from his vibrantly colored stories about it.

My father only got to see my house once, six months before he died with a bitter yearning for his native earth and language. Weakened by his heart illness and a twenty-year-old longing for what he had lost, mistaking the little town I was living in with the town of his childhood in northern Moldavia, he told me when he saw the house for the first and last time, "Good for you! I'm proud of you. You vindicated me for losing my parental house with huge orchards to the Russians."

The entire chain of tragic events in his life started with the day Russian soldiers marched into this mythic house in 1944, ravaged it and killed his favorite dog and then moved on to take away everybody's lands and properties. He never stopped longing for that house and its orchards and never tired of cursing the Russians and their killer tanks.

I absorbed his longing for the house with large orchards that I never saw but only imagined. I brought it with me in the Shenandoah valley, thousands of miles away from my father's native Moldavian town, lost amid the blue Appalachian Mountains, always looking for a center and still asking myself whether I really belong here in the space that had once belonged to a southern sheriff.

I still inhabit the house like a visitor expecting to encounter the ghosts of the past at night on the hallway leading from the front staircase to the kitchen. Apparently, the sheriff was famous in the area, as famous as a sheriff played by John Wayne or Clint Eastwood in their Western movies. Only this isn't the Wild West but the sleepy American South, relatively near to Scarlett O'Hara's famous Tara from *Gone with the Wind*, a novel my high school friends and I read feverishly and delinquently, sharing the library's single copy during the obligatory Russian language or Marxist philosophy classes.

"Tomorrow is another day" was often our slogan when we left the classroom guarded by the larger-than-life portrait of Nicolae Ceausescu hung on the wall above the door. We silently hoped that the glorious "tomorrow" might bring about Ceausescu's own death, the collapse of the Communist Party, or the punishment of its evil members. But that was only going to happen six years after my escape.

Welcome to America

My parents and I landed on American soil at JFK airport in New York on a dark December day, dizzy and exhausted from the ten-hour flight filled with turbulences. Our three suitcases were vigorously kicked around by the American airport workers who also graced us with several swear words as we tried picking our luggage up. We were not supposed to pick it up until the porters were going to place all suitcases coming off that plane in one place in the terminal.

Our refugee airplane had special treatment. Despite the rude awakening to American airport procedures, I was glad I could pick up the swear expressions "what the fuck", "get the fuck out of the way", and "motherfucker". The American gangster movies I had seen on our tiny black and white TV had served some good purpose. From the pay phone at the airport, I called Zoila to tell her we had arrived in America, in New York, and we were waiting for our plane to Chicago. She said she was so excited. "I'm going to wait for you at the exit. I can't wait to see you."

I called her "collect" because she had told me to when I called her from Rome, which to me sounded like Colette, the French writer. Despite my years of studying English language and literature, I still stumbled through many colloquialisms, and my knowledge of Shakespeare, Emily Dickinson, Thomas Hardy, or French writers like Colette was either a huge source of confusion or of funny coincidences, like in this case.

Zoila waited for us at O'Hare airport wrapped in a fluffy gray fur coat and screamed with joy when she saw us. Her sister Mirella was with her, and the two of them spoke Spanish to one another, the sound of which made me feel somewhat at home. Any of the Romance languages made me feel more at home than English, which still seemed cold and felt like I was talking out of a textbook.

We descended upon Chicago in the coldest winter of the century, and I had no words to describe that cold. I immediately realized that before I did anything else, I had thought I would do in America, I had to learn how to survive the cold of that historic winter. That was going to be a main job, surviving the cold.

The sheepskin winter coat that my mother insisted I take in my one suitcase and on account of which I was almost stopped at the border by the customs police, proved to be a lifesaver. My mother kept saying "I told you so" while she was herself shivering in her light woolen coat, as she had chosen to take the family jewelry instead of her warmest coat.

My father wore his sheepskin tall hat, which protected his head from the cold, but his trench coat lined with faux fur was a joke in the face of the minus twenty degrees Celsius roaring outside or the minus five degrees on the Fahrenheit scale, which I had no understanding of and which always tricked me in thinking it was warmer than it actually was.

There were also two kinds of temperature measurements, which added confusion to my will to survive the cold; one was the real temperature measured in the Fahrenheit system still foreign to me and the other one was the windchill factor that I understood as the "windshield" factor and imagined it must have been the force by which the wind hit the car windshields.

The linguistic confusions infantilized me and added humiliation to my struggle with the elements. Not even the sheepskin coat fully protected me from the metallic cold of Chicago with its wicked wind from the lake blowing through all my clothing all the way to my soul. Nothing was as I had imagined it.

The fancy suburb where our generous sponsor lived and where she found us a tiny temporary apartment for which she paid the first month's rent was deserted and lifeless. My father kept asking "where are the people?" Which made Zoila squeal with laughter every time we translated his question. The people didn't walk in the streets but drove everywhere.

After years of semi starvation in Romania, I was beside myself with excitement when visiting the supermarkets. Zoila took us grocery shopping the day after our arrival and told us to choose anything we wanted. My father filled the cart with toilet paper and cigarettes, as those were some of the shortages from which he had suffered the most in Romania. She laughed wholeheartedly and said there was still going to be toilet paper in the supermarket the next day.

My mother wanted to buy meat for a steak, and Zoila got her a prepackaged steak called rib eye steak, which I hadn't heard of in any of my English literature readings. As for me, I was so confused and dizzy at the sight of the different types of peppers, apples, hams, cheeses that I decided to pick something I had never seen or eaten before such as sun-dried tomatoes, hearts of palm in a jar, and marshmallows in a huge plastic bag.

When asked about bread, my father said none of it looked good and gave up on choosing any of the breads in plastic wrap. Zoila filled up the cart with cans, jars, items in plastic bags and paid for everything with a card. It all seemed unreal and sad. For an incomprehensible reason, the visit to the supermarket and the empty streets outside the supermarket made me feel more alienated and scared than the unbearable cold outside.

In fact, they made me fiercer in my battle with the Chicago cold, wind, windshield winds, for that felt adventurous and harshly real, while the suburban streets and the supermarkets were artificial and soulless. I knew my father hated everything, from the slowness in his gait that used to always be fast and brisk, to the film of sadness in his eyes. I tried to be cheerful and upbeat. I felt fake like the supermarket shelves with five kinds of giant peppers and ten kinds of tasteless breads in plastic bags.

We couldn't afford to be sad though. We had to put up a happy front for everybody who was helping us to get settled and integrated. Shiny cars, sparkling stores, endless highways with mammoth trucks, the little fragrant soaps and four different sizes of towels in people's bathrooms—all these were large and small signs of abundance and served as a cheerfulness drug, a happiness injection, an anesthetic for the soul.

My father mimicked the cashiers in supermarkets with a sideways movement of his jaws and a sound almost like a roar as they went "aha" in response to every "thank you". He had once been a charismatic university professor who now was reduced to mimicking the few words and an onomatopoeia that he understood in English.

Zoila was preparing feverishly for Christmas and telling every single friend and acquaintance about "the family from Romania, yes they escaped with God's help, I know, I prayed for them all the time and God answered my prayers, isn't it wonderful?" At first all the God talk I heard around me seemed nice, a proof of the famous freedom of speech and religion. But after hearing God invoked for everything, from large things such as our adventurous escape to the most insignificant detail of everyday life such as finding a parking place, I became uncomfortable and scared.

People were inviting us to their churches left and right, and out of politeness, we always said yes. Many of these people were also sending us bags with clothes and shoes and even checks written in our names which we had no idea what to do with, as we had never seen a check in our lives and didn't have a bank account yet. So, going to church with them seemed like the least we could do to show our gratitude. I was excited about the piles of nice American clothes sent our way and said yes to everything.

When we went to church the first time, my father kept asking "where is the church?" And "when does the service start?" He was expecting painted golden icons and frescoes, stained glass windows, incense, cupolas, and chanted prayers, like we had in our 400-year-old Orthodox churches. Instead, at church here, he felt as if we had gone to a meeting in an administrative building.

By our third incursion to one of our benefactors' churches, we started fearing that we were being drawn into a cult and started finding excuses to avoid these unpleasant incursions into suburban Methodist worshiping. I started spending more time with Zoila's sister Mia, the only one who didn't adhere to any of the religious fervor surrounding her, smoked cigarettes, cussed vigorously, and liberally drank vodka directly from the bottle. My kind of girl.

She made us laugh and took us on whirlwind tours along the dazzling Lake Shore Drive. She said she missed Cuba even though she was only three years old when her parents had brought her to Miami to follow the adventurous Zoila.

It turned out that the price of Zoila's American adventure had been her conversion to the religion of her adoptive missionary parents in Louisiana. I had no idea what missionaries were either, but it didn't sound good. Mia swore and gossiped, and I learned new cusses in the English language from her, for which I was infinitely grateful. She said, "America is plastic"; she talked of Cuba as her true home where food had real taste and the beaches were mesmerizing.

She was the only one who kept worrying about my father and stopped in the middle of the street to ask, "He misses his country, doesn't he?" Then she hugged him out of the blue. She won my father's affection instantaneously, and in her presence, he laughed all the time. Mia's wildness, her criticism of her adoptive country, the chaotic tours of the city she took us on, freeing us for a few hours from the stifling sanitized quiet of the north shore suburbs, her unrestrained laugh, smoking, cussing, refusal of her sister's adopted religion, were the first ties I established to America. Despite all her criticism, she loved living in Chicago, in America.

I understood that if you were young and knew the language, you could make your own America. I wasn't sure at all about my parents though. I wanted to live in her America, and I wanted nothing to do with the America of the Methodist suburban churches. Zoila negotiated it all and she navigated through opposing currents with the cheerfulness that had charmed us ten years earlier on the shores of the Black Sea.

On second thought, it was the combination of the two Cuban American sisters, their light arguments half in Spanish, half in English, that brought us solace from the physical and human coldness of that winter.

The Christmas party offered in our honor by Zoila's best college friend, now a millionaire and owner of a huge wax company strangely called Turtle Wax, was also something out of the Dallas soap opera we used to watch in Romania. We hadn't heard of Christmas parties either, as we just celebrated on Christmas Eve with gifts and carols around a fir tree my uncle had cut from one of the thick forests in the nearby mountains.

The enormous table filled with every imaginable kind of meat, cheese, vegetable, fruit, pastry and other edibles we had never seen, held more victuals than our entire family would have consumed in a year. We stared at it and didn't know what to do, what to take, where to start. My father asked Mia to bring him some whiskey, my mother went for the French cheeses, and I attacked the strawberries and chocolate desserts.

My face hurt from all the smiling I had to do. I felt clumsy and dropped everything on the shiny floors. I was trying to eat and satisfy years of pent-up hunger and at the same time tell all the guests so curious about 'the Romanian family', 'our story' and describe our country about which nobody knew anything other than the fact that Nadia Comaneci and Dracula came from there.

Suddenly, as I was talking about my country with my mouth full of chocolate pudding to rich people who didn't seem to give a damn about my or anybody else's country, it all felt unbearably fake and unreal.

I had no idea what America was all about. It seemed like a picture in a travel agency. The general din, the conversations, the Christmas music, the luscious decorations, they all seemed equally unreal, as if on a movie set. I was suspended between two unrealities, ungrounded and irrelevant. Why had I come to America? For chocolate pudding and strawberries?

I followed Mia to the balcony where she had stepped out to smoke a cigarette, followed by my father, carrying his whiskey glass like a precious goblet. The three of us lit up cigarettes and smoked heartily in the frigid night, staring at the starless sky, the sparkling Christmas decorations, and the shadows of the people milling around in the spacious and strongly lit rooms.

My mother was talking to Zoila and she was laughing. She seemed happy. I didn't know what happy meant any more. I didn't care about happy at that point. I wanted real. The cruel wind blowing from the lake was the only thing that felt painfully real. I swallowed it greedily.

My 'Roma Cita Eterna'

My life story moves in zigzags and disheveled circles, and is sliced in half by the day I left Bucharest for my great American adventure, just like my father's life story was divided into two separate parts by the day of the Russian occupation following Romania's coup of 1944: the before and the after. And then it was divided a last time when he packed up his suitcase, leaving all his life's acquisitions and personal histories behind, and got on a train to Vienna to follow me on my grand adventure.

By the time of his and my mother's departure to Vienna, I had already left the country on my lucky visa to Italy, one golden September day in 1983. Once in Rome, I asked for political asylum and submitted my request to immigrate to the United States. I stayed in a suburb of Rome in a one-room apartment with a former friend of my mother who had escaped a decade earlier, her seven-year-old daughter, and her mother.

Apparently, good affordable housing was hard to get in Rome, and she complained all day about the difficulties of life there, the expensive food, and bad schools for her daughter, although she was driving a nice Fiat to work and had an entire closet only for shoes. I was fascinated with her apartment and collection of shoes of all colors and for all occasions.

Even though the apartment had only one room, it seemed spacious and elegant, with its shiny tile floors and a balcony that was as big as the room itself and that overlooked the blue hills surrounding Rome as well as a whole bunch of flower-filled back yards of fancy brick houses. I would have stayed there forever listening to the melodious Italian conversations of the neighbors or passersby, gliding on the shiny rosy tiles, and staring at the hills of Rome in the distance.

The first month in Rome was a period of existential levitation, a dizzying balloon ride before hitting the hard and freezing earth of Chicago at the very end of that year. I was still on a tourist visa, so I acted and felt like a tourist numbed to the bone by the shock of leaving country and family forever. It was unreal and exhilarating.

Being poor and free in Rome as the summer glided into the golden days of fall was cinematic. I rambled on my own on the magnificent boulevards, between Piazza di Spagna and Fontana da Trevi, the Campidoglio and Via Veneto with only enough liras in my bulky Romanian purse to get me back to the one room apartment in the suburb. I was in the limbo of my life and it felt delicious. The memory of my life before I got on the plane from Bucharest to Rome was suspended in a watery abyss and didn't seem to matter anymore.

The future on another continent where I was supposed to start a new life, seemed like someone else's story. Not my own. I was removed from my own feelings, and it seemed entirely normal to stroll aimlessly down the rich and crowded streets of Rome. I had crossed over, and my reality was anything I wanted it to be.

For instance, my reality could be drinking an espresso in an adorable little café on a side street off the Via Veneto whenever I had a few extra liras. Going on an aimless stroll on a famous Roman Avenue window shopping as smiling vendors tried to lure me into their designer stores as if they couldn't tell I pretended to be rich and Italian in my clunky Romanian shoes.

A lot was about pretense, but really a pretense that was more about survival than about anything else. I was turning myself into my own fairy-tale protagonist, window shopping in Rome.

My hostess would sometimes pay me for babysitting her daughter while she went out with a boyfriend on a weeknight, wearing a beautiful pair of pink shoes she saved for going on dates only. The patent beige or red ones were for going out during the weekend. Her daughter Francesca would sometimes put on her mother's shoes when it was just the two of us and imitated her mother's walk, swaying her hips and pretending to smoke at the same time.

I rolled on the luxurious balcony laughing at Francesca's impersonations, until her grandmother, a bitter old woman who cooked most of the day, would yell at both of us to get back inside and not make fools of ourselves in everybody's view on the balcony. She also scolded me every time I took a shower and 'used up the water'. She must have gotten the habit of saving water from her days in Romania, and nothing could change her mind about it.

I would say to her, "There is hot and cold water here all day long, you know, this is not communist Romania where water is rationed!"

And she would answer back with infallible logic, "That's no reason to waste water with all this washing. Waste is waste." I vowed to myself that there would come one day when I would take a shower as often as I wanted, and my hair was never going to look greasy and unwashed. But in the end, even those little squabbles were part of my big adventure, which so far seemed to unfold smoothly.

My life was at a standstill, a game of playing house and pretending to be a Roman citizen. I quickly learned a variety of Italian mannerisms and gestures, which I used casually, and I picked up Italian quickly by repeating what everybody said to me back to them as a question or a confirmation. I enjoyed my new life until the day my mother called her friend's apartment with news about their passport situation.

We had settled on coded language to discuss their visa issue over the phone. If only one of my parents got the passport and a visa, they would say that they got 'the antibiotics', but if both of them did, the code was to say that they got 'the red shoes'.

Obviously, for my mother, shoes were more important than medicine, since she was the one who had chosen the codes and the red shoes symbolized the ideal situation, the complete flight of our family unit out of communist hell into capitalist paradise. I picked up the phone and listened to my mother's trembling voice as she delivered the message that they got the antibiotics for my father.

She sighed, then she said she was happy, my father had a chance to get over his illness. In code, that meant that only my father got the passport, and that at least he'll be out.

Half of me was happy that I was going to see at least one of my parents, while the other half drooped and withered at the thought of my mother being left all alone. Most likely, she would be fired from her job, would go through innumerable and unspeakable humiliations as 'the enemy of the people', as the Securitate would label someone who submitted an application for legal emigration to reunite with her family of 'traitors' abroad.

The people we knew who had gone through that process, ended up looking like concentration camp survivors from the psychological torture involved in the process, the loss of job and income during the period of their wait for the appropriate emigration papers. My mother's voice tried to be steady and strong on the phone, but instead it sounded shaky and frail. The thought of the possibility I might never see her choked me.

"That's perfect, you were able to get the antibiotics, Dad should feel much better now," I said instead.

Soon after I got the news of my passport that summer, my parents had also applied for a passport and tourist visa for Italy and France, hoping that given how common our last name was, our different files, submitted at different times, might fall in the hands of different clerks and be taken as unrelated. So, it was already something of a miracle since one of them got a passport.

But now, I was faced with the reality of further splitting my family, of seeing one but not the other of my parents and causing the separation between them. I worried for my mother having to endure trials and humiliations because of our escape. It all seemed like a cruel joke.

Francesca was pulling at my dress wanting me to play with her, and the neighbors were talking in loud Italian statements about their day. Families were together and not torn apart like ours was going to be. I said goodbye to my mother and told her to take care of herself. She did the same with another sigh. We hung up. I went back to playing with Francesca though I had no desire to do so.

The life from before my departure rushed at me like an erupting volcano. It was messy and dark, and it was burning and suffocating me. I had left it but was never going to get away from it. Not if my mother was on the other side. Rome seemed to lose its colors; the loud Italian words sounded shrill.

This was the language of people living in freedom and not giving a damn about those who didn't. They bantered about trivial things like the size of the spaghetti they were going to cook that night, the soccer match on TV, the special pencils required for one of the kid's drawing class and their outrageous expenses. I didn't care about any of that.

Suddenly, I was no longer a tourist on a vacation visa. The vacation was over, and I had just entered the refugee phase surrounded by Italian talk heard from a rooftop. The future was a vacuum, the present moving sands. Only the past sat unmoved, but I had lost it, and it didn't matter. I didn't hear anything from my parents for two weeks, time in which I moved through Rome like a somnambulist. Everything had changed from the first month of levity and joyful aimless rambling in the *cita eterna*. All the beautiful stylish Italians in the street were suddenly strangers and didn't speak my language.

Two weeks later, the phone rang at six in the morning, and I jumped instantaneously out of bed to answer as if I knew it was for me. I was having a dream about a train when the phone burst its shrill ring into the one room apartment. In my dream, I was seven or eight, and I had gone to the train station with my aunt and uncle to wave goodbye to my parents boarded on the train on their way to Vienna and then to France. The train was entering the station at high speed enveloped in thick curls of smoke and passed by without stopping as expected.

For a dizzying second, I caught a glimpse of my parents at a window waving and calling my name before they disappeared in the cool summer night. I was never going to see them again because this time they were going to stay for good, not just for a month on a tourist visa and come back with gifts for me that they had gotten at flea markets at the outskirts of French cities from the few dollars they had been able to smuggle out of the country. I stood on the platform screaming at the top of my lungs, holding my aunt and uncle's hands, heartbroken.

Francesca also woke up instantaneously at the sound of the phone ringing. I had a feeling something was changed forever in my life, that I was never going to be the same. I picked up the phone after stumbling over a chair and a pair of pink shoes. It was my mother who let me know that both she and my father had gotten to Vienna, and that they needed me to send them one hundred dollars at the Western Union in the station so they can get to Rome. She was laughing and said I wouldn't believe what had happened. I was speechless, happy, and curious.

Both my parents arrived at the Termini station in Rome the following evening with two suitcases that contained all their belongings, the most important and necessary items they could take with them from everything they had amassed in their lifetimes. It was November of 1983, and Western Europe was closing its doors to the floods of refugees coming from the communist countries of Eastern Europe, though they were still pouring in at an alarming pace.

African refugees from Algeria, Ethiopia, and Eritrea were now starting to arrive in Italy. We were part of all those waves and happy to find ourselves on the same side of a Western European border in the Termini train station amid the hundreds of passengers, travelers, or other confused refugees like us. It seemed unreal that both of my parents had been able to leave when only two weeks earlier, my father was the only one who had obtained the passport and visa to Italy.

It turns out that a small miracle had happened due to a mistake in the system of surveillance. The day my father went to the police authorities to pick up his passport, my mother accompanied him. The clerk called my father's name, and when he went to the booth to pick up his documents, my father was handed not one but two passports, one for him and one for his wife.

He called my mother, who rushed to meet him there, and they left the office in a hurry, not believing their eyes that what seemed like a colossal mistake had worked out in their favor. So anxious were they that it might have been a trap set by the secret police, that they managed to get two train tickets to Vienna within two days, which for everybody familiar with the bureaucracies of traveling abroad under communist rule at that time, would have seemed a real miracle.

Since they didn't have enough money to buy two train tickets to Rome, they got tickets to the first train station past the communist frontiers, which happened to be in Vienna. "And that's how we got here," concluded my father.

My parents were telling the story laughing as we walked through the station towards the exit. It was obvious they were riding the wave of their adventure, thrilled at the miraculous mistake made by the Romanian police. "We did it, didn't we?" said my father stopping to light a cigarette. "No turning back now!" he added with a smile that for a second made him look said. He looked as if he was trying to brace himself for the formidable road ahead.

They were happy they could smuggle out of the country my grandmother's precious jewelry, the diamond and ruby bracelets, the diamond broach, and a couple of other diamond studded items. My mother wore part of the jewelry herself, and she carried the remaining items nonchalantly in her purse.

On the train to Vienna, she had placed the purse on the table in front of her. "I told her to put what was most precious in the most obvious place, almost in full view, and it worked." My father couldn't get enough of the satisfaction of having fooled the customs officers notorious for rummaging every bit of luggage mercilessly.

My mother's eyes sparkled with a new light when we came out into the evening humid air of Rome. She was still bedecked in rubies, sapphires and star diamonds that her mother-in-law had left her while they didn't have enough money to buy themselves a sandwich in the Vienna station.

"Tomorrow we go to the organization that helps out political refugees from Eastern Europe and you submit your requests." I said all knowingly as I had already done that on my first full day in Rome.

"Oh, that soon?" said my father. "I guess we have to, don't we?" That no longer sounded like a man on a tourist visa, but one who had just realized the full enormity of what he had just done. "No going back now!" Indeed, there was no going back except for in memory and dreams and the road forward was an immense leap into nowhere.

Many Romanians we knew had fled the country to Western Europe. America however was a place depicted only in the movies, a fascinating and scary fantasy. And that was the place we were headed to, after the immigration papers for all three of us would be processed and our political refugee status established by the refugee organization.

On my first day in Rome, I knocked on the door of that organization, drunk with the excitement of my adventure and ready to take on the world as a penniless freshly escaped Romanian. I was reassured when I found out the name of the organization was no other than the Tolstoy Foundation, which I thought was the most extraordinary omen for my future.

The organization that was going to process my political refugee status carried the name of a famous Russian writer and a great literary favorite of mine. Not Soviet, but Russian before the Bolshevik Revolution. I liked interpreting symbols as if they were omens. I filled out a long application in English, proud of the ease with which I understood everything on it and thanking my Romanian teachers who had taught me such good reading comprehension skills.

I testified in a spacious office overlooking the piazza Navona about the persecutions and miseries I had experienced in my country, the secret police that followed me on a daily basis during my last year in the country; party officials at the university harassing me and pressuring me to become a party member; the doubling up of the secret police following me once I refused the offer to inform on my colleagues; the editor of the student journal where I had submitted a short story asking me to change the story to fit the 'inspiring' journal whose title was *Communist Convictions* and how he sexually harassed me during a meeting in his office, which he claimed was needed in order to work together on editing my story.

And then there was the whole 'freedom of speech' bit, the 'freedom to express myself' line. It suddenly seemed fake, a cliché language like any other. All of that said, there was nothing of the insidious fear, the grayness, and the lack of air I experienced going to my classes in Bucharest, taking the crowded buses, the black hole I saw in front of me when I thought of my future in my country of birth.

As I was speaking my newly acquired political refugee language, I realized the finality of what I was about to do and was hit by a brutal sense of longing. I was on the way of no return and instead of all the bad things I said I was running away from, everything that tied me to that miserable country at the crossroads of the Balkans bloomed in my mind in a chaotic kaleidoscope of images: the Black Sea at sunset, a Gypsy girl selling violets in the spring, a Bach concert in the majestic Athenium, the view of the highest peak of the Carpathians from the train on the way between Bucharest and Brasov, a dance under the full moon with the man I had loved. Too late.

At the end of the interview, I zipped up that portion of my psyche and promised myself to go back to the state of nonchalance I had felt before going to the Tolstoy Foundation.

After I took my parents to the office of the Tolstoy foundation and they went through the entire process of the political asylum request themselves, we walked slowly, in a daze past the monumental sites of Rome, the gurgling gigantic fountains, the churches, cathedrals, piazzas, pizza stands, and ice cream booths. We craved for everything and could afford nothing.

Nevertheless, my mother bought my father a slice of white pizza and me a cone of peach ice cream using the change she had left after purchasing their train tickets in Vienna. She didn't get herself anything. She seemed exalted. She was wearing her mother-in-law's turquoise broach that she had so skillfully sneaked past the draconian Romanian customs in her purse that sat on the table in front of her in the train compartment throughout the crossing of the border ordeal. Just because now she had it and she could wear it.

We sat on a bench at the foot of Piazza di Spagna. My father ate his pizza in silence, and I ate my ice cream while talking to my mother about the people at the Tolstoy foundation. "They were nice, civilized," my mother concluded.

The next day, I called Zoila Valdivieso. It was five in the morning in Chicago, and she sounded sleepy. Her voice was sweet just as I always remembered. I told her, "Zoila, we are all in Rome, we did it, we escaped. Can you help us? Can you be our sponsor? We need a sponsor to guarantee for us in order to be able to immigrate to America." I spoke in long and convoluted English sentences as if taking an exam.

Immediately, her voice became vibrantly awake and joyous. "Oh, how wonderful, of course I will, tell me what I have to do, and I'll do it. I'm so proud of you." Up to that moment, I had never thought that I had done anything to be proud of and the idea amused me.

In the state of confusion and emotional roller coaster I had been in, jumping from fierce excitement to desperation, to overwhelming melancholy and back to excitement, it felt more like I had done something out of whack and out of line. Something dangerous and sneaky. "You were so courageous, you and your parents, everything will be all right," she said, and I wondered how the weather was in Chicago that morning, where we would live. I hadn't thought of courage either.

The morning of my departure to Rome, when I was vomiting in our newly tiled bathroom in Bucharest and thinking why the hell had my parents bothered to have the bathroom tiled the year I was planning my escape, when I was regretting my decision, clinging to my past, shedding ridiculous amounts of tears, the idea that I might have been performing a courageous act would have made me laugh. It felt more like a profound betrayal, a terrifying mistake, a heartbreaking move. At the airport when the customs officers were suspiciously rummaging through every item inside my suitcase, all I felt was fear and a desire for revenge against those kinds of people: secret and non-secret police working in the service of the regime.

At the end of my conversation with our American Cuban cheerful benefactor, the thought did occur to me that maybe the decision to leave everything and everybody and the persistence to follow through with it despite the unbearable pain and existential mess associated with it, that maybe that act was the most courageous act I was ever going to undertake in my life and the gesture that would define me forever.

The gesture of a young woman, holding in oceans of tears, afraid and angry, walking towards her plane without looking back, not even caring about her suitcase, saying goodbye, getting on the plane, holding her breath until the takeoff, breathing once she saw for one last time the fields and the earth where she had grown up. That gesture would become her signature mark, a mark like no other, that held in it the reality of a kind of death and of a new existence all in one pulsing and unhealable wound.

Our departure to America was scheduled for a cold rainy day in December of that year. At the Fiumicino airport in Rome where I had arrived three months earlier with my forever suitcase, as we were waiting to board our plane to America next to a couple of hundred other refugees, we all cried saying goodbye to Francesca and her mother.

Leaving Rome where I was just starting to feel at home and speak the language was a heartbreak on top of another heartbreak. The refugee life came with an endless package of partings and separations, because once uprooted, you were loosened from your grounding, you became a nomad, an ever-rambling thistle.

The First Summer in Chicago, 1984

The first Chicago summer descended upon us as shockingly hot as the winter had been paralyzingly cold. A different kind of heat, not the dry dusty heat of the long Bucharest summers from which you could find refuge under the shade of chestnut or linden trees, but a gooey clammy heat that crawled into every corner, into all indoor or outdoor spaces whether shaded or not.

By June, we had moved into an apartment outside of Chicago, in one of the larger northern suburbs populated by more diverse groups, not just the Methodist millionaires where Zoila lived. There were new smells in the hallways, pungent, spicy, and Mexican music at all hours of the day and night. There was rapidly spoken Spanish in the street or bursting through the open windows, a colorful, fragrant, and noisy humanity that was comforting and uplifting.

A little farther down the street, there were Polish families that spread *piroshki* and *kielbasa* fragrances and the chunky rich clusters of their Slavic language into the neighborhood. My father cheered up every time he saw the Mexican or Polish families talking on the front steps of our building, having barbecues on the tiny back landings of their apartments, and he often engaged in truncated conversations with them, using bits of every single language he had some knowledge of, except for English. Some French and Italian and even Latin with the Mexicans, Romanian and bits of German with the Polish.

He was making up his own language and miraculously managed to engage in full animated conversations with neighbors and passers-by. I was taking summer courses at one of the big universities by Lake Michigan to finish my degree as fast as I could. All that was being paid by the financial aid I had received based on my refugee status and my nonexistent income.

When the beaches along Lake Michigan opened for the summer, Mia had the delightful idea to spend the first weekend at the beach, slathered in Johnson and Johnson's baby oil to get a bit of a tan. I got a sunstroke that sent me to the emergency room, as I became delirious and was shaking and shivering in the student suite where I was living that summer.

When my Ukrainian suite mate saw my crimson red face and arms, she exclaimed in horror at the sight. When I started running a fever of 102 and talking to imaginary Romanian relatives in my delirium, she took me to the emergency room of the university where the doctor lectured me for fifteen minutes about the noxious effects of the sun, before giving me a strong anti-fever drug and an ointment to cover my atrocious looking blisters.

At the beginning of my biology class the next morning, the professor felt compelled to also give me a lecture on the same subject in front of all my classmates who stared at me now not just because I looked and sounded foreign, but apparently also because I must have appeared like the most moronic person on campus, with my face and body all covered in repugnant looking blisters as if I had passed through a fire.

At least my blushing didn't show on my parched cheeks. I braved it all with impunity, pretending I was feeling great and mocked them as paranoid. By then I had learned idiomatic expressions like 'give me a break' and 'it's no big deal, leave me the hell alone', which everybody found hilarious.

I was something of a novelty among my university classmates, with my flowery gauzy dresses and skirts bought at weekend garage sales in the rich parts of the north shore suburbs, and my loud, accented, and hyper-correct sentences. I understood nothing in the biology class in the aftermath of my third-degree sunburn, a class I had no idea why I was forced to take in the first place, since my specialization was English literature.

I wasn't sure whether my obtuseness to the composition of the ribonucleic acids that formed our genetic structure was due to an irreparable damage of my brain in addition to the one of my skin, or to the never-ending culture shock that extended from the bitter winter into the sweltering summer.

And they were wrong, those who called it 'culture shock'. It was more like an overall physical and mental shock to everything that I experienced: from the tasteless pasty tomatoes, to the American mannerisms of rolling one's eyes and smiling incessantly even when one didn't mean it, to the strength of the sun, the consistency of the air I breathed, to the sound of the voices around me, to the exhaustion my jaws and head felt from speaking only English for hours, for days on end.

I delighted in speaking Romanian with my parents when we gathered in the evening for dinner, throwing myself into conversation the way one throws themselves into a cool spring on a sweltering day. My native tongue felt cozy and refreshing to my soul and in my mouth.

That same first long hot summer in Chicago, I also started dating an American poet in love with Romanian poetry, of all things. We had met at a conference of Romanian studies at Brown University earlier that year where he was the only American because he had translated poems by a contemporary Romanian poet into English.

Romanian intellectuals from diasporas around North America gathered to talk about poets and writers that I had studied and loved during my high school and university years and compared them to writers of English expression. I hadn't thought anybody gave a damn about any of those writers from a remote country only known for its one-star gymnast and a famous vampire.

While I was completing the degree in English literature that I had started in my native Bucharest on a campus overlooking Lake Michigan, Romanian poets and writers were the last thing anybody in that entire school of thousands of cocky American students and erudite American professors would have cared or known about. It took me about a week in America to realize that my little country in the Balkans with its entire horseshoe shaped arc of the Carpathians, the Black Sea shores, the Danube delta, its old cities, its two millennia of history, traditions, and culture was nothing but a tiny insignificant point floating in a nebulous of foreignness for most people walking in the streets of Chicago, taking the graffiti ridden trains or rushing to classes on the campus of my university.

That also happened to be the summer when Nadia Comaneci withdrew from competition, and her absence from the Romanian team that year at the Olympic Games was almost as sensational as her presence had been in years past. Nadia Comaneci took the shape of the entire map of Romania, and the image of her flying on parallel bars in the dark hole of Romanian history emerged in my mind with every new mention of her name that normally would occur during the first three minutes of every first conversation with an American.

So, the conference on Romanian art and literature and its relations to other world literatures at a major university seemed like something of a major cultural miracle for our family of three. My father felt at home for the first time since our arrival during the coldest winter of the century and prepared a glorious talk on his favorite Romanian symbolist poet, the first and last time he ever got to appear and speak in a function that came close to his charismatic lectureship at the university of Bucharest. He had high hopes that his participation in that conference was going to secure him a position at an American university.

Before we even arrived in Rhode Island accompanied by our indefatigable sponsor, Zoila Valdivieso who drove us in her grandiose Oldsmobile, he saw himself lecturing to American students in a university amphitheater about the currents and trends in Romanian and other European literatures.

Just as my fantasy of becoming a journalist for the *New York Times* and an author of best-selling novels within the first two years of my American life, his dream was in the realm of the fantastical. After the conference was over and no such opportunities arose from anywhere and he was back in the sweltering apartment in the larger Chicago area, he collapsed into irremediable depression.

He nodded with tears in his eyes every time Zoila or any of her friends would go on about the American opportunities and how he was going to eventually "do everything he put his mind to, once he learned the language". The falsity of such utopian statements, when translated from English in pretend cheerful tones by my mother or me, sent him even deeper into utter existential disgust.

In the very midst of that same sweltering summer, Aunt Mimi, my father's sister, died of a heart attack, news of which he received from my mother's sister, Aunt Nina. She was found dead after three days, with all her jewelry stolen, the entrance door ajar as if someone had broken into the apartment and ran away in a hurry. My uncle carried her coffin down five flights of stairs on his back, steadying himself by the walls with deep gashes and cracks left from the big earthquake of '77.

She was buried in the family plot that was already housing my grandparents' bones. They had to bury her on top of everybody else in that grave because they didn't have the money to buy another parcel next to the plot. Other than a couple of remote relatives and family friends, the funeral was attended by Gypsies desperate to receive free food given as alms and a Securitate man who followed my aunt and uncle everywhere when they came to Bucharest to take care of the burial, liquidate her apartment, and recover some of the remaining precious objects and books from our own deserted apartment.

America was not working out very well for my father that summer or any of the subsequent summers. The longing for his country tore him apart, the sight of him trapped in a language he didn't understand or want to and the enormity of an alienating land where the heat of the most sweltering summer felt metallic like a burning iron on the skin, made me wonder again and again whether it had all been worth it. Trading my father's life for my future? What future? It wasn't clear. The refugee trap! The American Dream trap! What were we to do now that we had all the freedom of speech in the world? What were we going to talk about?

The frostbites I had gotten during the unearthly cold of the previous winter were tormenting me in the torrid heat with red itchy swollen blotches on my hands and feet. The autumn afternoon I said goodbye forever to my native Bucharest and to the Gypsy girl who sold chrysanthemums in the University square, and to everything else I ever loved and knew, I couldn't imagine that climate, sun, cold air, hot air, humidity, food were all going to prove hostile in America and attack my body with such merciless violence.

I thought it was all going to be psychological and consist of commonly known difficulties: hard work that would prove too hard, financial worries, longing for the mother country. But it was my body that most felt under assault, ravaged by the unbearable heat, the slimy humidity crawling into our apartment, a ravenous itching of the body and soul, a feeling of pent up tears ready to blow up my skull into smithereens.

I moved from voracious hunger to nausea to bloated stomach and swollen limbs. I smoked Merit cigarettes, ate pancakes, steaks, marshmallows, orange cheddar cheese, pineapple, and drank large quantities of orange juice in indiscriminate order trying to satiate a hole that traversed from my psyche to my body and vice versa like a formidable tape worm trying to annihilate me. I was devouring in order not to be devoured. The American experience that summer proved to take place in the gut, a battle of ferocious cravings that happened in the very center of my physical body.

I craved the petunia aromas at the Black Sea, the smell of the espresso coffee from Rome, the taste of the watermelon from Brasov and of the cottage cheese made by shepherds in the faraway corners of the Carpathians, and the joy of having sex with the Romanian man I had loved at seventeen, eighteen, nineteen. Lots of sex with my Romanian boyfriend. And truth be told, as I was painfully aware that my Romanian romance was gone forever, any of the male classmates in my biology or religion summer classes would have been good enough for me that summer.

I stared at them from the corner of my eyes during class, the evolutionary biology theories of Stephen Jay Gould flying by me in incomprehensible jargon as I fantasized about the evolutionary equilibrium I would achieve, were I to hold between my scorched thighs any of those lads sitting with their legs widely spread in work out shorts in the stuffy classroom with a view of the enigmatic Lake Michigan.

That was when the arrival on a visit to Chicago of the poet I had met at the Brown University conference on Romanian studies proved to be a life saver, cooling my burnt bloated itchy self, down to some state of normalcy. He wanted to be romantic and talk about Romanian poetry, but all I wanted was for him to shut up and have sex with me. Maybe that was the ultimate American experience, the pounding, raw, unleashed sex. The American way, or what I thought the American way of sex was.

The American poet, seemed dumbfounded by my voraciousness but went along bemused. "You're one of those Romanian vampire women," he laughed. "Don't get me wrong," he said, "it's fine by me, great actually. Just that American women aren't so direct about sex, you know."

It was my turn for bemusement as I learned that it took a thirty-year-old American man an encounter with a traumatized, frostbitten, sun-burnt east European girl with ten dollars to her name to discover straightforward female desire and sexual needs.

During the time of his visit in my dorm suite, I lived on sex and hardly any food. My body regained some of its lightness and center. When we weren't entangled in sweaty embraces in my squeaky twin bed, we swam in the cold water of Lake Michigan and drank beer at the dive under the Chicago elevated subway at night as we watched the Romanian Gymnastics team without Nadia Comaneci at the summer Olympics in Los Angeles on the bar television.

One of those evenings he said that he had never met anyone like me, that he would marry me if I wanted to. I said, why not, let's! The owners of the Greek dive where we hung out happened to be Romanian Greeks and heard our conversation. "Yes, yes, you marry in Romanian Orthodox Church on

Paulina street. Very nice church, good Romanian priest. He was not Securitate, you know, like other priests in Romania."

Mark was amused by the high standards of integrity of the orthodox priest of the Romanian church on Paulina street and went along with the ad-hoc marriage plans.

It all seemed a hilarious joke, which nevertheless I took seriously, starting to fantasize an adventurous life filled with poetry and smoldering sex next to the American poet who was also a literature professor at a university in Cleveland, Ohio. How many chances were there that I would meet an educated sexy American man who loved and translated Romanian poetry, who had visited my country and loved its culture, who was in awe of my Romanian sexual appetite and my love of English literature? None, for sure.

I worked myself into a frenzy, told my parents that the American poet and I were getting married, and visited the orthodox Romanian priest on Paulina street. I told him about my father's grief at the death of his sister in Romania and asked if he could perform a memorial service for her, and then in the next breath I asked him if he would marry me to my American boyfriend. The priest was originally from Brasov, where my mother's sister lived, the city of my childhood, adolescence, and first love.

It looked like suddenly things were starting to click in the gooey heat of that Chicago summer. Turning on a dime. The life of a refugee! It all hung in the toss of a dime, heads or tails, one minute down to suicide with the homeless and the wretched, the next minute marrying an American poet and discovering the Romanian church with a priest from my hometown who was not a secret police agent. This was frosting on the cake.

I brought the Romanian priest to our apartment, driving him in the boat-sized Oldsmobile that Zoila had eventually given us. My father smiled for the first time in months, his high forehead framed by the wavy white hair relaxed from the deep frowns that had crossed it. On that same visit I broke to my parents the unusual news of my impending the poet marriage to the poet from
    Cleveland.

My mother smiled, the poet in her happy, the mother in her cheerful, the adventurer in her who had done every possible sport in her youth from mountain climbing to fencing was proud of her adventurer daughter. The priest scheduled a memorial service for my aunt Mimi and a month later an orthodox wedding for me and my poetic beau who had saved me from a rapid descent into sex deprivation hell.

The death of a loved one when you can't go back to mourn them, is like a lost-in-action kind of disappearance. It is immaterial and despairing. My father blamed himself and all of us for the cruelty of leaving his sister behind, knowing that she had a serious heart condition. She was all alone, nobody next to her to know what her last hours might have been like.

"She died all alone," he kept repeating, then punched a hole through the wall of our apartment with his fist, cried, cursed, called for God, talked of suicide, and the horrible mistake of having left his country forever. As bad as the communists were, it was better, he said. "I had a university job with a pension, my language, my country, my sister that I could have saved, cursed be Chicago and it's fucking sinister lake."

He hoped that both the communists who had made a mess of his country and the slimy capitalists who prevented him from being a university professor in America drowned in its cold and "filthy" waters.

The Romanian priest brought a modicum of solace to my father's delirium of suffering, longing, and alienation, and the rich orthodox service at the church on Paulina street a sense of relief. The church was a decent imitation of the hundreds of years old Romanian churches, even though the frescoes of saints were a bit too bold, too fresh, too American looking, so that they looked a bit like rock-star saints. But the powerful incense was as transporting as in any real church in my country.

My father cried throughout the service, the chanting about his sister Mimi being in a better place with green pastures and blinding light brought him to sobs and my mother and I to silent tears. Our refugee tears seemed to flow into a void between oceans and continents, useless, superfluous. My mother made the *coliva* food for the dead, a pudding made of cooked barley, powdered sugar, and decorated with chocolate candy in the shape of a cross.

The familiar taste soothed our souls after the service and the red wine we drank in remembrance of the dead gave us the necessary buzz to reconcile our pain with our immigrant confusion about where we were, who we were, and why we were there. The priest poured red wine onto the *coliva* in the shape of a cross, and the memory of a Romanian ceremony at my grandparents' grave in Brasov shivered though me like an electric current.

A cool eerie breeze traversed me, as if the Carpathian Mountains were sending me a message of recollection across the ocean. I felt the coldness of death through the deadly heat and a hot longing for native mountains.

The following day, my parents invited Marc to dinner to celebrate our engagement. My mother cooked all the Romanian foods she hated but knew were a hit for American intellectuals passionate about cultural diversity embodied in ethnic foods: the corn meal polenta with sour cream, the stuffed grape leaves and stuffed bell peppers, and the sweet cheese pie in filo dough.

My father cracked jokes and used the handful of English words he knew to reach out to the American poet of Irish origins. The "bad stupid communists", the value of American and German cars with "Mercedes very good car" as the king of cars, the hot weather, and Romanian poetry were central to the conversation.

In the middle of the lively dinner with my American poet fiancé who was also using his few Romanian words against my father's few English words, we were in for a surprise. My father produced a little black jewelry box out of the pocket of his pants and when he opened it, Marc and I were stunned to see nothing less than two wedding bands.

I remembered the rings as the gifts that my now deceased aunt Mimi had brought me a couple of years earlier from her epic trip to Jerusalem where she had gone mainly to visit the holy sites of Jesus Christ, as she was the one fervently religious member of our family. I was then surprised by the gift, as I had no one standing in line for my hand in marriage, but the bands made of 24-karat yellow and white gold were stunning, the special cut of the gold making the rings shine as if encrusted with diamonds.

I remembered wanting to get married then right away just to be able to wear one of the rings. "This my sister bring…From Jerusalem…For Domnica and you."

My fiancé's mouth remained wide open as bits of polenta and grape leaves were dropping from it. I was red to the roots of my hair and the nape of my neck, and my mother was shaking her head as if stunned all over again by the beauty of the rings.

My fiancé's mouth left him speechless and immobile on his chair. He wiped his sweaty forehead with the back of his hand. What had started as a joke under the rail tracks in the uptown of Chicago in a Greek restaurant owned by a Romanian couple several days earlier, was now an engagement scene with sparkling wedding bands that had traveled all the way from Jerusalem, having been blessed on the tomb of Jesus Christ, went to Romania, and traveled to Chicago in America via Vienna and Rome.

To break the bad spell, the embarrassment, the awe, and the immobility in which we were caught, I snatched the box from my father's hand and took out the rings. I tried them on playfully. Funny thing, they were both the same size and quite loose on my ring finger.

"Oh, look how they sparkle," I said with mild enthusiasm, sliding one of them on my left ring finger. My poet knight in not-so-shining-armor smiled almost with a grimace and looked back into his plate filled to the brim with the polenta, peppers, and stuffed grape leaves. I knew it then by his forced smile that there wasn't going to be any wedding and that the Israeli white gold wedding bands that had touched the tomb of Christ himself were going to go back in the box and back in the drawer of the dresser where my father had placed them, the way one does a priceless treasure.

I saw myself in the full enormity of my ridiculous naïveté and over-the-top behavior, a famished refugee from vampire and gymnast land, who in Marc's eyes must have looked desperate to grab onto an American man: a money grabber, a sex grabber, a manipulator.

My scorched skin was peeling everywhere on my body, leaving white flakes on my chair and the table, as if I were a snake shedding its skin, the new Eve. A heaviness of spirit and body hovered over us. The earth of that Chicago area neighborhood was going to open up and we were going to be swallowed up in its entrails and probably catapulted to the other side of the earth right back to where we came from.

At least the tomatoes in my grim country caught in the throes of dire poverty and dictatorial surveillance tasted better when you could find them, I thought and smiled at my thought. I imagined my mother bejeweled beyond belief in the ancestral jewels she had sneaked out of the country on the train to Vienna, sapphires, rubies, and star diamonds lighting up the sky on our flight back through the clouds that looked like the clouds depicted on the large packages of Downey's toilet paper. This toilet paper was "soft as a cloud" and available in abundance, unlike the scarce brown rough rolls of toilet paper we lined up for at the stores in my motherland.

The food made me queasy, and I wanted my American soon-to-be-ex-fiancé to leave the apartment. Sentimental Mexican music came in through the open windows, and aromas of burritos wafted in and mixed with those of our stuffed grape leaves. What a shocking mess it all was! Why had we come to America, I asked myself for the millionth time that year, knowing that I would have done it again, all over and over again. Come to America, that is.

I knew there was a thread, a life saving device that I needed to grab onto but wasn't yet sure where to find it. But what I knew then with certainty was that it wasn't going to come from the American Irish poet from Cleveland who had translated a volume of contemporary Romanian poetry into English.

My father said Romanian classical poetry was untranslatable, period. As was all the Romanian language, literature, the tragedy of a small nation at the crossroads. He was getting more and more heated up as if lecturing to a grand audience. As untranslatable as was the most important word in all Romanian language, *dor:* the very word for longing, yearning, missing something or someone. Untranslatable.

It wasn't fucking vampires and gymnasts that made any part of Romanian identity. It was the totality of everything contained within the rims of that one syllable word, the landscape, the earth, the language, the soul, the tomatoes, the bread, and the masterpiece poem by the Romantic nineteenth century national poet celebrating the morning star in immortal lines. I was translating his words into English. We were forever going to live a life in translation, cutting off the edges of meaning and nuance, rounding everything up in diluted approximations.

Soon after finishing his piece of the sweet filo dough cheese pie, my now ex-fiancé stood up to leave, and since he was staying in my dorm room by Lake Michigan, I had to leave with him. It felt awkward, like a farce. My parents stood in the doorway as the two of us went down the creaky staircase. They looked sad and exhausted behind their polite smiles.

I thought mine must have been the shortest engagement in the history of engagements, with two Israeli wedding bands that were sitting unused in an empty drawer in my parents' apartment. I was sure the wedding bands themselves felt embarrassed. The Mexican music erupting from neighboring apartments invoked lovers who couldn't live without one another, hearts that belonged to one another for life, *corazon, mi vida, esta noche, te quiero.*

The Spanish words poured into my soul with the full urgency of passionate love, as I understood them all and felt their urgency and their longing. The Romanian *dor* seemed smoothly transplanted into the melodious rhythms. The

72

Mexican neighbors all seemed happy and cheerful. I was leaking into a different language and country, melting into the languid melodies. I wanted to be Mexican; being Romanian in America was too lonely.

Love and Landscape

The man who was my first great love left me on a cold February day in Bucharest because he couldn't stand the big city life and was dying to return to his native town of Brasov in the Carpathians. He couldn't breathe in "the stinking capital", he said, he couldn't see the sky, he couldn't see the stars at night. I was "a monster" to hold on to my university degree and to not want to move with him to his beloved town where we had met and loved each other like the Romanian version of Romeo and Juliet under communist shortages.

It had taken me three years of the most intense studying I was ever going to engage in to prepare for the entrance exam at the University of Bucharest. People threw themselves out of balconies or overdosed on Valium out of despair for having failed the university exams, so fierce was the competition and so important was to hold a university degree in our country as it could offer you a modicum of dignity and leverage in the overall inferno of life in the worst dictatorship of Eastern Europe.

I loved my university courses in English literature and linguistics. But I was also head over heels in love with my mountaineering lover. Standing in the kitchen of our apartment, I held the phone receiver to my ear as if it were glued there. I was staring into the flame of the stove burner that was supposed to spread a flicker of heat in the frigid room.

The Party cut off the heat in apartments across the country to save resources so that they could pay off the national debt, and we lived in our cement bloc apartments like squatters, eating and sleeping in our winter coats. "You are a monster, really, to want to hold on to this stinking city."

"Yes, fine, I'm a monster, so are you to leave me for a bunch of mountains. I don't care, goodbye," I finally said and hung up. I wasn't attached to the "stinking city", but I wouldn't give up my university studies either. I stood and watched the gas flame on the burner until my eyes got bleary and I saw only the red and blue anemic flickering of the fire.

I wrapped myself tightly in my ugly brown winter coat that I was also wearing in the only photograph he and I had ever taken together, which was among the handful of pictures I carried with me in my purse when I left the country a year later. A street photographer had taken the picture one wintry gray afternoon as we were walking aimlessly arm in arm, he after his day of work at the factory of wheel bearings and me after my English Literature classes at the university. I was a frozen figure in a photograph. I melted inside my own photograph, tear-less, with a clenched heart. I felt my heart squirm and fold unto itself like an animal in agony, but I had no tears.

Scenes of the two of us during the three years of what we had thought was the most fiery and unbreakable love affair on earth passed before my eyes like a slide show. The first time we kissed under a shelter in a torrential rain on a one-day trip to a mountain peak near Brasov; the sun came out after the rain and the pink and violet clouds surrounded us above the old church steeples and medieval walls of the city.

A postcard with us as the protagonists: love in the Carpathians, visit Romania! Making love on a bed of leaves and ferns next to the ice-cold sparkling waters of a mountain stream. I remembered the wild berries he fed me and the cold water he brought me to drink in the tin cup he carried in his mountaineering backpack. Another postcard of love in the Carpathians, steaming, burning love to die for; there never has been a love like ours before. Visit the Carpathians. Communism is not that bad if you go to the mountains! Forever and ever, we were going to burn through the gloomy thickness of the stupid dictatorship we lived under and craft our own country. Fuck the communists. Our love was stronger.

The torrential rains we walked in, the fluffy thick snow we tiptoed and made love on, there had been no time of the year, no type of weather we hadn't made love in, fiercely, with no concern for the next hour, drunk on the delicious present. Love was all that mattered.

I now stood empty-handed, empty-hearted, staring out the window at the roofs covered in slushy snow. My mother walked into the kitchen also wrapped in her winter coat and stood next to me looking out the window at the point where I was staring as if interested in what was happening on the roofs. A row of shivering pigeons, a curious cat drinking from the gutter, dried leaves and slush. The roofs were teeming with life.

She knew what had just happened and said nothing. I saw her slouch slightly, suffering for my suffering. Even though I had raised such havoc in our family with my long-distance love, "shaming" them in front of the neighbors whenever I visited him in Brasov, "making a spectacle of myself", my mother still stood by me.

In fact, despite the draconian anti-abortion, anti-contraception laws, she had managed to obtain for me a package of contraceptives several months earlier from a friend of hers who was a doctor. I think she wanted to spare me the danger and humiliation of having to procure illegal abortions, which she herself had had plenty of, until she almost died once from a botched procedure.

There was one thought and one thought alone grilling through my brain, *he left me for a nicer landscape, I let him leave me for my studies. Landscape— studies, landscape—studies, landscape—studies.* Which was more important, who should have given up what for the sake of love? When love was all we had to lift us above the misery of living in a dictatorship with no hot water and no heating in the coldest of winter days, who should have given up what?

The landscapes were beautiful, and education was rigorous. And landscapes translated to space, place, lifestyle. Some version of a lifestyle. Education translated into career, profession, future. Some version of a future. Living where we lived, we couldn't really talk of either lifestyle or a hopeful future. Everybody waited in the same bloody lines for food at the grocery stores, restricted in what they could buy by the same stupid food rations and was being followed around by the same onerous secret police. And everybody had the same vision of a grim future, whether working in a factory or a high school.

More lines for food, more surveillance, more party slogans, diminished food rations, less ability to travel abroad. It was all a wash in the end. Ours was a country of miserable people whispering political jokes to each other to make life more tolerable. Even the secret police agents were miserable, as it appeared clearly from their frowning, angry faces and heavy walk.

It was so cold in the kitchen I thought I was going to die from shivering so hard. My bones and teeth were going to crack from the cold, and I was going to end up a pile of broken bones on the cement floor of our frigid kitchen. My mother lit a couple of candles, as if to warm up the kitchen. That seemed painfully funny. Or maybe she lit the candles to mourn my lost love, which also seemed perversely funny.

I went to bed at eight that evening. We conserved energy by sleeping long hours. Plus, there wasn't much to do anyways. There were hardly any foreign films and programs on TV, but mostly pieces of news and reports about the prowess of the Party, the visits to foreign countries that our leader made in the interest of world peace, the accomplishments of factory workers and cooperatives. You could also watch folkloric programs from the different regions of the country, featuring stars of Romanian traditional singing.

I had black dreams. Not black and white, just expanses of opaque black all around me. I was moving through this ocean of black like a ship through the night, having no idea where I was going. Occasionally the black was broken by a forest of fir trees, dark green against the black. I was being swallowed by the fir tree forests.

Until one night, about thirty nightmares later, when I came out into a clearing. I was a wild forest animal, and I found a magnificent clearing that looked like an image in a French book I had read when I was in second or third grade, called *Patte Bleue, Blue Paw*. The book was about an unusual animal with a blue paw that a kind boy had saved from being hunted down. It must have been a fawn or a fox. It turned out that the blue pawed animal had unusual powers precisely because it was not like the others, and because it was marked.

That morning, I woke up with an uncanny feeling of freedom. I had thrust through my nightmares, come out at the other end of a pretty picture in a childhood book, and survived what I had thought was going to be un-survivable.

Now that my great love ended, I could leave the country. For the first time in months, I thought of our American friend in Chicago, Zoila Valdivieso. I was going to call her and find a way of telling her in code that I wanted to leave the country and come to America. She had once promised me she would help if I ever wanted to go to America. Now I wanted it.

That day of the dream with the clearing and with me being transformed into an unusual animal, I also joined the Attic Theater on the last floor of the Communist Youth building, and I entered its make-believe universe which felt more real than anything else that went on below the theater and in the entire rest of the country.

For the following months, all through the rest of the winter, spring, and summer I acted in all the plays of their repertoire—I was a witch predicting ominous events in a Romanian nineteenth century play and making owl sounds, I had a supporting role as a street woman in a German play, I practiced the role of Gertrude in *Hamlet,* for a forthcoming production of that play, and even played in a Kabuki style play, a Japanese girl in love.

Then I got the part of Winnie in Beckett's *Happy Days*, which carried me to magical clearings and through the grayness of daily life and the numbing sadness of the loss of love until my departure.

Ten years later, I left my great American love, choosing again career over landscape, only in the reverse way to how I had done it on the cold February day in my freezing Bucharest kitchen. This time, I was the one leaving my first American city, Chicago, with its myriads of attractions, throbbing urban life, and my parents, for a university job in a town in Virginia, amid the Appalachian Mountains. Beautiful sunsets, rolling hills, thousands of acres of wooded areas crossed by impatient streams! This was the home of civil war generals. Come visit Virginia!

I was leaving the big city for the mountains, taking the route my Romanian lover had taken when he left me in Bucharest for a life in the Carpathians. Some kind of inverted curse! I was tearing myself away from everybody and everything that I loved to move to a place that seemed to me as foreign as the surface of the moon for all the natural beauty surrounding it. If I were to believe in Romanian superstitions, I would have said I was cursed to fulfill the journey that my first love wanted me to fulfill, namely to live in the country, in the mountains, in a provincial setting, away from urban life. Only this time alone.

I was parting a second, and a third time from my loved ones and from a space I had learned to love as my adoptive city. If I hadn't left Bucharest for love, it was damn sure I was going to leave Chicago for work. And alright, I was not really alone, but with a three-year-old child and an American husband in a crumbling marriage.

From the first and ultimate tragic character in western literature, the notorious Oedipus Rex, I had learned that our lives are guided by a wicked and unexpected destiny which crushes into our personal will and often makes a mockery of our choices. Again, I felt trapped inside a postcard—this time an American postcard: greetings from the Shenandoah valley, the Blue Ridge parkway, colonial houses from the time of Scarlet O'Hara. Smile!

Everybody smiled and was nice in a way that made me nervous, as if I owed everybody something. All the nice people in colonial houses, so welcoming of a new arrival in their pretty town; a new assistant professor, a

Romanian refugee with an accent, a married woman with a dark secret. Smile to cover it up. And smile I did until my jaws were about to fall off and the smile on my face turned into grimace.

I parted with my illicit lover on a sweltering humid summer day, not much different from the one of my broken engagement with the American poet. I had also heard it said, I think from my father, that "character is destiny." That our life's journey is dictated by our destiny which in turn is dictated by the character we are given. So maybe I was given a crooked character and my whole bloody destiny was going to be made of one crooked choice after another.

One thing I knew for sure though was that I hadn't chosen to be born under a communist regime and it wasn't me who had chosen to break up with my Romanian Prince Charming. The choice between love and my studies, which translated into my future, for whatever that was worth, had not been a fair one. Neither of us chose love. He chose landscape, and I chose university studies.

Now in the lush and humid summer of Chicago, which I had gotten to love like a hometown, I was again choosing career over love and over my parents. I was choosing a marriage that I no longer valued and a child I adored over a passionate love that came too late in my life and in his.

Everything had gotten so much more complicated since the breakup of ten years earlier now that my life was woven in an intricate design of relationships and ambitions of success. I was packing and crying with colossal tears, part of me not wanting to go, part of me drawn by the adventure and the attraction of a tenure-track university position I was selected for from among one hundred and fifty candidates.

I never forgot the suitcase I had left with ten years earlier, the sum total of its contents and its meaning to me: summer clothes, a winter coat that almost got me in trouble at the border, and tucked in the middle of a whole bunch of ugly Romanian tees and unfashionable shoes, my first volume of short stories titled *Yes but Life!* for which I had received a national prize.

I had somehow managed to sneak by the censorship in Romania, had my volume read and approved for publication by one of the rare, smart, and courageous editors of that time, a unique chance, and then had left it all. I wanted more: a larger suitcase, a bigger volume, a freer life.

Maybe I had misused my freedom I thought as I was packing and crying in our apartment in Chicago. My son was playing with a puzzle depicting *Snow*

White and the Seven Dwarfs right next to me. I chose the family unit over the passionate love. The domestic life I had loved at first, as if playing house, the husband I had loved at first, and our life filled with the totality of American domestic details that were still a novelty to me, now felt like an unbearable burden.

I had read and analyzed too many novels of tragic adulterous women; I was telling myself. I was even going to teach some of those novels as an assistant professor at the university that had just hired me. But I was only supposed to teach and analyze the literary value of those novels, not actually live them myself. That would have been taking the slogan "teach by example" a bit too far.

My husband had helped me with the job application process, which seemed like a bureaucratic labyrinth. In fact, I had only heard of the university that ended up hiring me when they called me for an interview. It turned out that my husband had seen a job ad that I hadn't, and he added the address to the list where my file was being sent out of his zealousness to help me find a job.

Forget destiny, my life was being made not only of my own, but of other people's choices, random decisions that were going to change the larger trajectory of my journey forever.

I had Chicago in my mind when I left Bucharest with my pathetic stuffed suitcase. Virginia wasn't even a place I had ever thought of settling down in. I didn't even think it was a real place in the world. My paternal grandmother was called Virginia, and I had never made any connection with anything American whenever her name was mentioned.

She was as Romanian as it gets, with the delicious walnut, rose petal and sour cherry preserves she made, the folkloric stories and anecdotes she told me when I was little, the soft accent from northern Moldavia that she spoke with. I had never heard of the Shenandoah Valley, the Blue Ridge parkway, or "the Generals" before I visited the university campus.

It turned out I was as much of an ignoramus about parts of the American geography and history as most Americans I met were about the entire geography, history, and culture of my native country. Tit for tat! I was moving to a different planet.

Those last July days of my life in Chicago I moved through a thick fog of confusion, regrets, and sorrows, aghast at everything I was going through as if it wasn't happening to me. I clang to every Chicago street I knew and loved for dear life. I took my son again and again to the park he had played in for the first three years of his life and where he had taken his first steps.

I cried with sobs of desperation in my lover's arms, then cried again softly in my husband's arms. I packed with my husband but offered locks of my hair as keepsakes to my lover. I had created a formidable mess in which I was wallowing, and which seemed to have a life of its own, to have taken a speed and force that I had not foreseen. It seemed I had sent the ship of my own life on a tumultuous sea and had no more control over it.

Was character destiny? Was destiny always at odds with one's choices? Destiny, character, choices, it was all a fucking mess. I blamed it on the communists. They had fucked up our whole life, and all my miseries had already been decided when I came out of my mother's womb that glorious June day in Bucharest in the era of communist dictators.

In the few moments of lucidity, I experienced at dawn when I was desperately writing the last pages of my dissertation, or during an afternoon moment of respite, I wanted to punish myself, slash irreparable scars on my body. I promised I was going to make everything right for everybody, that I would restore my marriage and my integrity, be happy in Virginia.

Visit my parents often. Be the best mother ever. Translate the short story collection *Yes but Life*! into English. Finally write the novel I had started a hundred times and was never able to go farther than the first two chapters, never farther than the death of the girl in the mountains in the hiking accident. Because my novel was about a love story that starts on a mountain hike in the rain, with a man whose previous girlfriend had died in a mysterious hiking accident. It was about leaving love and family and country in order to escape from a dangerous set up by the secret police.

In Virginia, I was going to have the time, inspiration, and mountainous landscape amid which to write the great American novel and raise my American-born son. Another new beginning, another bleeding heartbreak, another suitcase. On the road again. Bye-bye Chicago and parents, bye-bye little park where my son had played, just like in the famous *Goodnight Moon* book which I had read hundreds of times to my son before bedtime. And bye-bye, secret love.

A full life, somebody might have said. Why had I even come to Chicago in the first place if I was going to leave it? Why had my parents come with me if I was going to leave without them again? The departure with my husband

and son that July morning in the black Mercury Marquis that my parents-in-law had gifted us, saying good bye to my parents, the sight of my mother sobbing after her beloved grandson, all obliquely reminiscent of a September day in Bucharest—it all felt like I had murdered someone.

Another bit of myself maybe, carefully wrapped between clothes for all weather, parts of me bleeding all over my old short story collection written in Romanian, and the first pages of my novel about the girl who loved the man who loved the girl who died on the hiking trip, written in English. My suitcase was getting heavier with each new departure, more pages written, more crimes committed.

Graffiti and Chicago Trains

After the colossal engagement and marriage fiasco with the poet from Cleveland, I refused to date anyone for the rest of my time in college. I didn't understand dating, I had no idea what "to make out" meant, and I was embarrassed to ask as I was suspicious it might have meant to have sex. I refused all invitations to the parties thrown by my classmates. I worked three jobs and took six courses a semester, and when I didn't work or study, I hung out with Mia who was always a roller coaster of laughter.

We had wild little adventures such as the day she let me drive on Lake Shore drive without a license, or the evenings when we ate hamburgers in the loop, or the times we drove around the rich neighborhoods in the suburbs and commented on rich people's habits and fashion. Sometimes I took the train to unknown destinations in all directions of the city, south, north, east, west, just to see what the city was all about in the areas that were not glamorous like the "magnificent mile". This type of random travel gave me a wild sense of freedom and kept me in awe as I moved through all that swarming humanity of all colors.

I found out that my father did the same on his own, while my mother was teaching French part time at different colleges all over the city. He would return home with stories of people he met and talked to in bus or train stations, all of them strangers. Using the handful of English words he knew, he managed to ask for directions and talk about the weather or about his favorite subject: cars, American versus German cars, German versus Japanese cars, discussing which ones were better.

He had always answered himself that "Mercedes very good car". He referred to people as 'Mister, Sir' and 'Madame', using the French pronunciation. He took buses and trains to the end of their lines and reported to us how sometimes people on those buses or trains advised him to go back in the direction he had come from and to leave those neighborhoods as fast as he could.

He was fascinated with the Black neighborhoods and liked the adventure of being the only white person on the respective public means of transportation, while Zoila's friends always warned him to stay away. He didn't understand why and didn't care about what they said. Whenever we explained to him what these 'kind' warnings meant, he gave the same answer that he always did whenever we warned him of anything considered 'dangerous', including speaking against the Party and the secret police in Romania. He was never afraid of anything, "except for God", he would say. He had started English as Second Language classes and took the train to the college in the afternoon.

On one such afternoon during our second sweltering summer in Chicago, as I was returning from my own classes and transferring at the same Howard station, I saw him walking slowly towards the ticket turnstile. He was holding his English books under his arm and looked lost, in a way that was more concerning than not knowing where to go in space.

He looked completely alienated from the world around him. Such a deep sadness spread on his face that it was palpable, a thin glowing layer of sadness mixed in with sweat drops, like a child lost in his own misery and in the world. I felt so sad for him that I wanted to crawl on the subway station floor and cry myself to death. The full enormity of his loss weighed on me like a thousand-ton train. He had lost everything, and it was clear he couldn't make it in the harsh go-get-it-everything-is-possible world of a country he had nothing in common with.

And I hadn't achieved that much either in the two years of American living, to justify his sacrifice. A couple of frostbitten feet; three jobs, two of which gave me no satisfaction; an overload of courses, half of which made no sense to me, why I had even bothered taking them; and no money in my pocket. I was always too tired to write and too busy keeping up with work and study to think about the next steps in my life.

What was I doing with my freedom of speech now that I had it? Nothing, riding graffiti-ridden trains and going to yard sales on the weekends. What was my father doing with the freedom of expression now that he had it? Nothing, moving through hurried alien crowds on the verge of tears. He was trying to get through the turnstiles, but his ticket kept coming back out.

A line of irritated busy people stood behind him as if ready to pounce. One woman yelled at him to hurry up. I went straight to her and hurled all the swear words that Mia had taught me in an avalanche. Then, I used two of my tickets to get both my father and me through the turnstile.

Afterwards, I yelled back at the full line of busy people, "Shame on you, unkind American people!" It felt like I had stood up to the entire country in an assertion of universal revolt and independence.

All the pent-up anger I had gathered during the years of living under a dictatorship, added to the disappointments and confusion of my first two years as an immigrant exploded right there in the Howard subway station. An older Black man smiled as if he knew my frustration and patted me on the shoulder in approval. "You tell it, girl, people is mean and busy these days and don't care about nobody but themselves."

My father smiled back at him as if in mutual understanding and recognition: the poor, the tired, the lost, and the displaced people of America sticking together. The Black saxophone player on the platform was playing a sad melody that sounded like a smoldering wail. I took my father's arm and got on the train with him. I felt him frail and shaky and weighed down by nostalgia and despair.

On the train, we sat facing each other. Silent tears were streaming down his face. The train benches, doors and walls were scribbled with graffiti, sporting obscenities and the many names of male and female genitalia, sometimes accompanied by detailed graphics, almost like the porn comic book version of an anatomy lesson.

In between the drawings of genitalia, the words read 'cunt', 'cock', and 'motherfucker'. I was glad I understood them all. There was a heart pierced by an arrow, a sign of love, and names of people I didn't know: Jamal and Lakeisha, Carmencita and Rocky, Jose, Maria, and Jesus. I stared at the graffiti carefully and let out a simper. An entire community of people I didn't know felt the need to express their anger, lust, or attraction to one another on the train walls.

I wondered also when they might have had the time to scribble all that and whether anyone was watching. They may have done it late at night or at dawn, when the trains were starting their first journeys. It seemed like a thrilling occupation, and I felt close to Jamal and Carmencita, whom I imagined must have felt as angry and dejected as me. But unlike me, they were fiercely in love with each other, and they let the whole world know it. At least, that was how I imagined them.

I wanted to meet and talk to them, see how they lived. Maybe they were refugees too, poor, sad, and homesick. I felt closer to those strangers I had never met, authors of childish scribbles on the train walls, than to any of the white Christians in Zoila's Methodist suburban church who warned me and my father precisely against taking the kind of train we were on and be around the people that surrounded us: Blacks, Mexicans, Indians, Puerto Ricans, some loud, some poor and proud, some poor and angry. But most of them poor!

How come there were so many poor people in the country of dreams coming true and opportunities for everyone? At that point on the train staring at my father's tear-stained face, I couldn't see very far ahead into my future or his. I wanted to be Black and Mexican, Guatemalan or Jamaican, I wanted to meet Carmencita and Jamal, write graffiti on a city wall. Those people seemed to be confident in their own skin and members of lively communities that had fun despite the poverty. I wanted to be part of such a community; surrounded by poverty and graffiti and all the colors of the rainbow.

Accident with a Nun

During my second Chicago summer, I graduated with my BA degree in English. The day after my graduation, I got behind the wheel in our communal boat-sized Oldsmobile and drove to the closest city college of Chicago, looking for a teaching job. Given my excitement and my vague grasp of American traffic rules, I ran straight into a blue car at an intersection. It was a turn left only lane, and I went straight ahead towards my first dream job interview while the car on the turn left only lane next to me turned left violently blocking my passage.

The sound of crashing metal and glass in the middle of the famous Sheridan road on the north east side of Chicago electrocuted my brain into a wild frenzy. I was sure I was in the right and the blue car was at fault. Consequently, I got out of my car in my hot pink summer outfit with my monumental crown of curled hair rising to the sun like a mad rocket, and I started yelling at the driver at the top of my cigarette smoke-filled lungs.

It turned out the driver was a nun wearing her nun outfit at the sight of which I remained aghast in the middle of my barrage of deeply accented screams of righteous indignation. Her Catholic outfit was blue and white, with the headdress that looked like a miniature airplane sitting on top of her head.

Before I knew what was going on, a couple of Chicago policemen surrounded me and asked to see my driver's license, registration, and proof of insurance. The policemen didn't intimidate me because I only cared about making it on time for the job interview appointment at the city college a few blocks away.

Luckily, I was in the possession of all the requested documents. After inspecting them, the police asked me and the nun to please follow them to the nearest police station, two blocks away, for the police report. One of the policemen had a mustache like Officer McCloud in the American police series

I used to watch in Romania, and I thought he looked amused by my indignation and probably also by my hair spiking in all directions.

I smiled at him in the middle of my tirade but went on. Thinking I was in the good graces of the McCloud look-alike, I said confidently, "I can't come to the police station. It was not my fault, but hers. I have an important appointment. I have to go."

The nun commented in shock, "I can't believe she is the one yelling when it was her fault, the nerve!" I didn't know what she meant by "the nerve" and became even more belligerent.

By now a small crowd had gathered on the sidewalk to watch the scene like a show. It felt like an exciting moment, and I went on with my rant. I asked the nun with her airplane headdress to pay for the damage done to my car, I yelled at the police to leave me alone, and I gesticulated and pivoted in place in the middle of the Chicago intersection with impunity.

The handsome officer with a mustache blocked my access to my car and in a firm voice said that they were going to arrest me if I refused to follow them to the police station. Only then did I concede, and I got back into my car agreeing to follow the nun and the police car.

Instead of feeling scared, I was excited to see the inside of a police station in Chicago. It felt weirdly good to be a delinquent. I had just received an English degree from the university nearby and although I still didn't know colloquial expressions like "the nerve", I felt confident and invincible in my reckless revolt at members of two revered institutions: the Catholic Church and the Chicago police.

It is likely that my accent, my gestures, and all the other ways that revealed my belligerent foreignness inspired everybody at the police station with a sense of compassion and forgiveness. After filling out some forms and explaining to me calmly why I had been in the wrong in the accident, both the clerk filling out the form and the policeman who had threatened to arrest me a few minutes earlier, sent me on my way, with the warm warning to "drive safely".

After being assured that my insurance was going to cover the damage done to her car, the nun followed me out the door with a profoundly puzzled expression. By the time I arrived at the office where I had the interview, I was sweaty and red like the proverbial lobster and my hair had achieved an added level of frizz and unruliness due to the sweat and wind blowing on the way there.

The director of the English as a Second Language program stood up from her desk when I entered the office and shook my hand firmly, welcoming me. She was statuesque and strong and appeared as a force of nature. She took one quick look at me, and I immediately gathered that she understood everything about me, my fierce will to survive, my desperation, my ambition, and my confusion.

She said, "So you want to teach here! Why do you want to teach?"

All the phrases I had prepared about my qualifications and aspirations flew out of my overheated head in a millisecond and I said, "I would love to teach here, I would be a good teacher, I know it. Just please give me a chance." I felt proud of the spontaneous English that flowed out of my mouth.

Then she asked me about my "story". I didn't know what story she was talking about. She asked me where I was from and how I got to America and wanted to know everything I had done during my two years in America. I poured out the story of my escape, talked about my previous jobs that I had hated, the English literature courses I had loved, settling first in a suburb of Chicago, then in Chicago itself, I told her about my parents, about my family back in Romania.

At the end of half an hour, she got up from her chair and asked me if I was OK with teaching evening classes. She told me what the pay was going to be and said, "You can start tomorrow! Be here at five, classes start at six." I smiled the entire drive home, and this time I watched carefully the double left lane intersection where I had driven full force into the blue Chevrolet of a Catholic nun.

Mango – Very Good Fruit

Around the same time that I got the job at the city college of Chicago teaching English as a second language to refugees from South East Asia, my father got a small job through the Berlitz School of languages, tutoring Romanian to an American woman who lived in a rich suburb and owned a tiger for a pet. It wasn't clear why she needed to learn Romanian in an accelerated way and why she owned a tiger, but my father thought it was because she was in the CIA. He was probably right.

The eight months during which he went to her house twice a week for the private classes were probably among the happiest months in his American life. He never ceased to talk about the docile pet tiger who stared at the window of the suburban mansion and whom Sandy, his student, often stroked during the lesson. He got used to being in the presence of the tiger and ended up being quite fond of the majestic feline purring at his feet while he was passionately explaining to his pupil the nominative and accusative cases of Romanian grammar.

In the meantime, my Cambodian, Vietnamese, and Laotian students brought me back to life. I threw myself into their immigrant stories, lives, and cultures with a vengeance. I made them chant and sing all the irregular forms of past tense, compete for the best conditional phrases, and perform real life conversations in their aerated deeply glottal English to roars of laughter.

Our collective journey through the basics of English communication felt joyous, colorful, and gritty, equally a journey through the basics of life and survival. It was a wild love affair with language and trauma that gave me a sense of purpose and the community I had yearned for when reading the cryptic graffiti stories on my train rides.

I was now driving the first American car I had bought from my first few pay checks, an enormous Córdoba with leather seats and automatic windows and laced with layers of rust on the outside, like most of the older cars that had survived several of the fierce snowy winters in Chicago.

I frequented all the Vietnamese and Cambodian restaurants in the uptown neighborhoods with my fellow teachers after work, went to dances at the Laotian Community Center where one of my students tried to marry me to her son until I told her I was engaged to be married, accepted dinner invitations and ate Cambodian food sitting in a circle on the floor of tiny apartments surrounded by all generations of refugees having escaped the massacres of the Pol Pot regime.

I fondly remember the spicy pungent foods, the syncopated consonant clusters of Asian languages flowing like tiny drumbeats in my ear, the Hmong tapestries telling stories of mountain village people living among colorful birds and exotics animals that I hung on the walls of my room, and the unlikely stories of survival about running through the jungle, sailing in crowded boats and being attacked by pirates. They all became the center of my universe and the key to my own survival.

One student stole my heart and forever changed me with her story of love, horror, and kindness. I can only tell this story in the present. This and a few other parts of my life never became the past, but they stubbornly stick to the present as if they are all still happening in parallel with my life. One day, my wisdom teeth get infected. Some Romanians I know say all new refugees get tooth infections during their first years away from home, from stress. I must have two of my wisdom teeth extracted on the same day.

I don't want to cancel my class, because I never cancel classes. I walk into the classroom biting on the bloody gauze the dentist had fit into my mouth. I try to teach my lesson, the "if" conditional: if I were rich, I would travel all over the world; if I were rich, I would buy a new car and bring my mother from Cambodia to Amelica—they can never pronounce the r's.

I say, "Amerrrica, repeat after me"; they laugh and say, "Soly teacha, can't speak English well." I taste the blood gushing out of the two holes inside my mouth, raw, sour. I swallow it, and I say, "To hell with the conditional, why don't we just talk about you." They laugh and say, "Aah teachaa say hell."

But they tell me about the mango trees and "mango very good fruit", and they tell me about the mountains in Laos, very big mountains. I want to know more, I want to know what they ran away from. I'm still trying to understand my own story and why I ran away, and I want to know why everybody runs away.

An old woman, plumpish and smaller than the rest, with no front teeth, stands up in the middle of the classroom and starts to recount her story. She ran away with her family, her children, and grandchildren, walked for many nights and days through the jungle, "very tired, no water, afraid of soldiers shoot and kill and cut to pieces, give children round little fruit which make them sleep all night so no cry. If children cry, soldiers hear and shoot everyone. Pol Pot very bad man, Pol Pot kill everybody. Older son behind with children and wife, we walk ahead through the jungle, soldier catch my son and his family and kill everybody."

Her mouth is open in a huge, toothless grin. "Kill my son and grandchildren, take out hearts, we see from the trees." I bite onto my bloody gauze. She's crazy, I think, nobody cuts out people's hearts, except for the evil stepmother in Snow White who wants Snow White's heart on a platter. I remember how I used to draw Snow White and the seven dwarfs the way my father's artist friend had taught me, but this is impossible. This can't actually happen in the real world.

I had thought my parents' stories about the horrors during the Stalinist period when people were "accidentally" crushed by cars and political prisoners were tortured or sent to Siberian camps, were just about as deep as evil could reach. But there seems to be no limit to evil, I learn from the toothless Cambodian woman.

The other students get up and are gesticulating. They want to tell their stories too about how they ran away on boats, with pirates attacking them, through storms, and how many people died, and others like the old woman, escaped through the jungle. "We lucky," one says, "soldier don't get us."

The old woman with the slaughtered family is standing in the middle of the room smiling. I bite hard onto my bloody gauze and taste the blood in my mouth. I take the hand of the old woman and hold her.

The other students say "No, not impossible, they cut up people and Pol Pot even kill people with glasses because if they have glasses, it mean they study, and take out people's hearts." My little story of escape to Italy seems so puny, so insignificant.

I don't know what to do next. We are all standing in the classroom now, and I ask the woman about the rest of her family. She says she escaped with her other son and daughter. "I very lucky," she says, and the blood coming from my extracted teeth is filling my mouth.

It tastes sour, and I'm glad I'm tasting blood when I hear the story of the old Cambodian woman and the stories of endless escape walks through the jungles and about pirates in Thailand waters, cutting off people's throats, and especially the stories about people's hearts being cut out of their chests by Pol Pot's soldiers. I don't know how to end the lesson, this lesson that should have been about the "if" conditional.

I write on the board, "Mango very good fruit. If I went to Cambodia, I would eat many mangoes." The students laugh.

Then I feel it coming back; the ease with which I used to draw when I was seven and eight years old, an irrepressible desire to draw a fairy-tale image on the board overtakes me. I draw Snow White and the seven dwarfs, the way I used to draw them on the board in my father's university classroom: Snow White ahead, in a long skirt and a ruffled blouse, and the seven dwarfs lined up behind her.

I even use colored chalk for Snow White's red lips, and for the dwarfs' costumes. I use a different color for each of their long hats, blue, yellow, orange, green, violet. I desperately color the dwarfs' hats while tasting blood in my mouth and feeling the tears well in my eyes. I color the last hats, red, red, red like the heart.

All the students laugh as they recognize the characters. Then they sit down and retrieve back into silence. They laugh some more at my drawing and say "teacha vely good dlaw".

I say "see you tomorrow" but they linger in the classroom, as if reluctant to go. I ask them all to accompany me to my car, as I'm trying to deter their thoughts from the stories they've just told me in syncopated English, but I know those stories are with them all the time, no use pretending, just trying to go on, learn English, buy a new car, bring mother from Cambodia.

I say I've never eaten a mango fruit, and many offer to bring me a mango the next day. I say OK. I know it makes them happy to offer gifts. "Mango very good fruit." The name of the toothless Cambodian woman is Pho, like the Vietnamese soup.

Overworked Working Mother

Bestselling novels typically unpack glamorous or sensational subjects: a murder, a revolution, a crime of passion, a formidable escape on water or land in the dark. Abuse stories and weirdly dysfunctional family stories are good for bestselling novels too. A woman torn between raising the children she loves and the work she also loves rarely forms the substance of such a novel. And if such a woman is also torn between a husband and a lover and she loves them both, then it's subject of fierce gossip and litigation. And it might even be too lowly a subject for the great American novel, neither very sensationalist, nor very "down to earth".

The female protagonist is "unlikable". Only a nineteenth century French novelist like some of the ones I am teaching would venture to pick up such a topic and write such a character. Leave it to the French and their obsession with triangulated love. And if this woman happens to also be torn between countries, languages, cultures, forget it then! She is beyond the bounds of both accepted reality and fiction, from whatever century she might be.

In fiction, this woman is "too confusing for the reader", an unlikable and "self-centered" character. As a real woman she is reprehensible, and other mothers don't let their children play with her children. They are afraid she is "a bad role model" for their children and that she is going to "steal" their husbands. Really, forget the role model part; they are just afraid she'll steal their husbands.

This woman with an accent will come one night when the entire happy family of mother, father, and three children are asleep, she would tiptoe near the bed where the mother and father are blissfully sleeping in their spacious and recently remodeled bedroom, she would be wearing a mask like a burglar, and in one move she would swoop the snoring husband from his slumber and carry him on her back to her den in the Shenandoah forests where she makes her potions for beguiling and bewitching good American husbands like this one.

He becomes her sex slave until the righteous wife, with the help of the devoted local police and a detective with a southern accent and with a passion for hunting, recuperates her lost husband and carries him back to her whiny children. Then the good wife testifies in court how the "foreign woman with an accent" stole her good husband with witchcraft brought over from her country, and the happy family is restored back to its original bliss, while the husband-thief woman is sent to prison for life, and she might even get the death penalty. Not to mention that she loses her hard-won tenure-track job. Serves her right! Such convoluted fantasies sometimes cross me as I race between work and daycare to pick up the children.

I am not sure anymore where the "real" woman ends and where the fictional one begins, where my story starts, and the story of that other woman ends in this town of very nice people and their many nice children. And the reason I am so confused about this woman is because I only get four hours of sleep at night if I am lucky, and I run and work like a maniac all day to keep my job and to keep my children.

Or, as the one idiomatic expression I like so much goes, "to keep body and soul together". I still interpret some idiomatic expressions literally in my head, and the image of my exhausted body trailing behind my wildly confused soul like a lost child trailing behind his mother, makes me laugh as I am vigorously pumping milk from one of my engorged breasts to leave with the babysitter for my six-month-old son while I am teaching the French subjunctive to first year university students from rich southern families.

The fall mornings are foggy and damp, the valley seems indeed like a bewitched place. I wouldn't be surprised if a cortege of warlocks wearing the academic regalia robes that we wear at graduations and convocations were to emerge from the thick woods on the way to my classes.

My husband and I separated and are having the divorce litigation of the century. I got what I deserved. This woman is not a worthy topic for a bestselling novel, and *The Scarlet Letter* has already been written. Plus, the topic of a woman's work and her struggle to make ends meet every month is not an exciting topic for any agent or editor to want to publish such a novel.

At the end of each month when all the bills are paid and I have to put the groceries on my credit card, which is almost at its limit, I imagine two ribbons stretching around my cute little rented house keeping my family together. If only I can make the two ends of this magical ribbon meet and tie them together! Then we'll be OK, and we won't burst like the messy contents of a box stuffed too full.

Living in the literal realm of idiomatic English expressions helps me feel light when I am having a hard time just surviving. But invariably the ends of the two magical ribbons don't meet, and we burst through the seams and past the edges of the little house in the town with very nice people.

That's when I have to ask my babysitter to hold on to her paycheck until the last day of the month, when I write checks against an empty bank account hoping the electric or the gas company will take a few days before cashing my checks, so they don't put my account in the red.

That's when I start spinning in place, asking neighbors to watch my kids when the schools close because of snow, accidentally bumping my car against curves in town because I doze off in the middle of the day from lack of sleep. I nurse in public places with no worries. I chop the head of a garden snake with a hoe while wearing my one pair of pink pumps on my way back from work.

I get a beautiful white cat from the local SPCA so she could scare the snakes in the garden and eat the mice in our house. I join the local episcopal church, and I correct hundreds of pages of French exams a week, which sometimes get stained with breast milk and baby vomit. Out of a sense of professional ethics, I scrub the stained exams with rubbing alcohol and dry them on a chair in our backyard.

When I'm at work in my office, I think of my children, one of them at home with a local babysitter, the other in daycare. When I'm with my children, I worry about the lesson plans I still have to write for tomorrow, my end-of-the-year evaluation, and the results of the recent court motion in my divorce trial.

When my lover visits from Chicago to see me and the baby and we make love in the secrecy of the garage, so that we don't break the court order that does not allow any visits from unrelated males, I worry about my children all over again and about everything else that is beyond the red doors of my garage. Am I being a good mother, how will I make it until the end of the week, let alone the end of the month? It seems I am always in the wrong place, thinking of the wrong thing at the wrong time, in reverse order, in out-of-sync order, gasping in superhuman efforts to pull the two ends of the ribbon holding our existence together, and get my worn-out body to catch up with my yearning soul.

Everything is now unbearably in the present, all crowded at the same time as if no past has ever existed behind and no future will ever unfold ahead. Only the present exists in a perpetual static rotation, and it is raw and incoherent: a messy toy box filled with junk from lava lamps to unpaid bills, to dirty diapers, to nasty court motions, to every possible beanie baby animal, toucan, tarantula or penguin, to a walk in the park shuffling through the russet and scarlet leaves, scarlet like my past that keeps pouring its shameless contents into the present.

I'm all alone in a southern provincial town with two small children and a full-time teaching job. That's the bottom line, and I see the bottom, and I see the line. They are black on black, or red on red, dark. I am the most foreign person in town and am even foreign to my own self.

The fairy tales help a bit. I read them every night to my glowing blue-eyed children, fairy tales of all nations. The pattern is always the same: monsters and fairies with the prince and princess in the middle, trials of endurance and courage, long journeys through inhospitable forests and a reward in the end, a castle, a kingdom, or just a happy house with no witches.

But no fairy tale tells you about the children and the work, about how to pass that trial of endurance, how to keep your attention focused on the target and not collapse in the middle of the kitchen floor or run straight into a wall like a dizzy bird. Maybe you must read through the lines and learn how to interpret them in a productive way.

For instance, you must make yourself invisible and glide effortlessly between your colleagues as they whisper wicked gossip about you, float proudly and imperceptibly among the mothers you meet in daycare or in the park and who stare at you and judge you because you are a working mother—studies show that children of working mothers…blah, blah, blah…end up criminals and psychotic and engage in delinquency…blah blah…studies written by male scientists, of course.

How many of those social scientists writing articles about the development of children of single working mothers had to rush home from their precious research to feed their kids, drive them to soccer practice, math tutoring, or piano lessons, make dinner, help with homework, write notes to obtuse teachers, or worry about organizing the upcoming birthday party for one of their kids while an angry pile of unwashed laundry is staring at them?

And how about the judge who threatens you with loss of custody because you work, and you put your children in daycare? And how about the lawyers who eat up all your money? Oh them, they will eventually collapse by the side of the road like a bunch of dirty flies if you keep going, if you just keep walking through the rain and the sun, your children tightly next to you, a pile of French papers tucked inside the baby carriage, the groceries all neatly packed in a basket on top of your very head, like the baskets worn by African women walking through the Savannah.

And if you just walk proudly through the hot sands and the stormy rivers, through the snow and the flowery meadows, you might just make it past the finish line. Because there are also flowery meadows in this fairy tale, where you take the children on the weekend to the park with a magnificent view of the layered chains of the bluish Appalachians and wild geese flying in happy flocks. There are also the times when you write scholarly articles, fascinated with symbols of femininity in the French novels you teach, and you love teaching those novels too.

The students love you; they don't judge you and your litigation. You love speaking French to get away from the English of dreary faculty meetings, and you love speaking Romanian to your children to get away from the English of the court hearings and the English of faculty meetings. Basically, you are overflowing with love, you just have too much of it, it seems.

In the local bookstore where you take your children some weekends, silly titles of new books pretending to solve the drama of overworked suicidal wives and mothers grate your brains, *Women Who Love Too Much*, *Women Are from Venus, Men Are from Mars*. You just want to take a break from all this love and your Venusian existence and write your own damn book for a change.

Your children are growing up bilingual despite the curious looks of the locals. It makes you feel less foreign, and now that they are older, they have fun speaking Romanian to each other so that the babysitters don't understand them. The babysitters, some selected from among your own students, are amused by the children's bilingualism and admire you. You keep a positive attitude even when your colleagues criticize you for doing a good job teaching your classes and when they schedule meetings at times when you have to take care of the children.

You already know that everything is topsy-turvy both in fairy tales and in the men's world, in general. But it all turns out OK if only you keep your eyes on the target, like the huge stuffed animal at the carnival of the country fair that you won for your children by simply keeping your eyes focused on the target, the bull's eye, the basket in which you threw the ball like an athletic pro.

The children are ecstatic about the gigantic stuffed elephant from the carnival, and you eat funnel cake and cotton candy with them with a furor until you get dizzy on the sugar high, and you have a tiny fleeting memory of a time when your own mother bought you cotton candy in a big park by a lake in a city called Bucharest. That's another fairy tale that you don't really want to revisit right now. It's so far away. Was it even real? Are you even from there, or did you just make that up to amuse the children?

It must be real because you speak the language, you didn't forget that, and now your children speak the language, and you can read to them Romanian fairy tales from a book that your aunt from Brasov brought you when she visited America last year.

The Romanian fairy tales are funnier and gorier than the Western ones. A princess almost drowns in her own tears because of longing for her valiant Prince. She swims through the sea of tears until she reaches a forest of birch trees where she has to massacre the mother of the dragons and cut her to pieces and spread the pieces in the forest, so the trees move aside for her. Only in this way can she get to her lover, the prince who is slaughtering his own set of dragons. The prince and the crying princess work together to deceive and kill the dragons, called *zmei* in Romanian, and the mother of dragons, *zmeoaica*.

You look up from the fairy tale book with Romanian drawings of dragons and dragonesses that vaguely remind you of your own childhood on another planet, and you realize your two sons are listening aghast at the story, without moving in their identical pajamas you bought at Kmart. The three-year-old is holding the tricolor teddy bear and sucking his thumb, and the seven-year-old is sitting calmly with his hands on his knees, a worried look about the slaughter of the Romanian dragons disturbing his beautiful face.

"Mama, I like the dragon and the mommy dragon. I don't want the prince and princess to cut them to pieces." And the three-year-old starts howling in distress at his brother's humanitarian comment. They are both crying now. I have darling sensitive boys who don't play with guns and who speak a second language that hardly anybody in town has ever heard of, except for my one friend, the beautiful Spanish woman with a PhD in Classics and a son, the age of my older one. We are the only ones among the mothers in daycare who smoke, have a PhD, and speak a different language to our children.

She approached me once when I was hugely pregnant a few days before going into labor. I was picking up my four-year-old from the same daycare that her son was attending. She looked at me, and I knew she saw everything about me in an instant, that I was going through a hellish time, that I was wickedly confused and desperate. She was as beautiful as I had imagined Spanish women to be while growing up in Romania and hearing passionate Spanish music on the radio.

With her spontaneous laugh, her huge round hazel eyes, she reminded me of Zoila Valdivieso, though she had an edge of irony, a power that Zoila did not possess. She told me that once my baby arrives, she would love looking after him if I had trouble finding someone right away. She must have understood that I was single too. When my newborn was a week old and I had nobody I could trust to leave him with as I was still interviewing for babysitters, I called her and asked if she could look after the baby for a few hours.

She greeted me with an adorable bassinet that had been her son's, all ready and fresh-looking for the new bundle of life I was holding. Handing her my baby to place in her tiny bassinet was a perfect moment, ethereal and feathery, a tiny oasis of comfort in the indescribable mess of my predicament. In that second, I felt connected to her for life. I had a fleeting glimpse into my future, with husbands and lovers coming and going, but the brunette Spanish friend still in the picture of my life.

As my children both howl in distress about the killing of the mommy dragon, I know I would give my life for them in a second and am terrified of the brutal passage of time. They are already three and seven, they are growing up, and I'm still groping through a thick existential fog trying to make the two ends of that ribbon meet and tie them together to keep us safe and well fed.

I say, "Forget this story then. It's too brutal. I'll read the one about the cunning rooster." They like this one and roar with laughter when the rooster finds a little purse with two golden coins and the two evil boyars who steal the purse from him; the rooster chases after them going "cock a doodle-do, give me back my purse" until he gathers a mountain of golden coins on the road and retrieves the purse with the two initial coins on top of the pile of coins.

I bask in the heat emanating from their bodies, smiling to myself about the stubborn perseverance of the Romanian rooster and his two golden penny purse that turns into a mountain of golden coins. I fall asleep between my two children. It turns out also that the dragoness in the other story puts herself back together out of the many pieces scattered throughout the forest because the princess pours the magic water of life over her pieces and thus brings her back to life. Happy ending for everybody in the story. All this is very heartening. I identify with the dragoness more than with the weeping princess.

I promise to myself I'm going to take care of myself, have a healthier diet starting tomorrow, and no longer skip lunch and gorge on spaghetti at night. I vow to pour the water of life over all the pieces of myself and make them all one again. I whisper to myself in Romanian to be strong, to not give up. I am also the princess to my own dragoness, *zmeoaica*, a dear Romanian word with so many vowels and a triphthong—3 vowels pronounced in the same syllable—that consoles my brain, my jaws, and my vocal chords, giving me a break from all the English spoken throughout the day.

My therapist said, "Talk to yourself, embrace yourself, and forgive yourself." I now see a therapist because I want to get it together the American way. Good idea, I shift everything to the second person and start living with myself like a good partner, like a caring but firm lover, mother, partner, whatever. You are your own best friend, you got what you wanted, now sleep in it, deal with it, you make the bed you lie in, so you shall not cry over spilled milk.

You mix up the American and Romanian proverbs to spice up your work on yourself and to provide some humor for your own wellbeing. I can get mad at myself too, but just not judge my being mad at myself. It's in the therapeutic prescription of cognitive psychology. This way I am gentler to myself and can better cope with the "guilt". The truth is I don't experience any fucking guilt, I just need sleep.

I turn to the French fables and their harsh lessons of the law of the strongest, "oh you sang all summer, well now dance!" Well put, dance through the rows of unfair colleagues who are deciding your tenure and your future peeking critically at your file because you write too much, you attract too many students, your French is too good and doesn't coincide with the incorrect in-house written grammar book they make you teach from.

It turns out that what you thought was good is actually bad. Your talents are your hubris; your knowledge is your tragic flaw. Who would have thought it? It's not much different from where you left, only the salary is in dollars. But go ahead, dance! Dance through the rows of lawyers, settle the divorce, it's not helping the children to drag it on, lick your wounds like some lion in one of those fables once did.

Own up to the mess you made, dance to your classes, dance to the Edith Piaf *La vie en rose* and *Non, je ne regrette rien*, the two heartbreak songs you play for your students blasting through the hallways in the historic building where you teach. Dance through bankruptcy, dance through the rows of American stay-at-home mothers you don't understand and that stare at you like you are a feminist KGB spy who speaks a foreign language to the children; who knows what you might be telling them!

Take a vacation. Go to the ocean with the children during spring break. And write your damn novel. Remember the suitcase too, take it out of the basement, put all your manuscripts in order, cull through the crap, keep the pearls, make more pearls, you're a clever oyster, you're a fucking dragoness. And don't forget to smile!

From now on, you decide you are going to pay more attention to details and grasp as many precious moments as you can before the children are all grown up and it's too late. You don't want it to be too late. A line from one of your favorite French novels you teach haunts you. "At eighteen it was already too late." It's a novel about a first love written by a woman writer, and you stress that now in your classes: that it's a *woman* writer.

You are starting to understand that something is off about the balance of power and the balance of everything. The thousand-page French literature anthology you teach from includes only two women writers, and you know for a fact that there are more French women writers than the two here.

For instance, Marguerite Duras, the French woman writer you like so much who said, "at eighteen, it was already too late" and who is not included in the magnificent anthology. Maybe if you ever become the writer you always wanted to be, and if the tiny writer you snuck out in your suitcase across the communist border ever comes to life and becomes real and published, you won't be included in any such anthology either. So, what's the point?

You have unbearable quick flashes of understanding of why your favorite American poet, Sylvia Plath, killed herself putting her head in the oven one fated February morning. The fact that it was a cold February morning when she killed herself is mentioned in the encyclopedia entry you read about her. You know everything about that last stretch of grayness of an endless winter when you don't know whether you are going to make it till spring or not.

You would never do it like Sylvia Plath though, you would take a whole bunch of pills...No, wrong, you would never do it period! You are an East European tough woman like the character in a Romanian story who gives birth in the field, in the middle of the working day, as she seeks shelter under a tree in the shade. All by herself.

Then she wraps up her baby and goes home to cook dinner for her husband. The truth is, like hell she does. She smashes a rock right on her husband's head while he is sleeping in a drunken stupor on the floor. There are two versions to this story: the idealized one about the strength and endless endurance of the East European woman, and the feminist version about the real strength of the East European woman who is also a murderess. You don't want to be either of the two. You want to be a writer, and for now you just want to make it through the month of February without any attempts at taking your own life.

You notice all the ugly portraits of old men hanging in the main building of the university where you teach. They are founders, donors, deans, dead professors, trustees, famous alumni, presidents, all with proud looks on their faces as if they did something that the posterity must always recognize. There aren't any women. You somehow feel it in your bones that for you, too, it might already be way too late.

You are already in your thirties and haven't written anything other than literary criticism, more than enough of it to get tenure in the department where in three years you have exceeded all your tenured colleagues in the number of publications. But it's not what you were really dreaming of when you sat all snug by your suitcase, waiting to get put on the plane to Fiumicino airport in Rome.

Maybe for you, too, it was already too late when you were twenty-two and walked on the campus of that Chicago university in your overdressed outfits bought at garage sales, feeling a hundred years old with your communist dictatorship past and the heartbreaks and the frostbites, so out of place next to the careless and carefree students in tight jeans yelling "hi" in high pitched notes at every step they made. That's why now you are determined to start a race of sorts against time and against your own foreignness.

Despite your lack of sleep, this resolve added to the two strong cups of coffee a day and the multivitamins you take catapult you into an energetic spell. You are determined to remember more and not let the children's childhood years slip by you like a flash of lightning.

You prepare extravagant birthday parties with many guests, ice cream cakes, and generous party favors and bring your credit card to its limit with the expenses. A child falls and has a nosebleed, and the mother tries to be nice about it when she picks up her hollering bleeding child, but you know she is thinking you are careless because you work full time. Another child makes fun of the Romanian words you and your birthday son who just turned eight exchange amid the racket, and he asks why you are speaking Spanish all the time.

Thank God for the Spanish friend who laughs with you and makes you feel better because indeed, she does speak Spanish to her son and proudly so. When your son blows the eight candles on the ice cream cake while your almost four-year-old who is tiny like a two-year-old stares at his brother in admiration breathlessly, hoping he will blow off all eight candles in one breath, your eyes fill with abundant tears, which hasn't happened in a while. You've been too busy and too tired to cry. He does blow all eight of them, and everybody cheers. You are happy he is loved and blows all his candles on the cake in the pretty American house in the little town with nice people.

You lived in a minuscule apartment in Bucharest when you were eight and ten and fifteen, and only one friend came to your birthday parties instead of the ten you had invited, while the meringue raspberry cake your mother always ordered from a special pastry shop melted with the June heat as you waited for the friends that never came.

For a second, the image of the girl you were at your eighth birthday party swells up in your head like a bubble in a comic book, and you squish it quickly and give yourself your own pep talk just like your therapist advised you to do. Your son is growing up in America and not in Romania; he is not living in a pathetic apartment smaller than any of your other schoolmates, but in a full-fledged house with a back yard; his birthday is in the spring when everything comes to life in bright pinks and reds, dogwoods, red-buds, yellow daffodils, in the small southern town where everybody smiles.

You are living the dream. Smile! Don't forget to smile and take a happiness pill. You take lots of pictures with your disposable camera, but the truth is you can't wait for the party to be over and the game of putting the tail on the fucking donkey to be over. You are hoping to take a nap after the party because your Spanish friend, the only one you have, promised she will take the children to her house for the rest of the day.

You gather more happy moments and pictures in the huge album that your babysitter had covered in a tacky red cloth with teddy bears and ruffles. The album has pictures of Halloween parades and of your boys wearing fancy costumes of knights, pirates, harlequins that you now buy from a costume shop in a different town thirty minutes down the road and mothers think you made them yourself. "Your children are beautiful no matter what" is what you father always said.

Now he is happy to have two grandsons, never mind the mess in your life, the boys' two different fathers, a divorce, visitation rights. Nothing is perfect. You have a professor's job and two beautiful children and are living in a pretty house. Your father is proud and supportive as always and unlike you, he likes the small town where you live more than he likes Chicago; he always tells you that on each visit. Your mother is practically co-parenting with you whenever she has a vacation from her many part time teaching jobs.

Together, you two teach the children how to swim and bike: you take the swimming, she takes the biking. In one picture that is your mother's favorite, your two boys are sitting on a towel on a beach cuddled next to each other in front of a lake surrounded by hills and pine trees glowing in a golden sunset. It was taken when your younger one learned to swim and floated in the water like a tadpole.

They both look dreamy, a bit wimpish, and alone in the middle of an empty lake beach at sunset, like two lost children on a deserted island. You took the picture right before leaving the beach, on a summer afternoon when you felt at peace and content. The summers give you some respite. You swim, you write, the children are growing, and you are pretty sure that you are going to make it.

The divorce is over, and the father of your youngest child, your great American love, can now come over to your house with no fear of court motions for "immoral influence" on the children. He still lives in Chicago where he works at the prestigious university where you met. But at least now he doesn't have to sleep in the shed when he visits.

You work and take care of the children. You are two years away from tenure and things are a bit tidier in your life, though you're still not getting enough sleep, but you've gotten used to it by now. Things are looking up. Soon you might even have a bit of time for a good cry of relief, letting go of all the pent-up tears and rage gathered over the last several years of "paying" for your mistakes and working yourself into a raw pulp. But you're not there yet. Better wait till tenure to cry.

Marriage on the Blue Ridge

The winters are raw and majestic in the valley. A familiar air seems to move in with the solid cold as if traveling all the way from the Carpathians to visit you here in the little town: a fairy tale with fir trees and pine trees heavy with snow and the streets un-passable, the blue mountain ridges layered in white blankets in the distance. Everything closes and quiets down.

It is on such a winter day that you get remarried, this time in a white dress and a white faux fur coat that you bought at the thrift shop in town. You get married at an overlook against the majestic view of the mountains. The park where you first wanted to have the tiny wedding ceremony is closed because of the snow, so you drive higher to the overlook place on the Blue Ridge parkway, with the justice of the peace woman who is going to marry you riding in the backseat of your car, and the cars of your friends trailing behind you.

By now, you also have a Russian friend and her husband, and a French friend and her boyfriend. You stick with the European women, each the only representative of their country in the small town so that your wedding party looks like a miniature UN gathering. You are in tears though because you left your younger son with your hairdresser friend that you had met at the local city pool a couple of years ago, and because the park where you had planned to have the outdoor wedding is closed.

You cry as your soon to be husband keeps driving around the valley looking for an appropriate place for the ad-hoc ceremony. He passes by a deserted bus factory, a closed general store, a cemetery with confederate flags. You are crying with big fresh tears and you let yourself cry. You couldn't wait till tenure to cry. This is as good a moment as any to let it all out as you are searching for a place to get married.

You are thinking out loud, *Sure, everything has to go wrong in my life, upside down. I can't even find a fucking wedding place in this whole stupid valley. Why don't we just get married here in this cemetery, here by the side of the road, why don't we*! The woman justice of the peace laughs heartily in the backseat of your rattling Nissan Maxima.

You remember a sweltering summer day in Chicago, when you were at the dinner table in the small apartment where you were once living with your parents. You were engaged to a poet who was your fiancé for two days. You remember two Israeli wedding bands that had touched the tomb of Jesus Christ from where he was resurrected, too large for your fingers. What was your aunt thinking when she got oversized wedding bands from Israel?

Your attempts at getting one marriage right and real in your life all seem to crash in pathetic failures. But after an hour of driving around with the tiny UN cortege of female friends and their partners in the cars squeaking their way on the snowy roads, you say, "Here, look it's beautiful, a gorgeous view, isn't it? Let's do it here, all right!"

You wipe your tears and look for the champagne glasses and the champagne bottle. You are thinking that the strenuous search for the place to perform your second wedding is a metaphor for the obstacles you had to overcome in your life, but now it's over, you have reached your mountain top, you can just enjoy the view, you are a hopeful woman and an optimist after all.

The ceremony is lovely against the range of the Blue Ridge Appalachians, sort of movie-like. The champagne is bubbling in the crystal glasses your Russian friend has brought for the occasion, and a huge hope for happiness fills your soul as the mists in the valley rise abundantly over the white stretches of land all around.

After the ceremony, you pick up your son from your friend's house, newly married in your white fake fur coat and wonder why you hadn't taken him with you after all. You feel clumsy and regretful for a second. You have a fleeting doubt about the whole thing, but you brush it off with your last tear of happiness. Your son slides inside the foot-high snow in front of your friend's house and collapses laughing in the fluffy layers. "Mommy and Daddy just got married, isn't that exciting?" your friend says.

He doesn't care. He is eating snow and rolling in it, laughing. He wonders if now that you got married, he is still going to sleep in your bed, and you say, "Of course, why wouldn't you? Dad is still going to commute to Chicago for his classes, it will still be you, your brother, and mommy, the happy trio."

"Then why did you get married, Mama?" he asks as you are strapping him into the car seat. You laugh and kiss his flushed cheeks, cold from the snow, and the truth is you can't really answer that question yourself right at this moment. You shelf the question for another day. Right now, you are possessed by a renewed and wild desire to be happy in the most fundamental and basic ways: to be in love, to be good at everything you do, to dance to the moon and back and sprinkle a little of that moon powder magic over everything.

In the evening, your older son arrives from his weekend visitation with his father. He has the sadness of the-in-between-the-people-he-loves mood, the separation from one, the reunion with another, readjusting every time. You feel friendly and warm towards your ex-husband. You smile, and ask him how the weekend was, he congratulates you on your marriage, and you congratulate him on his, even though his was six months ago; he beat you to it.

You have the crazy thought of a big family and of an extended family reunion with all the parents and the stepparents of the children, a party of the exes and the present spouses to ensure a process of healing after the three-year-long divorce that led to absolutely nothing except for a lot of heartbreak and pushed you into bankruptcy. Your older son relaxes and embraces his brother after his father leaves.

But then your new husband becomes all glum and resentful because you let your ex-husband inside the house, and he stepped on the antique Persian rugs that had once belonged to his mother, and you were nice and smiling to him, to your ex-husband.

You tighten up into a knot of anger and confusion and another crazy thought crosses your excited mind of a second-time newlywed; that you made a real mistake by marrying again. Your life isn't going to improve much. You'll still be a single mother in practice for most of the time, with short periods of respite during the visits of your husband. His obsessive jealousy isn't going to get any better, and you want to hurt him and break china on his head every time you notice that he treats the two children differently, favoring his own flesh-and-blood son.

The hell with you, men, what good are you? You tell yourself on this day of your wedding that just took place at the very top of a beautiful peak in the Appalachian Mountains. But still, you tell yourself you are not going to care, you are going to be happy, and that's it.

"Let's go sledding down the street, boys!" You tell your sons, and they cheer at your idea, put on their snow boots, coats, and hats. They both look picture beautiful, and you know it again that there is no one and nothing you will ever love more than these two creatures that look like two adorable munchkins all wrapped up for the below-zero evening in the snow.

Your husband cheers up too, and you all go sledding down the street from where you live on the little hill behind the elementary school that your kids attend. A demented moon casts a wide strip of light on the snowy hill. The smell of snow and wood burning stoves in the vicinity, the moon flooding the earth, the swooshing of the sleds through the cold wind, the yelps and laughs of the children conjure up a memory of your own childhood a century ago and on another planet in Brasov when you did the same.

Your husband looks at the three of you amused and loving as you are gliding past him on the small sleds you bought at Kmart. Maybe this time you got all the pieces together, and it's going to work. You confidently take refuge in the cliché American expressions, like "you're going to make it work, you will make it", as if you were talking about a factory machine that became dysfunctional and it's going to be repaired and be alright.

Somewhere in the combination of moonlight, solid cold, iridescent snow, the smell of wood burning stoves, and children's unhinged shouts, you find a place in yourself that is luminous, solid, and unbroken, the place from where you love and imagine. And in that very place of light and imagination, the memory of you sledding as a child in the Carpathians marries this full to the brim moment of you sledding with your own children in the Appalachians. It cleaves the past *you* with the present *you* in a seamless grounded glowing piece of You. All of You is right here right now under the full winter moon.

Abortions

At some point during my childhood, before I have any idea of how babies are made, I start noticing a lot of whispering around me. It's mostly between my mother and other women in my family or between my mother and her women friends. I sense that these whispers are not about the Securitate or the party or my father's job, but about something else, something dangerous and shameful. Something that is not allowed.

I catch bits and fragments of conversations between my mother and Aunt Nina or Aunt Mimi, or some of the women friends who visit us often. Some of these bits of conversation terrify me and incite my curiosity like nothing else does. "But you might have a heart attack from it..." or "Yes, a lot of aspirin and a very hot bath"; "high quantities of coffee, but it might cause a heart attack"; "the injections are hard to find"; "maybe Neli can procure them"; "it could be dangerous though, I heard it's very strong"; "the doctor lives in the blocs...very far...very expensive."

I put my ear to the bathroom door whenever I see both my parents going in together. I spy and eavesdrop on every single conversation that my mother has with her women friends or her sister. I know it's something medical and dangerous, and once I catch half of a whispered story late at night about a woman who died because of this thing that has to do with large quantities of aspirin or some special injections or a visit to the doctor who lives far away. I try to interpret all the information I hear like a detective and realize it all has to do with my mother, something that my mother must do, that it's dangerous, and it's a secret, and one woman died from it. It could be my mother next.

I am terrified about my mother's life and watch her carefully throughout the day, wait for her to return from work, my heart bursting out of my chest with emotion. I try to stay awake and wait for her to go to sleep first and make sure she is breathing regularly when I sleep next to her at night. Then the whispering goes away for a while, and everything is fine. I only have to worry about the political whispering now: Securitate, the bad leader, someone that my parents know who lost his job because something he said, and someone else was interrogated in a basement for hours.

I've learned to deal with these kinds of whispers, plus they are sort of boring. I calm down and focus on my dolls, my French kindergarten classes, the girl that moved next door from us who is Jewish and pretty, the forthcoming trip to Brasov when I get to see my cousins and play outside all day, someone else who left the country while on tour with an orchestra from my mother's workplace. And then the other kinds of whispers start again.

One day, there is a big commotion around me. My parents leave me with Aunt Mimi for the whole day, and my mother looks deathly pale when she returns in the evening. She lays in bed for the rest of the evening, and my father goes to the pharmacy to get some medicine that she needs to get better. I go to bed by myself praying that my mother doesn't die like that woman in one of the stories I overheard.

I wake up in the middle of the night because I hear a lot of voices in the room behind the glass door. The lights are on, and I recognize the voice of the doctor who is a friend of my father saying, "We just have to wait and see. The antibiotic should start working soon."

I am sure that my mother is going to die tonight, and I get enough courage to get out of bed and go into the other room to see my mother one more time before she dies. My father, Aunt Mimi, and the doctor friend push me back out of the room and tell me to go to sleep. "Everything is all right," they say.

My mother is lying in bed on one side, covered in two blankets even though it is warm in the apartment from the radiators. The room smells like rubbing alcohol, and the doctor friend has his medical kit out on the table. I go back to bed and cry myself to sleep because I am sure my mother will die any minute and I won't have a mother when I wake up. But when I wake up, I hear my father saying, "You were so lucky." I hear my mother's weak voice answering that if it wasn't for Bogdan, the doctor, she might have died. She calls another doctor a charlatan. I'm old enough to know what that word means.

After the night when my mother almost died but was lucky enough to survive, I never again heard any of the kinds of terrifying whispered stories about injections and doctors and other such dangerous things. Later in our lives, during the period of my great love affair with my mountaineering prince charming, when I confessed to my mother one evening that I might be pregnant and she needed to help me, she too had a few confessions to make.

The whispered stories that had sent pangs of terror throughout periods of my childhood became clear as did the terrifying night when my mother almost died from an illegal abortion, the only ones a woman could get in our country. The electricity went off during the procedure she was having in a doctor's house, and he had to finish the procedure in the dark. Something went wrong in the dark, and she developed a deadly infection, septicemia. My father's life-long friend, Bogdan, the doctor from Brasov who happened to be visiting Bucharest at the time, saved her life. Now it was my mother's turn to be terrified about my life.

After the initial shock at the news, she gathered her wits about her and said that I should wait another week to be sure. If indeed I was pregnant, she was going to talk to someone and see what could be done. I was in my last year of high school, preparing furiously for the entrance exam at the university, working with several tutors, and studying all day until late into the night.

The overall shortages and poverty were rampant among all of us who did not corroborate with the party or the secret police. The thought of a baby at that point in my life made me think of suicide. I was going to have to drop out of school, forget taking the university exam, and live in a two-room apartment with my parents, freezing in the winter and following a semi starvation diet. Death seemed better. Suicides were frequent among the young, so taking my life didn't seem like such a big deal. But for the sake of my parents, I had to live, and it had to be without a baby.

The week of waiting to see whether I was pregnant or not was worse than any other week in my life to that point. Nightmares of bleeding to death from a mishandled procedure filled my days and nights, counterbalanced by fantasies of carrying around a malnourished baby without any goal in life other than standing in lines for food.

Luckily though, I started bleeding at the end of the week, just the day when my mother was getting ready to call the acquaintance doctor for the "procedure". Never had the sight of my own blood been such a source of wild joy, and never did I wait in line at the corner pharmacy to buy menstrual cotton in a happier mood. The future seemed less dark, and it even had a tiny bit of light in the distance, now that I didn't have to either commit suicide or die of septicemia from an illegal abortion. The joys of womanhood under communism were bountiful.

Fifteen years later, as I am juggling the care of my two sons by myself, my pre-tenure work, and the daily microaggressions from my "very nice" colleagues who find something wrong with my performance at every step of the way, I get accidentally pregnant. At this point in my life, there isn't room in my schedule for anything, not even for something the size of a needle or a dot, not even a minute for another activity, chore, obligation of any kind.

My daily schedule is filled with activities, chores, errands, games, and tutors to take the children to, papers to grade, and documents to peruse. I feel like an overstuffed suitcase that you can barely close. I am my own overstuffed suitcase. I visualize myself as this overstuffed suitcase whose buckles burst open one day, and it explodes right in the middle of Main Street in our very nice town, across from the cemetery where the "Generals" are all buried.

The whole town is staring at the stuff that bursts out of the suitcase, like they do at the Christmas parade, when everybody picks up the candy and the lollipops left by the side of the road by the proud parade participants: two husbands, two fathers, one for each son, one ex, the other barely present, the babysitter who tells you one day that she doesn't even believe he is the real father and you fire her on the spot, your recent divorce, lots and lots of papers, settlement papers, court orders—like you can't leave the bloody town until your older son is eighteen if you want to keep him—bankruptcy papers.

The lawyers ran you dry, and you got nasty letters from "nice" French or theater colleagues telling you off in writing, as you always seem to be doing something wrong, whenever you think you are doing a good job, an even better job than just good. They criticize you for writing and publishing too much, for drawing too many students to your classes, for not being a good colleague when you organize a theater conference on your own. They write you threatening letters of reprimand.

One such letter that you still keep as an important relic of your mistreatment starts with "how dare you?" A daunting pile of French exams and papers bleeding red with erroneous subjunctives and partitive articles is staring angrily at you in your office. You watch with envy the carefree freedom of the family of sparrows that come and go as they please from the cozy nest they have made in front of your window, right below the imposing white columns of the colonnade. You can recite French grammar rules in your dreams. You know them better than you know any of the rules of your own life and definitely better than the stupid grammar book they are forcing you to teach from. You didn't need to leave your country for this, but you did anyway. And the suitcase is the proof.

Just at this point in your life, the pregnancy stick shows the two blue lines, and you take two more minutes than usual in the bathroom to cry over the two blue lines and deplore the fact that apparently, the contraceptive suppositories didn't work. You are among the 2% that gets pregnant while using them, you are fertile like a goddamn bunny, equally fertile as you are productive at writing scholarly articles that your colleagues hate and reprimand you for.

You can't even cry for too long, sitting on the commode, staring at the pregnancy test because you hear the boys fighting over who was first on the swing. Loud noises are coming from their racket outside, a ball against a window and the sound of glass crashing. The sleep of the fucking generals in the nearby cemetery seems rather enviable too, just like the sparrows' freedom.

If only I could be a dead general, then I would sleep. A perfect conditional that would sound even better in French. And another perfect conditional is that I would rather walk the seven hundred miles to Chicago barefoot than have another baby right now. It all went down into chaos for me since I left Chicago, the city of my immigration, of my American education, of my American fucking dream, and I moved to this town here in a cradle of the Appalachians. "Such a great town to raise your children!"

Everybody says that about this town from hell whose lawyers and judges I got to know in the full glory of their sexist wickedness. I throw the pregnancy stick with its two blue lines in the trash and run outside to check on my energetic sons and the damage their squabbles might have done, and in that flight from the bathroom to the back yard I know for a fact that I am not going to have another baby, no way. I'd rather sue the pharmaceutical company for their unreliable contraceptive suppositories.

Maybe they are made by a "pro-life" asshole who intentionally diluted the contraceptive substance to get desperate working single mothers pregnant to raise more children to populate pretty small towns such as this one right here. I wouldn't put it past them and their "Jesus loves you" ideology. Let them raise my third child in the name of Jesus. In my feminist inner rant, I step over one of the children's toy trucks and almost fall on my face. I run outside and see my two boys now peacefully throwing basketball hoops in the ring that my husband attached to the red door of the garage in the back yard in one of his moments of supreme fatherly enthusiasm.

I am happy with the two angels I have, and I want to be good enough for them and survive the next year till tenure. I hold and kiss them both and tell them how much I love them in the Romanian we speak to each other, while in my head I tell myself I am going to look up the nearest Planned Parenthood clinic after I put them to bed tonight. I read to them one of the Greek myths about one of the wild metamorphoses of the gods, and the one about Perseus cutting off the Medusa head.

I always choose the right story for the right occasion. *Poor Medusa*, I think to myself, and the children feel sorry for Medusa and her severed head too. "Medusa is not so bad," says the older one.

"Yea, she is cool. I don't like it that he cut off her head. Can he glue it back, Mama?" the little one agrees. *Yeah, well, too bad she was beheaded. It's what happens to cool girls*, I think, and finish the bedtime readings with a couple of pages from *Through the Looking Glass*. We read the garden scene and the conversations Alice has with the flowers, to finish with something lighter and more whimsical and to erase the memory of the beheaded Medusa. Nothing like stories emerged from the imagination of people flying high on hallucinogenic drugs to take away the bitter taste of female immolation.

After the children go to sleep, I call my husband and leave a message on his office answering machine, the only phone he has, as he refuses to install one in his apartment because he needs his quiet there to be able to rest and meditate. I also need quiet and sleep like a parched throat needs water on a scorching day.

He calls later, and we both agree that we cannot have another child. "I can't give any more money or time than I already am," he says, and I laugh to myself at the irony, because if he were to give any less time to domestic and child-rearing obligations, he wouldn't be giving any whatsoever. And if I were to have to give any more time to anything other than sleep, I would finally enter the psychotic state that my therapist has already warned me of. She said, "Sleep deprivation reduces brain function and can lead to psychotic episodes."

You are telling me! It already feels like I am functioning on half my brain as the other half is struggling to stay awake for nineteen hours a day. Just imagine all the things I could achieve with my full brain fully awake! Only now it's not about my brain but about my uterus and the unwanted embryo produced by the tricky mischievous spermatozoa that escaped through the slushy foam of the contraceptive suppositories.

When the unproductive phone conversation with my husband is done, I look up Planned Parenthood clinics in the area. There aren't many. The closest one is seventy miles away, probably the other ones having been blown up or closed because of the "life loving" people who are also crazy about Jesus and his teachings about love. But at least there is a clinic an hour and twenty minutes away over the mountain, closer to Washington DC.

There were no clinics anywhere within ten thousand kilometers at the time my mother was of childbearing age in our native country of Romania. I'm lucky I can have a legal abortion and not die or end up with a hysterectomy from the illegal kinds of operations that my mother had had, and like my aunts, and like every woman who survived or died, whom I knew or didn't know while I was growing up in the communist regime.

The next morning, I call the clinic and set up the appointment for the exact first day of the seventh week of pregnancy which is the earliest I can have the abortion according to medical policies. I drag my nauseated body with its half-asleep half-awake-on-the-verge of-psychosis brain through the next month of work until the blessed day of the appointment mercifully arrives. Whenever I feel weak and sentimental about the growing life inside my tricky uterus, I look at my two dear sons who cling to every precious moment they have with me and I with them, and I get over my weakness fast. They are the ones who matter, and I am the one who matters too because I need me and because they need me. It's a perfect equation.

It's beautiful fall weather, and we run through the crimson leaves and roll in them after school, on the hill behind the elementary school where we go sledding in the winter. On the weekend, I make bread from scratch with the help of the children who love playing with the raw dough and stick it into each other's blonde hair. I learn a new recipe for butternut squash soup which my older son vomits after the first two spoonful.

I also want to vomit every bit of food I take a bite of, except for Gala apples and Gouda cheese. They constitute my new diet. On some nights after I put the children to bed and finish my preparations and corrections for the next day of classes, I take hot baths and swallow a few aspirins, remembering potential recipes for causing a miscarriage that I must have heard in low whispers growing up in our tiny apartment in Bucharest. Nothing happens, except more nausea. It's a stubborn embryo.

Occasionally, I fantasize about the ideal life situation in which I would have to be in order to want and be able to have another child. The father would have to live with us and equally share in everything, not just "help" on his monthly visits. He would have to take all the night and early morning diaper changes, so I could make up for the five years of sleep deprivation.

The university where I work would have to give me at least two months of legal paid maternity leave so I can rest, recover, take care of the older children, and nurse the baby. They would first have to have such a leave in place, which they don't. And even with all that, would I really want to start over? Not really.

What I really want is to have time to write, to wake up and use to full capacity my semi dormant raw brain. I want to take long vacations by the sea with my two existing and growing sons, have regular safe sex with my long-distance husband while I still can. I'm a greedy girl. A sea of melancholy washes over me that things are so messy and the balance of my sanity so fragile. That the world is so lopsided and cruel.

Before my grandmother had my mother, there had been a stillborn baby girl. For some macabre reason, my mother kept a picture of the dead baby sister in the family album she left with her sister in Romania, all dressed up in white ruffles with a white baby bonnet like a baby bride. That image of the dead sister looking like a sleeping baby bride enters my wobbly brain and painfully sits there for a little while.

Maybe this embryo here in my belly is the return of the dead baby who would have been my aunt, except that had she lived, then my mother wouldn't have been born and neither would have I. The game of "what if's" applied to ancestral lives and the wheel of cosmic occurrences messes with my mind to a degree that I get a series of blasting migraines over the next several days. I survive the migraines; I'm used to them.

Apparently, I have the migraine gene from the women on my mother's side. We are all tied by such unbreakable solidarity that we share everything from mother to daughter to daughter. I inherited the blue eyes and the unusually blonde hair for a Romanian from the same side of the family. We share migraines, blonde hair, and a fierce streak.

For a millisecond during one of my migraines, I wonder what sex this child would have been, and would it have been blonde or brunette, blue-eyed...*don't go there*, I tell myself and apply tiger balm to my throbbing aching head as a last resort.

My husband arrives from Chicago the day before the procedure, and we have a lovely family dinner that I make from scratch with fish and fresh vegetables. The children are on their best behavior, and tomorrow I am going to have an abortion. A legal one, lucky me.

In the morning, a late fall chilly, blue-eyed morning, my husband and I are on our way to the clinic, after taking the children to school and daycare. We drive in silence for an hour as the sharply contoured range of the Appalachians is lining up with unusual clarity in the distance. We pass by several trucks with bumper stickers that say, "It's a life, not a choice".

We pass three ominous metal crosses the size of the Eiffel Tower that supposedly were built in memory of the "killed babies". *They are fetuses, you morons*, I argue in my mind with the crowds of Jesus and fetus-lovers, the crosses, the Christian truckers on the road.

"It's a life not a choice"; *it's a fucking choice! How about the babies dead of starvation, the children shot in gun violence, the women killed in acts of domestic violence?* I develop an entire feminist lecture as we pass the glorious dark blue Appalachians just in the off chance that I may have to give such a lecture if ever I was to be judged for 'murder' by a jury of devoted life-loving Christians with gun collections in their living room cabinets, in the eventuality of a fascist take-over of the American government. I am prepared for everything.

The so-called clinic is more like a small set of offices like those in the dental practice in my town. Three tired 'pro-life' protesters sit in front of the building: a bearded long-haired man that looks like the Appalachian version of a Jesus Christ impersonator and two women with crazed looks as if they had been chased by wild animals and just barely escaped, holding their 'abortion is murder' signs and displaying science fiction pictures of bloody twelve-week embryos on their truck.

I look one of the women straight in the eyes and tell her, "Calm down, woman, you don't have to get an abortion if you don't want to!" She stares at me with total disbelief as if finally, only now, she found out that no "abortion-loving people" were going to kidnap her at night and force her into one of the clinics to abort her fifth embryo.

For a second, I think that maybe actually the Jesus people do teach their childbearing women that abortionists are capable of such hideous deeds as forcing life loving women to have abortions. Maybe without such teachings, these women would be proud pro-choice feminists. The thought makes me laugh, and the bearded man gets close to me as if ready to pounce. My husband gently pushes the protesters away from the door and keeps the door open for me. I see he is profoundly annoyed by the scene, and I feel great affection for him as I enter the clinic.

Some of the mad passion I had for him when we first met, with which we recklessly conceived our son, and which lately has been muffled by exhaustion, stress, a million worries and chores, lights up in my not-for-long-pregnant body and mind. I feel we are partners "in crime".

I feel no remorse, just a twinge of melancholy, while the nurse guides me into the waiting room where only women can enter. Ironically, I think this is one of the few places on earth where men are not allowed, and women have a place of their own. But it's likely that before too long these places will disappear. There is a comfortable silence in the waiting room where I am greeted by women of all colors and walks of life.

I feel reassured among them, in this sisterhood of "sinners". "You are going to be all right. It's not bad. The doctor is very nice," the young woman next to me whispers. I notice that she has a Spanish accent like my friend. Next, we are being shown a video with all the post procedure care guidelines, the risks, the potential after-effects. It sounds less scary than the list of potential risks after the kidney stone operation I had a year ago when I almost fainted from fear as I learned that anything could have happened to me, from never waking up from the general anesthetic, to having my urethra punctured and suffering of life long incontinence.

"It's all over. You did great," I hear the doctor say after fifteen minutes into the procedure. With the post-surgery instructions list, he hands me a pink round box of contraceptive pills and says, "These work better than whatever you were using before."

On my way out of the clinic, I pick up a pamphlet titled "One in Three", which refers to the statistics of women having had an abortion in their lifetimes in America. "One in four women gets raped." And every minute on the planet, a woman gives birth to a baby.

I am focused on these mind-boggling statistics trying to make some meaning out of them, and the best I can come up with is provided to me by my whimsical memory, the graffiti line I used to see everywhere on Chicago trains and bathrooms: "life's a bitch and then you die".

But also, every so often, a more optimistic person would have the kindness to counteract the hopeless slogan with a more life affirming one such as "life's a beach". Period. I used to work on the length on my vowels, the difference between the sound of 'I' or 'ea' in the words 'bitch' and 'beach'. I focus on "life's a beach" and visualize long white beaches by the turquoise immensity of a sea somewhere in the world, where I am going to take a vacation with the children and my husband the summer after I get my tenure.

Right now, my husband holds me tenderly in the parking lot of the clinic where a swift and refreshing wind is blowing. I feel suddenly relieved of the nausea that had poisoned my gut for the last seven weeks. "I'm starving, let's get Mexican food," I say.

I know he is also thinking what I am thinking, *We've been through a lot together, a miscarriage before we had our son, the birth of our son in the middle of divorces on both our sides, now an abortion.* I eat the hardiest lunch I have had in months at the Mexican restaurant nearby, and I think, *Never in my life have nachos tasted so delicious.*

I feel grateful that my abortion took place under all the appropriate and necessary lights, with no electrical shortages and blackouts, which is how my mother had the one that left her with a massacred uterus. A woman's life is full of "blessings" of some kind or another, regardless of the country she happens to be born or live in. That night all four of us slept together in the same bed, me holding the two children and my husband holding me. The night felt compact and comforting. The blood that was starting to flow out of me as expected was reassuring, a cleansing flood, and the sleep in between the three guys I loved, rather merciful.

Coming Out of the Six-Year Hangover

The spring I obtained my tenure, from a committee consisting of colleagues who had harassed me for six years just to show me they could, I tell my boss to fuck off, I quit smoking, I leave the episcopal church, and I faint on the kitchen floor in a pool of blood of my own doing, all in that order. Or so it appears, since my memory about the incident is blurry as are so many memories from that period when I only slept four hours a night.

I had reached and crossed the limits of stress and exhaustion from working myself to death in a department where they didn't seem to care much about the work I did, although they had asked for it when they hired me. The strain from the single motherhood, the cracks in my new marriage, the clash of Zoloft and Irish Bailey's cream I mix one evening when the kids are too loud, my mind too worn out and my husband too absent, cause a tiny short circuit in my brain, and poof! Before anybody can do anything about it, I am lying on the floor with a bad case of whiplash from the fall and blood squirting from cuts in one of my arms.

In the moment between holding on to the kitchen sink and falling, I remember thinking of Sylvia Plath, and saying to myself that she did it because she was overtired, not because her asshole husband wasn't there. She wanted to write poetry and was all alone with the children all day. She didn't have a moment to herself, and that would do it.

My children are puzzled when they come inside the kitchen from playing outside and see me lying on the floor, and I feel infinitely sorry that I let them down. My husband who arrives panting behind them says, "Your mother had an accident while cooking, but she will be all right!"

My older son asks, "How did she have an accident while cooking?" His question remains unanswered. The kitchen is a dangerous place for overwrought mothers. My son takes paper towels and tries to stop the blood. He runs across the street where my French new colleague and friend lives, to bring her over. She knows what to do. My little one is sitting on the floor, staring at me, guarding me, holding his red, white, and blue teddy bear, and sucking his thumb.

By the grace of my friend, I end up at the emergency room where the doctor, who also happens to be the father of my older son's best friend, stiches my cuts with meticulous care and asks lots of questions about the incident. I am petrified with shame. It's a fucking small town, you can't even slash your own wrists in anonymity. He is kind and does a great job sewing me. I start addressing myself in the second person again as my therapist had advised. She had a point. It's comforting. You distance yourself from your own fucked up self and you feel freer.

Then you must see the hospital social worker before they can release you. This is how you explain your messy state of mind to the social worker. Here is your brain, you say, drawing a large circle in the air. You have a large brain, the size of the entire little town. And here in the middle of your brain is the novel you've wanted to write for ten years but haven't had the time to do so, and it's red and swollen like a raw tumor ready to explode, begging to get out.

Here next to the novel tumor are the children you love so much but whom you are obviously letting down. They look sad and agitated. They are sick of the same soup and pasta you've cooked the tenth time in a row. They cuddle next to you at night hoping you will read to them their favorite story from the book of Greek myths, the one about Zeus transforming himself into a fly. He is the king of the universe and can change into everything he damn wants, in order to sleep with the women he lusts after.

Your head falls on the book as you doze off in the middle of your reading. Here in this other region of your brain, you gesticulate to the patient hospital social worker who is looking at you like she cares, here are the French subjunctive and the conditional and the passé compose screaming their many different forms in exasperation at all the students who won't get them and who make a mess out of the orderly ranks of these perfectly shaped grammatical forms.

They have a point to be mad, but you are doing your best with all sorts of games and fun activities. You know the French subjunctive and conditional are hard, and the students are doing their best. Everybody is doing their goddamn best, and the world is still a big fucking mess. Then you move on to the yet other side of your brain. You've got an infinitude of sides to your brain, and this is the side where your colleagues who finally voted for your tenure and a few others from across the campus are all sitting in a meeting, looking at your file and griping about it.

The social worker is confused about my use of the first and second-person alternation while telling the story. I tell her I often talk to myself in the second person, and that I'll change it to the first person only if it's easier for her to understand, I say, while thinking, *Goddamn moron, why are you a fucking social worker and you can't even get the therapeutic interchange of pronominal forms in my inner conversations with myself?*

I change the whole confession entirely to the first person to make it easier for the social worker and to think of it, I'll write my novel in the first person too. It's a good person. Whenever that may be. But back to my brain. My colleagues are all making a terrible riot inside my brain too, whoever invented colleagues anyways? The colleague who didn't talk to me for two years because he was mad that I was getting a divorce and he was losing my husband as his new buddy, goes on and on in a droning voice about the grades I give my students. They are too high, it appears.

The colleague who told me that I destroy the department because I draw too many students into my classes is complaining about me and about what a bad colleague I am while twisting and writhing in his chair like a deplorable character in a Charles Dickens novel. I think Uriah Heep. For some idiotic reason, I remember the name of the abominable character in Charles Dickens with wet sweaty hands and a continuously writhing body and unctuous speech. He is a bad man hidden behind creepy humility just like some of my southern colleagues who speak with a drawl.

And here comes in the colleague from the business school who once came into my house with his wife and started yelling and hurling cuss words at me as I was sitting on the sofa in the living room reading to my children; they are yelling and swearing because I lost two screws from the crib they had lent me when I had the baby four years ago. They are asking me to write them a check in the amount of two hundred and fifty dollars as compensation for the two screws in the crib, or they will complain to the dean of an honor violation.

They actually do just that: tell on me to the dean of the university that I lost their fucking screws, and the dean makes me pay the two hundred and fifty dollars as I feel like the criminal thief of the century on the holy grounds of the university for southern gentlemen where I work. I got screwed over two

124

screws, I think to myself and smile at my clever pun. These colleagues are making a huge riot inside my brain, filling it with a greenish poison-like bile, or maybe it's cyanide, the organic all-natural version of cyanide obtained from the health food store.

Just when the social worker who is yawning by now thinks the story of your brain is mercifully over, you go on about the judges and the lawyers in the trial that ended two years ago, but who are still sitting somewhere inside your brain, in the legislative and judicial branch of your brain, judging your mothering, your past, your present, your sex life, your morality, and deciding you owe them ten thousand dollars.

Among them is also the woman lawyer whom you hired because you thought she was going to understand and respect you better as a working mother and because she was the one who got the policeman who had killed his wife a few years before your trial, convicted of murder. Only that this valiant lawyer ended up suing you for more money and asking you if adultery was a thing in the Romanian culture.

Good thing you filed for bankruptcy the very day of the court date. It was one of the most satisfying moments of your recent years, imagining the face she must have had when she heard she was going to get zero money from you because of the merciful bankruptcy. The entire nation of Romanian vampires and adulterers felt vindicated through you that day.

And then there is the romantic branch of your enormous brain stretched to the very limit from one corner to the other pretty corner of the quaint little town where you landed six years ago, pregnant with your second son and ready to impress the entire confederacy with your knowledge of French literature and psychoanalytic theory applied to that literature.

The social worker is tired by now, yawning like mad without covering her mouth like every bloody American you see. If she thinks she's tired, she doesn't know a thing about tired until she's heard you through and through. In the romantic branch of my brain, there is my second husband who is a brilliant man and scholar of a thousand disciplines, with whom I fell madly in love seven years ago, but we got married only two years ago at an overlook at the very top of the Blue Ridge Parkway in the snow.

He does what he can, he commutes from Chicago, he can't leave his job, of course not, I am not leaving my job either, hellish as it is because I just got tenure, and I worked hard for it. We have excellent sex and excellent conversations about literature, art, and the human condition, I say to her.

At the part about the human condition, her eyes glaze over. However, my second husband isn't perfect either, who is, right? In this part of my brain, my second husband is throwing jealousy fits about my first husband. I have no idea why, maybe it's an older man thing. I wish he were more aware of what is going on in the house, more attentive with the children when he comes to visit, that he pays equal attention to both kids, not just to his flesh and blood.

I love him madly though. We dance to the music of Patsy Cline sometimes when the children are asleep, and when I had had enough coffee to keep awake the entire town of ten thousand nice people. I really want it to work this time, this household, this marriage, and this family.

I think I'm running a fever, I say, maybe I just need to sleep for a hundred years like sleeping-fucking-beauty in her pink coffin with Disney designs of flowers and butterflies all over it. I am going to wear my best red dress and red pumps when I go into that coffin for my hundred years of beauty sleep, no pink, just red. By this time, the emergency personnel are all getting fidgety and tell me that if I need anything anymore, I should call them. "Don't hesitate to call us if you need anything, honey."

I have no idea why I must call them when I'm right here and haven't finished my story yet. The social worker fills out the insurance paperwork and signs me out. She tells me I need to go into couple's therapy with my husband. Yes, right! Like that's really going to work, I say, and I also say I haven't finished my story yet.

I still have to tell her the part about my father who had a heart attack recently and my mother who is taking care of him all by herself in Chicago while teaching French like me, yes, she is also a French teacher! Like mother, like daughter. She spends the night at the hospital, sleeping on the floor next to my father's bed, and in the morning, she goes to her university to teach her classes. She writes poems in her spare time, between three and four in the morning.

My mother, for some reason, can deal with sleep deprivation better than Sylvia Plath and me. She wouldn't be caught dead lying on the kitchen floor in a pool of blood. The social worker says, "This is your mother's problem. Maybe she needs to seek help and go into therapy as well."

Yes, I get it. The social worker needs to move on to her next patient. My story is endless and so is my brain, holding the entirety of my story in it. My French friend is still waiting for me in the waiting room. She says, "ça va?" and I go, "oui, oui, ça va beaucoup mieux".

Thank God for the bit of French and the beautiful French friend. It adds some glamour to this small-town hospital. The nurses and doctors were much kinder though than many of my PhD colleagues. I'm all covered in bandages like the Romanian version of the Phantom of the fucking Opera, slightly dizzy from the pain killers for the whiplash, but it's not too bad. I'm going to sleep in tomorrow and ask my husband to take the kids to school. He owes me that much.

But no, I can't, I promised my older one I would go with him on his school field trip to some special caves or caverns near Washington DC. They are famous deep caverns apparently with stalagmites and stalactites and the works, and I can't let him down. I'll feel better in the morning, and it will be nice to take a day trip. No rest for the weary because tomorrow I start *da capo*. Now, though, I just take a chill pill as my older child has started to advise me. I just chill!

Come the first summer of my recently tenured self, I start the meticulous work of putting the scattered pieces of my own person together, bit by precious bit. Like a puzzle of a hundred pieces or more. My parents visit me in the summer as usual, and this time I ask them to take care of the children throughout the day, so I can sleep.

After I make up a fraction of the lost sleep, I feel like I am waking up from a six-year-long hangover. Latent energies are coming to life in my brain and body in disorderly waves that bring with them neglected desires, longings, ambitions. Ideas about a book on the tragic heroine and a new theory of tragedy blend with voracious sexual urges that leave my husband spent but radiant with masculine pride by the end of his summer visit.

My brain feels like my vagina and my vagina still feels like my vagina. I am driven by two insatiable organs like two hungry forest animals in search of their prey. I devour stories of tragic women, murderous women, mourning mothers, and vindictive wives from the beginnings of history. Murders, suicides, sacrificial deeds, the fierce Medea, the fiery and devious Phaedra, the pure and immolated Iphigenia.

The whimsical resilient Winnie from Beckett's *Happy Days*, my favorite female character buried in a mound of earth while singing, reminiscing, and putting on lipstick, the one who carried me through the last year of my Romanian life and through the very last minutes of my valiant and definitive escape, returns to me with a congratulatory smile and an American thumbs up like "you made it girl, how could you ever doubt it?"

I say to her, "Yes, but look at me, I'm a fucking wreck. I haven't slept properly in six years, and my brain is my vagina. I gained weight and I look like shit. My urethra was almost punctured by a goddamn stone that grew out of the minerals and garbage I put in my body with all the frozen precooked meals.

"My uterus was scraped off from an unwanted pregnancy. My arms have wound marks from a moment of temporary insanity. I can't hold one full thought for more than a minute at a time, and I have no idea what I want from life anymore."

"So what?" Winnie says. "Look at me sitting here in this fucking mound of earth for a thousand years. Do you think it's easy to be a female character in a man's play? So, write your own play, start your goddamn novel, get your fat ass to a pool or a gym, throw all the frozen meals into the garbage, make peace with both your husbands, plant a tree or a tomato plant, whatever, take your kids to the country fair. Did you know the circus was in town? It's a good circus with a ballerina on a trapeze and all. Go to the fucking circus," she says, "take your parents on a road trip. You're a big girl now, you're a tenured professor in an American university, take charge!"

Winnie has a point. I just need to get myself better organized, start exercising, plant some tomatoes so I don't have to rely on the supermarket. Write my novel, yes, write my novel, open that suitcase and see what I may find, maybe some new wisdom from Romanian ancestors, my old manuscripts, and a bit of my lost youth.

The mirror shows me a very different face than the one I remember from six years ago when I moved to this small town in the middle of the Shenandoah Valley. It's a puffy face with two new lines going from the base of the nose to the corners of my mouth that deepen when I try to smile. The eyes have a slightly crazed look like they are out of focus, and my hair is screaming for a haircut as it falls in wild strands all over my forehead like I'm the human equivalent of a poodle.

I did make it after all, yes, I did. Let's see how things go from now on. I take my children to the municipal pool and am surprised at their grown beautiful bodies, already five and nine years old. How did it all go so fast? The older one already knows how to swim, and I remember it was me who taught him that. It was me who nourished and cared for these lovely bodies, cuddled them at night, read to them the goriest and funniest fairy tales and myths, cleaned up their diarrhea and puke when they were sick, sat with them in the emergency room at two or three in the morning when they were burning up with fever from some virus they got in daycare.

I have no idea how I did all that. Some special magic force I must have inherited from my grandmothers who survived World War II bombs and famines, who survived both the Nazis and the Soviets. Maybe there was another magic streak that the Cambodian woman who lost half her family to the Khmer Rouge massacres gifted me in exchange for the English I taught her.

And maybe this was still another magic power from the homeless man with whom I sat talking for a full hour in downtown Chicago during my first year there. It must be the love of the Romanian ancestors combined with Cambodian magic, combined with the prayers of the Chicago homeless that gave me some of the strength to do it all. So, I give myself the American thumbs up and tell myself, *you made it, you are fucking superwoman.*

It's time to teach both my children some world geography now. My parents and I divide the duties and by mid-summer, both my sons can show Romania, Finland, and Chad on the globe they got for Christmas last year. They also know that Romania and Chad have the same flag colors—red, yellow, and blue—only in reverse order.

A channel of memory opens in a flicker, the colors of the flag, the national anthem about the tricolor flag that a little Romanian girl has to sing in school in a chorus led by a balding teacher of music in an outdoor school celebration. She doesn't mind the song. It's melodious and uplifting. Not everything is bad about her country. The fall leaves are swirling to the ground in the school yard. She misses her mother. That's the worst part.

My parents drive back to Chicago. We all wave tearful goodbyes to them as my mother takes off in her Toyota Corolla and my father waves back from the back seat where he always sits on the long trips. My father's face from the back window of the car is only semi sad from leaving us. He is proud of the

129

new car they have now and almost looking forward to the trip back to Chicago through the ravines and mountains of West Virginia, the blue grass rolling hills of Kentucky, the corn fields of Indiana. He is weaker after the heart attack that he survived a few months ago and might even need open heart surgery later in the summer.

My heart goes through a spasm of sadness when the car is out of sight. The goodbyes, the slow waving just like six years ago when I left Chicago, and like fifteen years ago when I left Bucharest, and all the goodbyes on the platforms of train stations, to my first love, to aunts and uncles, to parents going on summer trips to Western countries, to my great uncle come and gone all the way from the Soviet Union and back, to grandmothers and grandfathers, one long current created by hands waving goodbye through the thirty seven years of my life, from the little train station in the Carpathians, to the gritty crowded train station in Bucharest, to the bewildering airports in Rome, New York, Chicago. Final and definitive goodbyes.

And then here we are—my children and I moving our hands like tired seagulls on the front porch of our little house in a southern state of the past confederacy that still hasn't gotten over the fact that the confederacy is in the past, and they lost that war.

As the current of goodbyes crosses me, it comes to me: the heroine of my novel is a girl who leaves her country on a train. Forever. She plans to escape Romania through Yugoslavia to Italy. As she looks at the landscape of her childhood and youth rushing by her, she thinks of her lost love and everything else that she is about to lose in the monumental escape she is embarking on.

She waves goodbye to everyone and everything. This departure and her waving final farewells are the gesture that defines her character forever. Her gesture of defiance and ultimate self-inflicted heartbreak. I see her sitting by the window in the train compartment, she has no idea what lies ahead, she has torn herself from her past because she is focused only on this moment of her escape, her only chance, it's now or never, she must succeed. This is when I start writing my novel for real, at the point where I receive the wave of all the goodbyes of my life fully face on, a merciless gust of the past. I'm ready for the heartbreak of longing, yearnings, and the return.

Yes, I got just enough rest over this summer to be strong enough for a new heartbreak. I'm ready to dive into it and pull out bloody pieces of self, past and repressed fantasy and make it all into a new story with a new shape. The shape of an exquisitely broken heart, re-broken, mended, broken again wrapped up in the words of my new language, of English as a second language, the language of immigrants and refugees of all nations.

As I am coming out of my six-year long hangover, I start paying attention to politics. I make up not just for sleep and unwritten pages but huge chunks of life, memory and news that I missed. The Clinton presidency has passed by me almost unnoticed. The Monica Lewinsky scandal and Clinton's impeachment trial strike me as hypocritical at best, and I read about them mostly in the French news as I am traveling for a brief vacation with my husband in France, while my parents are taking care of the children in my Virginia house.

It's our first vacation together as a married couple or as anything. The Parisian and French sites, from Montmartre to the Loire castles, glide by us and through us in hallucinatory slides of color. We take in everything: the Gothic architecture, the medieval forts, the unctuous rivers and dreamy Normandy beaches, *velouté* soups and creamy deserts, prolonged love making in tiny provincial hotels with majestic views and jovial concierge.

We smile with the French concierge at the front-page news about the American president's disclosed sex scandal in the newspaper that lays on the table in the small dining room where we are served *café au lait* and almond croissants. Now the French like President Clinton even more than before because adultery is sexy here. As for us former adulterers, who are we to judge the president and his White House "indiscretions"? We laugh with the concierge and every other French person.

Apparently, President Mitterrand had a mistress and a child with that mistress and was doubly loved by his people for that. We feel part of an international solidarity of sinners. We are in very good company: heads of state besides characters in French novels. The word indiscretion baffles me with its fake connotation of offended secrecy, as if it were the breaking of the secret itself and not the action ensconced in the secret that is the actual "sin".

Parts of my atrophied heart open in romantic passionate outbursts towards my husband, the world, Europe, and its old-world charms that I had missed without even realizing it. It feels dizzyingly close to "home," only a short flight or a long train ride. It has been fifteen years since the day of my definitive goodbyes on a golden September day in Bucharest during communist times.

The French trains are similar to those I travelled on during my Romanian youth, only more luxurious. The street signs are written on the same dark blue ceramic square plates on the sides of buildings, only they point to rue Richelieu or rue Lecourbe. The parks have similar seesaws and green benches, colorful flower beds, and rich chestnut trees providing cool shade in the late summer days. Waves of melancholy, yearning, confusion and joyfulness sweep over me in unpredictable order.

One evening, we are having dinner in one of the outdoor cafés in Montmartre and a familiar tune played on an accordion floats by our table. I startle because the accordion music unhinges a sealed compartment in my heart like a burglar, violently, recklessly. Paris is romantic alright, with its fancy cafes and *bouquinistes* and portrait artists, but the accordion music speaks of an even more sentimental Balkan corner, an even older Europe, a messy Europe of bazaars and brooding forests, of stolen dances amidst harsh regimes, food rations, and deep potholes. *My* corner of Europe.

I am sure the accordionist is Romanian. I give him a few francs after he finishes his song, and I ask him in Romanian what part of the country he is from. My husband smiles, enchanted by my unexpected leap into my spaces of origin. The accordionist smiles, delighted and surprised to hear me speak his language. He is from near Bucharest and just arrived in France with his family to make some money in the streets.

We buy him a glass of wine; his wife comes over from the other side of Place du Tertre with an armful of roses that she is trying to sell to tourists and lovers. My husband buys me a red rose, and I talk Romanian to the couple about the present situation in Romania. I want to know how things are after the revolution.

"Now you can find everything, but people has no money to buy it," he says.

"People is leaving the country like crazy," says the wife with the roses. Wild inflation, street children getting high on glue, stray dogs everywhere, and the old Securitate turned to new government positions. I don't care. It sounds like fun.

My heart is splitting and my brain exploding. I spill my glass of wine all over my pink dress, and it looks like blood. The accordionist says it's good luck. He stands up and plays me a Romanian heartbreak tune, a drinking song, then a tragic love song with a murder of passion at the end, then a happy

132

drinking love song. The people at the other tables and cafés are looking at our table, some amused, some disdainful.

I tap my feet and shake my torso to the rhythm of the songs. I find my first post-revolution Romania in Montmartre, and it's all messy, bloody, and melodious, a shameless celebration of heartbreak and longing with wine and roses and accordion music that I didn't even use to like very much while living in Romania, but now sounds delightful, raw, and necessary. I miss everything, and I want to go back.

Turns and Returns

As soon as I'm back in America and in my small house in the Virginia town, I start planning my return to Romania for the following summer with my children. They are delighted and ask if everybody speaks Romanian in Romania. Finally, they will be able to practice the language in its country of origin and realize it's a real language and not a code I made up so we can speak whatever we want to say crazy things in front of strangers.

"Mama, even the children speak Romanian?" asks my younger one, worried he might not be able to speak his mother's native language with other Romanian children.

"Are we Romanian, Mama?" They also ask.

"You are half Romanian, half American," I say with great certainty.

"But what are you, Mama?" The question of the century! What am I?

"I'm an American citizen of Romanian origin," I answer in official language. My children can't figure it out why I am not also half and half like them.

"Are you more American or more Romanian?" By now they think this is an extremely funny exercise of interrogating their mother about who she is and what she is. "Why do you have an origin and we don't?"

"Your origin is Romanian American, you have both equally, you were born here. I am all Romanian but also American since I live here forever."

It hits me that there is a chasm between me and my children. I am practically a visitor in their country, on their continent. I have no earth and no heritage to hand down to them, only a brand of kitchen Romanian, simulacra Romanian holidays, and a few Romanian books of fairytales.

They are at home, I'm naturalized. They are natives, I am country less. Their childhood is nothing like mine was, not even in a remote vicinity of my childhood. I am light and rootless, but they are at home. How will I ever overcome that? That's why I make detailed and frantic plans for our trip next summer. I hold to some delusional hope that they will feel at home there too, that they will be contaminated by fragrances, colors, sights and gestures of my past, so we have a commonality of origins that does not consist in just our common DNA package.

I don't teach this year, and I have time to grieve, mourn, worry about everybody and everything and remember a lot. I have time to watch my children grow, improve their language skills, and to cook fancy dishes from Indian and Italian cookbooks. The girl sitting by the window on a train that is taking her out of her country forever comes to life with a vengeance. She starts growing a past, a complicated life plot with a twisted love story born on a stormy day with a rainbow on a mountain top in the Carpathians.

It's about remembering smells and views, sensations and feelings, a preferred street, a mountain alley winding through pine forests, the taste of a kiss, the stinging pain of a parting on a train station platform. The 'me' turns into 'she' and then back to 'I' on a journey of the self where the girl watching everything go by from the train window takes over the story.

Through her, I leap backwards over the years and over the colossal distances that separate us, and I let it all flood over me in waves that choke me in tears at times or send me into painful ecstasy. I stalk and corner her, I let go of her, then she comes back to me imperiously asking for attention just like my two sons.

Maybe this is my first truly content American year, and it took me fifteen to get here. Yet not so fast, because my father is getting sicker, his heart is giving up, and my mother is breaking from the effort of teaching and caring for him by herself. His open-heart surgery was successful, performed by a prestigious heart surgeon who in his spare time goes on safaris and hunts tigers.

For an entirely incomprehensible reason, my father's destiny seems to have a draw in the direction of tigers and the people who own or hunt them. He was still remembering Sandy, his former student from the CIA learning Romanian and petting her tiger when the heart surgeon talking about safari tigers came into the picture, distracting him from the ominous prospect of having his heart sliced open and one of his valves replaced with an oxen skin valve.

In between field trips to pumpkin patches and forest reserves with my children and their school mates, daily, worried phone conversations with my mother about my father's condition, the encounters with the tragic heroines of world literature who draw me into their bloody sacrificial or murderous lives, and learning how to cook Indian curries, the girl sitting on the train is persistent, stubborn and omnipresent.

She is sometimes cruel and illusive, beckoning me on dark alleys in my native Bucharest, taking me back to scary places with scary men, at other times playful and wild, drawing me into New Year's Eve dances, love scenes in secret meadows, quarrels in the snow, suspicions of betrayal. It's a wild carousel, a roller coaster where she tells me *it was like this*, and I tell her *no, it was like that, no, the color of the dress I was wearing in that first love scene was blue.* I say *no, it was rather greenish with yellow striations,* but she says *no, there was no such thing as yellow striations on any dress in the country I grew up in.* I give in and let it be the blue dress. I do what she says, I say what she says because she knows better.

This winter comes with magnificent giant snow falls like the ones I grew up seeing in the Carpathians, and everything quiets down to a deep fluffy silence. Even the children's yelps of joy in the snow are muffled and rounded up, no edges, just white fluff. I step into it to my knees, and so does the girl in the story, only a continent away, in the back yard of a provincial town in a country so far away it would take a month to get to it by ship.

I once lived there just like the girl in the story, though it seems so distant and hazy like it never even existed. Like it didn't exist, even though I recently got my birth certificate from my mother just to make sure I was born there. And on the certificate, it says such and such female infant was born on such a day in June of such year in Bucharest, the Socialist Republic of Romania, to such and such parents. Red, yellow, and blue like the Republic of Chad. These are exactly my parents' names, and of one of them is dying in America, on foreign land covered in foreign snow.

The snow of this year of my sleep recovery awakens new wild energies in my mind, body, and maternal instincts. I take the children to a nearby ski resort and teach them the basic skills on snow and ice. We start with ice skating on the round rink nestled in the Appalachians next to a formidable two-hundred-year-old hotel for the rich. We cannot afford the hotel as the price of a room is the equivalent of my entire food budget for the month, and we would have to either starve or stay for one night at the monumental hotel.

We stay at the edge of the resort in an inn owned by a Turkish man who looks like he has recently descended from the Ottoman Empire, with a turban, large black curled mustache, and a raucous voice with a deep accent. I delight in foreign accents. The foreigner the better. They overshadow my own foreignness.

The inn is filled with antique overly ornate lamps, sofas, sculpted lacquered wooden and wrought iron furniture like those from a Gothic story I once read. Like those in a house in Bucharest I once visited. I remember that the Turks are one of the ethnicities still living in Romania. Some Romanian deserts are Turkish, and some Romanian words and foods are Turkish too.

Maybe Romanians are also Turks. I am looking for connections in everything like mad, and I seem to be finding them without much difficulty because you find every country in the colossal bazaar that is America.

I recover my ice-skating skills with joy. I am gliding forwards, backwards, in pirouettes like nobody's business. I remember that my father loved to ice skate as a young boy and once he fell inside a hole in the ice in the pond underneath the ice and almost died, or he had jumped in to save someone who almost died. This happened during the war, as most of his teenage memories are from the war: moments of stolen joy or close escapes amid German or Russian tanks and American bombs.

Now he is almost dying of heart disease. I should be next to my mother and father right now in Chicago, helping them, but here I am with my children, teaching them how to skate. Who would do that if not me? Who would take care of them if not me? Where is that husband when you need him?

We move on to the ski slopes, but I can't afford a ski instructor, so I proceed to teaching them this sport too, though I'm much wobblier on my skis than on skates. This is winter wonderland, and the children take to the skiing too. We are having the time of our lives. My younger son insists on carrying his skis up and down the bunny slope himself and not using the baby lift to get him to the top. He is a tough and stubborn little blonde bundle of loveliness and teaches himself how to go up and down the slope.

I decide to take my own skis on my back as well instead of using the ski lift on the adult slope, from a mixture of fear of heights and a desire to just exercise and shed the pounds I had put on in the six years of my sleepless life. People lean over their chairs gliding above the slope to ask if I am OK. It's not clear why I appear that there might be something wrong with me, but I yell back that "yes, I'm fine, thank you"; *just going up the fucking slope*, and *mind your own fucking business* is what I mutter into my snow-covered scarf. My older son who courageously got on one of the ski lifts on his own waves at me from the air.

I look with pride at my boys, one red-faced like a blonde carrot struggling with his skis on his own, one in the air proudly holding his skis and ready to fly down the slope. I see myself at their age on a steep slope among dark brooding fir trees and tall rocky peaks carrying my heavy skis on my shoulder. They weigh a ton. My cousins and I and the ski instructor stop at a turn in the path for a break from the strenuous ski lesson. We eat our sandwiches and drink the tea from the thermos that our parents had prepared for us.

The fir tree branches are heavy with snow, and we shake the lower ones to make the snow drop on our heads to peals of laughter. The butter and salami sandwiches for which our parents must have spent an hour in line are delicious, and the tea with lemon and sugar is warming us up. I have a slight hallucination on the American slope that I am a child and my children are my buddies. We are all learning how to ski. Or is it that I am hallucinating on the Romanian slope and having a vision into the future about children I will have one day and whom I take skiing to a resort in the Appalachians next to a historic hotel where President Nixon, Frank Sinatra, and Grace Kelly once stayed?

I know that because we snuck in earlier in the day for the afternoon tea, pretending we were hotel guests. We partook of the free refreshments served by Black waiters and waitresses in uniforms and looked at the black and white pictures of celebrities that had once stayed there. All the customers were white, and all the servers were Black.

I live in the fucking southern confederacy and in places it still looks like we are on a plantation. I stared in anger at the bratty children screaming at the top of their lungs in the grandiose hallways of the hotel and had a desire to slap one of them as he knocked into me and my tea while the mother in a snowman and Santa sweater called him "sweetie, come to mommy".

I wanted to slap the mother even more. The Black waiter who was all smiles came over, cleaned the floor, and replaced the tea. I leaned over to help him wipe the tea off the glossy tiles, and he said, "That's all right, ma'am." He talked to the children, asked if they enjoyed skiing.

"We don't ski so well yet," they answered.

"Oh, you're alright," he said and gave them each a lollipop candy from one of his uniform pockets. I felt like every single one of the mothers in snowmen sweaters and the fathers in turtlenecks were from another planet and the waiters and waitresses were from my planet.

The scene rolls in my hallucination as I am exerting myself on the slope and for a second, I am sure I am on the Romanian slope hallucinating about a strange future in a rich people's resort in confederate land with women in snowmen sweaters, pictures of Frank Sinatra, and kind Black waiters serving the snowmen people.

I get hit by a snowboarder coming down the slope. I am definitely in America in my new stage of doing all the missing and yearning and idealizing every bit of Romanian past life that I haven't done in my fifteen years of immigrant life. I lose my balance and roll a few feet down the slope. My ridiculous white fake fur hat flies down the hill. My clothes are too hot. I am red, sweaty, and a hundred years old, out of sync, out of touch, and out of whack. My eyes fill with tears.

I win the clumsy refugee of the year award for sure, but my sons are waiting for me at the bottom of the slope satisfied with their skiing downhill performance. They are happy to see me and don't laugh at me, for which I'm super grateful. I am getting them all the hot chocolate and muffins and doughnuts they want at the little café at the bottom of the hill.

When we get to our hotel room with antique furniture in the Turkish inn, I have a premonition of disaster and call my mother. She doesn't answer, and I leave a message on her answering machine with the phone number of the inn. I am seized with panic, but the children are happy with their day, and they cheer me up as well.

We all fall in an afternoon slumber; the winter light is rosy and eerie at dusk. The dream of running among black fir trees and then reaching a clearing in the shape of a wild animal returns to my sleep this afternoon, from eighteen years earlier after my Romanian boyfriend left me for the mountainous landscape and its fresh air.

I am running with great difficulty through the deep snow in the clearing, because this dream has snow in it too. I am running in the shape of a wounded deer, a female deer like in the song "doe a deer a female deer".

I am bleeding from a wound in my side from a hunter that shot me but didn't shoot me properly and left me running and bleeding. I will run in the snow and the clearing until I die. If only I could get to the edge of the clearing under the pine trees, I might be alright and survive. A huge twelve-wheel truck is approaching from somewhere and in another place of the clearing is a box with the bloody body parts of a woman that was just murdered and cut to pieces by the Romanian serial killer that haunted Bucharest in the seventies and massacred nurses and waitresses.

I am desperately wondering as a doe woman if the box might not contain the body parts of my own mother. At this point in my dream, I am pulling myself out of the trap of my own subconscious and hear the shrill sound of a phone in my room. When I pick it up, my mother tells me that my father reacted badly to a test that they did on his heart called angioplasty and went into a coma, she is waiting to see what happens. The name of the procedure sounds all wrong like a science fiction machine, and the word coma strikes my brain with a heavy thud.

A blizzard has started during our slumber, and the heavy snow falling outside makes me panic. How will we get out of here and out of the Gothic Inn with the Turkish owner? The children are sleeping blissfully next to each other, their cheeks flushed from the day in the snow. A melancholy bluegrass melody is trailing from a radio in an adjoining room, and I am feeling like the wounded female deer in the dream as she is trying to get to the edge of the clearing, under the pine trees. I am wondering what the significance of the parceled woman in the box at the end of the clearing is.

We can't leave the resort or the Inn because the snowstorm is raging, and the roads are closed. I have to stay in the room by the phone for news about my father, as they are waiting to see if he comes out of his coma. The doctor had to perform resuscitation on him to get his heart going again. The heart, the heart, the heart, it's always the heart in my family. My children and I are trapped in snow land in a Gothic castle with winding creaky stairs and absurdly ornate furniture.

All the objects in the cavernous entrance hallway look like they could come to life at night and could start moving and talking and maybe telling scary stories about the previous lives of the Turkish Inn owner who, for all I know, may be the thirtieth-generation reincarnation of an Ottoman prince that had once invaded one of the Romanian provinces, got impaled by Vlad the Impaler, and is now after me looking for revenge.

In the night, I hallucinate again; not dream but hallucinate. Maybe I'm running a fever. There are strange people walking into our room with turbans and snowmen sweaters trying to take away my children. I fight them with the

Swiss knife I have from my father, or from my husband, maybe two Swiss knifes, one from each.

An old woman with a black babushka scarf on her head that looks like an old schizophrenic friend of my parents who used to read our future in the coffee dregs on the inside of the Turkish cups in our Bucharest apartment, comes into the room. There is a recurrence of Turkishness as well as of the tiger motif all around my room. There are mysterious signs everywhere and wild animals, tigers and female deer roaming around the snowy hills, because our room is now open onto the snowy fields, and we are for sure going to freeze to death in an avalanche like a student once did on a hiking trip in a country occupied by Turkish people.

The schizophrenic woman with the babushka whispers in my ear that my father has died, and I never got to see him before he died. I must have screamed or talked gibberish because my children are shaking me and asking in Romanian, "*Mama, eşti bine?*" "Mama, are you alright?"

I am sweating from the heat that I had turned on too high and from what feels like a fever and tell them that their grandfather is very sick, and we won't be able to go home tomorrow because of the snowstorm. They are ecstatic about the storm because that means no school and ask if their grandfather is going to die.

I don't answer but take a double dose of the cherry-flavored children's Tylenol for the fever and cuddle next to my boys in the king-size bed with ornate wooden posts at each corner. I say don't worry, we are going to be alright, alright, alright, everything always comes out alright in America and in snow fairy land.

What a relief, the snowstorm might just be a great boon. Everything stops and stands at a standstill. In a Romanian poem that my father loved and wrote about, the lovers are watching the snow slowly bury them in the small cabin where they are taking refuge, apocalypse by snow, and they are just alright with that. We are going to sleep late and do nothing but listen to the snow fall until the roads clear up.

My mother calls late at night mercifully waking me up from the carnage of another nightmare to say that my father has come out of his coma and is regaining consciousness. They also called the tiger-hunting heart surgeon and, together with the resident doctor, he brought my father to life. His heart is still working. My father has the strength of the tiger, for sure. I am going to sleep for the next fifteen hours if I can. I want nothing but snow and sleep.

Big Return, Big House

Am I the girl on the train looking out the window at the landscape passing by or am I the girl on the platform waving at the train rushing by? Am I the girl swimming away from the shore or am I the girl on the shore looking at the swimmer in the sea? As we are getting closer to the European trip which will conclude with the return to my native land after sixteen years, these questions haunt me incessantly.

It is the last year of the millennium, and everybody is making lists about the one hundred best this, and the ten most important that of the last century. I have no idea why I should care and why the news channels do not care more about the war going on in the Balkans than about Marlon Brando being the best actor of the century. An ironic thing it is too, that my return happens to be at a time of war, when American and UN bombs are blasting over Belgrade, practically next door to Bucharest.

There were bombs also four years ago over Belgrade that President Clinton had ordered to stop the killings of Muslim Bosnians by the Serbs. That was during my no sleep years when I was struggling to survive an abortion and tenure files, bankruptcy, kidney stones and divorce procedures, my soul trailing behind my body, or the other way around or both trailing behind everything else in the world. I wouldn't have known or cared if there were UN soldiers camping in my own backyard.

Now the bombs are meant to stop the killings of the Albanians by the Serbs. The hell with Marlon Brando and Katherine Hepburn being named the best actors in the universe by *Time* magazine. I want to know why Romania is now a fly zone for American and UN war planes on their way to send smart bombs over Belgrade.

My mother's best friend left the country to Italy via Belgrade when I was seven years old and worried about all the whispers and secrets swarming around me. Belgrade seemed like a good place when my mother's friend escaped and went to Italy from Belgrade and to America from Italy. She took trains, hitchhiked in cars, took planes, all the means of transportation to get to where I am right now, in America. Only she must be in Arizona or somewhere in the Wild West. There are Romanians in every American state and in every European country and city.

Now that I am jotting down ideas about my novel and preparing to go back to Romania, I find it intriguing that the bombs are back in the vicinity of where I'm from. I'm almost excited, and it makes me want to go back even more. But mostly I try to figure out whether I am the girl on the train or the girl on the platform, the one on the shore or the one swimming away.

This seems very important in the construction of my novel and in the future construction of my life, really. Should I live in the first person or in the third person? The second person seemed good too when I was bursting at the seams like an overstuffed suitcase and conversed with myself to invoke the last shred of sanity lost in my hopelessly entangled psyche. I must make important choices again.

So, I choose the first person, then I can't blame anyone. It's harder though to choose between the girl on the train and the girl on the platform. I want to be both. Sometimes I am looking into a compartment from the platform and see a blonde girl embracing a dark-haired man goodbye. They kiss passionately for a long minute, then he puts her suitcase up on the luggage rack, takes her in his arms again, gently pushes a strand of her hair off her forehead and runs out onto the platform just when the train is slowly starting to move. He lights a cigarette and waves at her one more time.

The thing is though that he is standing right next to me and just like him, I see the girl on the train wiping away a tear, putting her face against the window pane, and looking at him through her tears as the train catches speed and here we are: the dark-haired man and me standing next to one another on the empty platform on a late summer day when the leaves are just starting to turn russet and fly aimlessly through the air. Only that he doesn't know it because I am the one writing him.

However, and this is the weirdest thing, I now am also the girl on the train watching the mountains, forests, rivers, ravines, peasant houses, yards, sunflower fields all rush madly by her. I see it all through unstoppable tears, so everything becomes blurred. I'm not sure of my destination, but one thing I'm sure of is that I am going far away and not coming back. Not for a long time, not for another sixteen years but I don't know that when I'm riding that train and staring at the landscape through my tears. Right now, in 1983, I think it's forever.

My children have no idea about the girl on the train or on the platform, but they wonder why sometimes I stare aimlessly, mutter to myself, or am distracted more than usual, being already used to their mother's regular leaps into reverie. I say I'm excited and nervous about the trip back to Romania. It's been sixteen years, which is exactly the sum of both their ages.

At this same time when I am booking plane tickets and hotel rooms, looking into euro rail passes for France, Italy, Budapest, and Bucharest, I find a new babysitter for the children that speaks an unusual and at times incomprehensible brand of southern English and says things like "we done making a cassage with the kids", which by the looks of the art projects she proudly presents to me at my return, must mean a collage of pictures and paintings.

She takes extra care in every detail of the children's activities and safety, which reassures me greatly, and sometimes she tells fascinating stories of which I only understand parts, but which the children seem to get in their entirety, much better than me. They are the native speakers and are now adjusting their English to that of the locals whenever in contact with them. She tells the story of how she hit a deer on the road one evening. The windshield glass broke and now some of the broken glass is coming out through different parts of her body through her skin including from her behind.

She smiles wide through all the stories, and I tremble at the image of the glass shards spiking through her puffy white flesh and possibly cutting through my children's flesh when she touches or picks them up. She also tells the story of babies switched at birth in the same hospital where my younger son was born and the very same year, a switch which only now, six years later, has been discovered. It turns out the story is true as I heard it on the radio and the mother of the exchanged babies is part of the family of this important dying sheriff who owns a beautiful house two streets away from us. It also turns out it's the same house I had been staring at for several years whenever I visited my Russian friend who lives across the street from it.

It's a damn small town and everybody is connected to everybody else. It's a compact settlement just like the three-hundred-piece puzzle that my older son put together and then taped into one solid picture of adjoining houses, yards, streets, one park, and a tiny center, all tightly linked by an invisible circle within the cradle of a section of the Appalachians.

The stories of kidnapped and switched babies and of accidents with deer freeze the blood in my veins, and I start bringing more of my work at home, so I am in the house when this new babysitter watches the children in another room. Her round glossy pink face with light blue eyes that seem too light makes me nervous like many of the people around here do.

Behind their unctuous drawl and honeyed niceness, there seems to be a hidden rancor, a secret motif. Plus, she has glass shards coming out of her skin and orifices, and it sounds scary.

The raving, grieving, hair-tearing heroines I follow through the demented waves of ancient tragedy all the way to the romantic and suicidal neurosis of nineteenth century protagonists aren't helping my anxieties regarding the local babysitter and all the kidnapping possibilities that seem to be lurking around either.

Photos of children who have disappeared posted in the local grocery store are sending me into throes of panic, to which I respond by enhancing my vehement surveillance of all the babysitters, schoolteachers, day care teachers, neighbors, and even some mothers that seem to stare at my children a bit too much when I pick them up from a play date. Forget the playdates, sleepovers, and other such frivolous American child pastimes. America is a dangerous place full of children kidnappers.

In my more lucid and relaxed moments, I wonder whether the time I now have on my hands during my leave might not be detrimental after all. I don't seem to have found a balanced relation between all the parts of me and the American environment yet. The maternal, professional, social, artistic, erotic, wifely, filial parts of me seem to be more jumbled up than ever now that I have caught up on my sleep.

How did my mother manage to raise me in communist Romania with no day care available, shortages for every possible item needed for our daily existence, secret police swarming all around us, no contraception, no access to legal abortions, in a tiny apartment the size of my kitchen? And with that question swirling madly in my brain, the longing for that pathetic place of hardships and shortages where I grew up frees itself and explodes from its sixteen-year long prison of pent-up tears.

My return seems necessary for my survival right now, or I will entirely lose myself in the mire of American activities, overstuffed grocery lanes, play dates and plastic niceties. The girl on the train watching the landscape pass by is stuck in a fold of my imagination and she desperately needs me to free her.

It helps that my husband is equally excited about our trip and is learning Romanian under my guidance while I am learning Homeric Greek under his guidance, so I can read the Greek heroine texts in the original. It's a sexy exchange in which we recover our tenderness for one another. He grounds me in the part of America that I like and that fulfills my refugee soul, its gritty romanticism and irreverence, intellectual rebelliousness, the rush of the endless expanses of land, horizon, highways, the idiomatic expressions, the pies. It's the end of April and the dogwoods are madly in bloom in the Shenandoah valley, the surrounding mountains laced with red buds at their magenta peak.

The babysitter with the scary stories and bizarre vocabulary, glass shards coming out of her skin, arrives one afternoon a bit earlier than the established time with a wide smile on her face. "The sheriff died, and the house is on sale," she blurts. I know what house she means, the one with the wide front porch ornate with delicate pillars, a red door and green chimneys, the house I have been staring at on each visit to my Russian friend's house across the same street, while her daughter and my younger son would play refugee camp on the front lawn.

Whenever I stayed over until late in the evening, the lights would be on and the house across with the large bay windows, the elegant façade, and delicate posts framing the enormous porch would appear magical and unattainable. A dream house! My Russian friend and her husband would tell me as we all admired the house from her side of the street, "It belongs to a rich sheriff, it must be crazy expensive, unaffordable."

The babysitter seems quite excited about the sheriff's death, and it takes me a few minutes to make all the connections: that she is remotely related to the family, that she has heard me talk about the house and about how much I admired it. "Them children of the sheriff is looking to sell the house right fast," she says, "they don't want to post it with an agent, don't want to pay no commission."

She is excited for me and the possibility that I might have a shot at the house. "I'm sure I can't afford it, Laura," I say, uttering her name for the first time since she's been babysitting this year.

"Oh ma'am, the sheriff's kids are right eager to get the money fast on their daddy's properties. Why don't you just go and talk to the woman who's been caring for the sheriff and see how much they want for it. Say I told you to do that. She is mean, and the kids hate her, but she is the executor of his estate and done taken care of the old man until he's dawg gone dead."

Suddenly, Laura doesn't seem like the babysitter from the dark side, and her light blue eyes and round face are alright. I cringe at my own hypocrisy and prejudices of the past couple of months towards this local girl trying to please me with the art projects and 'cassages' she has been making with the children, suffering the after-effects of a bad accident and now revealing to me before anybody else she might know who may be interested in the house, the secret path towards obtaining it.

"Just make an offer and see what she says. If I was you, I'd go right fast before anybody finds out about the house." I embrace her and she blushes to her ears. It is through my children's babysitter Laura that the shield of judgment and apprehension I've held between myself and a side of America that she is part of, shatters to smithereens to my own shame and relief. My educated PhD colleagues who have put me through a slow burning hell for six years aren't one iota better than this girl trying to finish nursing school at the community college and doing her damnedest to entertain my kids with projects and fun activities.

I've had sixteen years of American life, have obtained a PhD, a tenured job, become a mother of two, and I understand so little of the country I'm a citizen of. I've wrapped myself up in my European refugee superiority and indulged in my foreignness out of fear and self-preservation. It's time for yet another page in my refugee saga: the page of breaking the southern dialect code and owning the old sheriff's estate. Not to mention the part about self-reflectiveness and tolerance.

The next day, I wake up determined to knock on the door to the sheriff's house while the children are in school. I jiggle the knocker on the red door and stand waiting on the wide porch for a long time. A porch swing is moving imperceptibly from the spring morning gusts on one side. A wicker rocking chair is gaping open at the other end of the porch waiting to be rocked. There is a flair of times long gone quivering about the house. I knock one last time and turn around to leave when the front door opens abruptly, and a short woman looking a hundred years old appears in the doorway, smoking her cigarette.

I peek inside the house and am stunned at the curving ornate banister of the staircase leading to the first floor and mostly by the long hallway that opens in a straight line towards the very last room of the house in the back, a deep perspective towards one room after another, a chandelier sparkling timidly at the other end of the hallway, a wide room with curved bay windows on the side next to the staircase.

I have entered a Dutch painting, a Victorian abode, with detailed woodwork, layered perspectives, and an overpowering cigarette stench. I take it all in within the first couple of seconds as I say, "Hello Ma'am, Laura said I could stop by and see about the house. She told me it's for sale."

The woman says quickly in a clear voice that sharply contradicts the intricate web of wrinkles on her tiny face, "It's not for sale yet, we haven't advertised it anywhere. The sheriff's children have to decide which properties to sell. They said they want to sell this one first, but I don't know, because they keep arguing among themselves." She puffs from her cigarette deeply and then crushes it in the ashtray she is carrying with her. "But you are free to look inside if you want."

Of course, I want to. There is nothing else I want more in this moment than to walk throughout this house. She leads me in and shows me one spacious room after another, two symmetrical rooms with deep bay windows letting in the morning spring sun through gauzy curtains blackened by smoke. I don't care about the smoky curtains or the peeling walls, I don't care about the ugly linoleum in the two bathrooms, the even uglier linoleum in the large kitchen with a view of an immense back yard and a majestic oak tree ruling over it, a couple of apple trees bursting in pink and white blooms, a magnolia tree with luscious white flowers and budding maples around the edges of the yard.

I ask, "Does the yard belong to the house?"

"It does indeed, all two acres of it." She lights another cigarette. "The sheriff's wish was that the house goes to someone who ain't gonna sell the land."

The word land circulates through my excited brain and opens onto memories of stories of land and orchards and elegant houses once owned by my grandparents before the Russians and the communists took them. It's a compact and steady word that comforts my agitated soul. "No worry there," I say breathlessly. "Why would I sell such a beautiful piece of land and the gorgeous oak tree?"

I already see myself having a picnic with my entire family, children, husband, parents right under the shade of the proud oak tree on a balmy summer afternoon, our lives harmoniously balanced once and for all. After stormy seas, I land on a benevolent shore.

We go back into the house, and she shows me a second living room with bay windows turned guest room. This was the sheriff's bedroom where he died. "Right here was his hospital bed," she points to the space in the nook of the rounded bay windows. "I took care of him until the last minute," she says lighting the umpteenth cigarette while a delicate tear is making its way down the labyrinthine path of her wrinkles.

I realize she was the sheriff's lover, partner, caretaker. "The kids all hate me, but I was the one caring for him, and that's why he made me the executor of his estate. The family has owned this estate since the war, 1943, I think."

The heavy Victorian furniture cluttered in every corner of each room gives off a somber air and a musty smell to the entire house, a smell of lives lived and gone, children running up and down the winding stairs, grandparents dozing off by one of no less than eight fireplaces, one in each room downstairs and upstairs. I think she must be referring to the house and the land when she mentions "the estate".

I had always thought estates must have forests and oil fields on them for some reason, some awkward reminiscence from the Dallas soap opera. The world is a never-ending field of surprises, large and small, particularly when one is a constant and a stubborn refugee, because once a refugee, always a bloody refugee, at times a hundred years old heavy with too many experiences and memories and at other times reduced to the infantile stage of a child learning the alphabet. Nobody in generations in my family had ever owned an estate and I might just be the one to do it.

I ask about the price, and that she has no idea of. "If you are really interested, just make an offer, and I'll see what the children say," she tells me as we are now standing by the front door, and I am getting ready to leave. "They want to sell it without an agent, so they don't pay commission."

I am ashamed to ask, "how do I make an offer?" so she doesn't think I'm gullible and can be easily persuaded to pay some outrageous price. So, I say, "I will consult with my husband"—I need to mention husband as around here, women are taken more seriously if they refer to a husband for every decision— "and get right back to you."

That seems too vague I think, and I want to own this house with sudden desperation despite its rotting gutters, peeling walls, disgustingly old greenish stove, crummy linoleum, that can all be changed. But the bay windows, the pine floors, the eight fireplaces with ornate wood carvings, the two acres of land with the majestic oak tree in the middle, that cannot be replicated. "I'll call you and make an offer in a couple of days," I say.

"If you want to make an offer, just write it down in a letter," she says, clarifying my confusion about how to make an offer.

The following day I go on a school field trip with my older son to the house of the famous Thomas Jefferson, a creamy luscious mansion with a million and one gadgets that the founding father had created, and lots of tiny stone cubicles the size of dog houses where the slaves lived next to the abundant gardens. The woman guide goes on and on about the Black young girls who served in the house and did all the weaving, cooking, house chores.

She doesn't say "slaves" but makes it sound like these young girls were having the time of their lives cooking and weaving for their master and then going to sleep in the dog houses on the property, on the magnificent estate. I stop her from her droning high-pitched platitudes and ask, "Weren't these girls slaves, or what were they?"

The tour group stops to stare at me. All the children are curious about what the lady with an accent has to say. The woman guide mutters some falsity, and my son blushes to his ears. I get fidgety about the word estate and remember the sheriff's house. I don't want to lose it. I don't want someone else to snatch that house from me. I run to the public phone at the entrance of the Monticello estate after I say to the guide, "You need to tell the truth about the slaves. He was a slave master and that Sally Hemings' story, yikes, she was a slave girl, for Christ's sake"; and then I say to my son in Romanian, "Don't worry, I need to make a phone call, I'll be right back, *da bine*, OK?"

"Yes, alright?"

I call the sheriff's house. When the cavernous voice answers, I say breathlessly, "I'm going to buy the house, I'll make the offer tonight when I get home. Please don't tell anyone about it, that the house is for sale, I mean!" It feels like a mafia movie. I'll make the offer she can't refuse.

I must get the money for the down payment first. Forget consulting with my husband! He doesn't live with us anyways, so it will be my house, my estate. The cavernous voice says, "Just write the letter with the offer and bring it by."

On the way back home on the school bus, I go on and on to my son about how the schools and the museum guides need to be honest about the slavery thing. I tell him I am going to buy the house across from my friend's house. "You know, the sheriff's house, the one with the columns? It has a huge yard in the back. You and your brother will have so much yard to play in."

"Yes Mama, but do you have the money for the house?" Good question, my son is more practical than I am. I have to get the money somehow, that's all. *I'll rob the local bank*, I joke to myself.

I should get some money from the house we are living in right now, which I bought for eighty thousand dollars from the woman who was renting it to me last year, because everybody says: "you have to build equity", which I have no idea what it means. I am also embarrassed to ask.

I think jokingly it must have to do with being equitable and just, which I know I'm doing my best to be, though I have no idea why they are saying that to me, as if because I'm a refugee, I might not be equitable or what? It must be a technical term about house buying, and I realize it would be a good idea to use the Webster dictionary occasionally, the language teacher that I am. Now that I'm on leave, I can work on enriching my practical English vocabulary further as well.

As I see a four-wheel truck with a sticker of the confederate flag on its rear, it strikes me that I'm going to buy an estate in the land of the confederacy, where they had tobacco plantations with slaves on them around here like the one of the famous founding father whose house we just visited. The famous Scarlett O'Hara's line about the land, "Tara, Tara, I'll never be hungry again" from *Gone with the Wind* pops in my head on the bumpy school bus ride back to our house in the small town where I have lived already for six full years.

That book's falsity about the conditions of the slaves strikes me in its full enormity. Still, it's not like I'm buying a plantation with slaves on it, I tell myself trying to calm the unease I feel at buying an estate in this land of the civil war, the generals, blah, blah. The first president of the university where I get my paycheck from was a confederate general. It is what it is.

Everywhere you look, the world is contaminated by some awful history. It is where I am living now and got tenure and my children are growing, so I might as well live on a goddamn gorgeous estate. My ancestors were thrown out of their houses and estates by communist pigs and made to live in tiny one-room apartments with shared bathrooms.

I have to vindicate the honor of my ancestors enslaved by the communist criminals as my father likes to call them. He will be so proud to see me living on the beautiful estate with the big oak tree. For sure it will remind him of the house with the orchards that was ripped apart by Russian soldiers at the end of the war.

I rush to the typewriter when I get home. It's the year 1999 and people still use typewriters. I write a letter of offer to buy the house for the sum of…I have no idea what to write, so I calculate that since I bought this cute small house with borrowed money through my university mortgage program for eighty thousand dollars and the whole property of the sheriff is about five times the size of this one, not counting the land, but it's in a mess of a shape, with peeling walls, rotten linoleum, rust filled leaking gutters and roof, I write down the sum of one hundred thousand fifty-seven dollars, almost twice the price of my house but not quite.

The next day I go back to the house and hand the woman executrix of the estate and former lover of the big sheriff my letter. She says she'll show it to one of the children, the oldest son, Billy. She mentions the son's lawyer and it turns out it's also my lawyer, the last lawyer I had in my divorce, the nice and honest one who advised me to file for bankruptcy to get out of paying more thousands to the woman lawyer from hell.

After I drop the letter, I rush to my lawyer's office and I say, "I really want to buy this house of the sheriff whose son you are representing. Help me out. What more do I need to do to get this property estate?" It turns out there is conflict of interest, but he'll think of a way to go about it. "Please do, please do," I repeat, "we need to hurry so nobody gets to it before me."

The former battle instincts from the days of standing in line for every bit of food or household item where people sometimes got into fistfights for messing with one's place in line, surges its ugly head like the black snake I decapitated with my garden hoe a few years ago, to my children's horror and awe. I'm first in line for this southern estate, damn it! The lawyer smiles, tells me not to worry, compliments my red dress, and says that everything is going to be alright.

The house negotiations and the preparations for the upcoming trip to Romania are going on at the same time, like two opposing roads. Passports for the children, hotels in southwestern France, then in southern France and northern Italy, and then more trains all the way to my birthplace. I want to get back on land since I left on air. I'm crafting it all like a novel. My glorious return with children, husband, a university professor's job, and American clothes, must be exquisite.

The girl on the train has been stuck in that deep fold of my imagination for weeks now, begging me to get back to her and find the direction of her journey. I'm prepared for my big return but also fiercely eager to set deep roots in southern land of former sheriff. I'm dividing myself across continents and ripping myself apart again, one side to the east, one to the west. I'm like the dragoness from the Romanian fairy tale who was first chopped to pieces and then put back together with the help of the water of life, and apparently, she emerged from that experience even stronger.

By the time we all leave for our big European adventure, I have put my little house on the market, have drafted a contract for the purchase of the sheriff's house with my lawyer, and have given him power of attorney to close the deal in my absence. Two homes, two continents, going after old roots, growing new ones, a messy rainbow across the Atlantic! My children are more excited about the trip than about the house.

They say it's too old, and I say, "Yes but the yard is stupendous." It has two acres of running and playing space. I show it to them from the back of the field. "Look, see how big it is and look at the beautiful big oak? We might even plant an orchard one day!"

"The yard we have right now is nice, Mama," they say, "and what's going to happen to the swing in the back? Are we going to leave it here? Why do we have to move?"

My younger son who at six is still fiercely sucking his thumb starts crying over the swing and the arbor vitae in the front where he and his brother have built a treehouse, while the older one is all gloomy and says he doesn't want to move.

154

"You are each going to have your own room and be able to invite friends overnight, and there will be lots of trees to hang the swing on. I wish I had these problems when I was your age." I go on and on about how lucky they are to even live in a house at all, and how I lived in a 'matchbox' apartment with my parents throughout my entire childhood.

Their eyes glaze over at the story of my childhood misery, and the older one says, "Yes, Mama, but we are fine with the small house, and you are the one who wants to move to the big house, not us."

I am stunned at his logic, but I end up imposing my own illogical will on them, and I say, "Well, it's too bad. You are going to have a big old house whether you like it or not. Maybe I want a big old house alright!"

I leave everything in the care of my lawyer, the sale of one house and the purchase of another. One depends on the other. And we are off to the old world, my children's first travel abroad, each with their own backpack, no suitcases.

Our travel through the immensity of space at thirty thousand feet above the North American continent and the Atlantic Ocean is equally a travel in time for me. I am taking the journey back full circle to the destination of the minuscule place of my birth, barely visible on the airplane television map, bunched up with Warsaw, Budapest, and other European capitals, almost insignificant, the place I thought I might never return to.

My suitcase is carrying gifts for the family I left sixteen years ago and no short story collections, but next to me on each side my second American husband and American children each sleeping, snoring, mouths wide open. A new me, the girl on the plane, the girl on the train, which one am I?

I travel in time to the point on the Black Sea beach where I met Zoila Valdivieso in her brightly colored clothes and scarves and to the point in her hotel room the afternoon when she said: "if you ever want to come to America, I will help you", then giggled over the voice of Nicolae Ceausescu on the television set. I didn't want to go to America then but in the end, America chose me.

If I had known then what I know now, would I still go through everything I have been through? Who cares! For here I am on this Air France flight trying to figure out what distinguishes a refugee person from a non-refugee person, someone who ran away from their birthplace to a different corner of the world for safety, freedom, a loaf of bread, whatever, from someone who has grown up and lived their entire lives in the same place where they were born.

My kids interrupt my philosophical musings as they wake up briefly, kick each other, and call each other retards as they fight for more sleeping space in the small airplane seats, to which I respond by reprimanding them in Romanian, to which they respond back in Romanian saying, "*nu fac nimic*"— "I'm not doing anything"—which makes the flight attendant passing by and several of our airplane neighbors gasp in indignation.

The Romanian word for doing "fac" sounds exactly like the American versatile "fuck". *Such pretty young children cussing in the worst way, what bad upbringing*, I hear the thought circulating in the dry air of the airplane. I want to tell them all to fuck off. These are bilingual kids on their way to being trilingual. That's right, they are the kids of a refugee and speaking another language, do you have anything against that?

My husband wakes up and repeats after the kids "*nu fac nimic*", because he is learning Romanian and repeats almost everything we say. I feel tremendous love for him right now as he repeats the children's Romanian words. *Here everybody, look, this is my American handsome husband, tall, hazel eyes, dark graying hair, sure a lot older than me but so what, aren't I a lucky girl!* The people around us look disgusted, just as well. *How many languages do you speak?* I want to ask. We change seats, me in the middle and a child on each side, and I go back to musing over the differences between a refugee and a non-refugee.

I give myself a multiple-choice exam on this fundamental question with the cautionary note that in the past, I had flunked the GRE exam for graduate school and was accepted solely on the merit of my personal statement and the transcripts of a year and a half of American college, that I had barely passed the GED exam which I had to take in order for my college diploma to be released since I had left Romania with no high school diploma, and couldn't get one without the other.

Thank God and my Romanian English teachers that I had passed the TOEFL English proficiency exam with the grade for native English speakers, or I would have ended up as a non-US citizen with no college diploma, not to mention without a PhD, a bum in the streets instead of the associate professor of French that I am.

To think that so much depends on so little, filling out the wrong or the right bubbles in a multiple-choice test! Multiple choice exams are definitely not my forte, but I am really tempted to try the refugee non-refugee one since I can get no sleep squished as I am between the kids and my snoring husband.

A refugee is someone who: a) speaks with an accent; b) is divided between two languages and cultures; c) ran away from a bad country and moved to a better one; d) is poor and wants to be rich; e) has no home; f) leads a nomadic lifestyle and is sexually promiscuous; g) has two homes; h) cannot go home again; i) is a con artist.

I stare at the list that I wrote on the back of my boarding pass and smile at how ingeniously I combined bogus answers with true answers to confuse the student, meaning myself. I can only choose one, and although there is something to be said about the truthfulness of almost each one of them, I am drawn to the last one: is a con artist.

I know there is something more to being a refugee than just the cliché lines about searching for a better life, running away from oppression, the American dream, being uprooted, living between cultures blah, blah, blah…But that's not all and not the very bottom line of what distinguishes a refugee from a non-refugee. There is something else, even more mysterious.

A refugee is a con artist, because you are no one in the new country, a non-entity, and then you have to choose what and who you want to be. Then you must stick with it if you are to make it, play the game, smile, pretend you know the rules even when you have no idea what the fuck is going on, while deep inside, you try desperately to keep a shred of who you once were in the original place where everybody knew you and saw you grow up, as opposed to here where there are no witnesses to your history.

As you learn the con artist thing, that shred of your deepest core becomes thinner and thinner, and you almost become the one everybody thinks you are in the new country, but not quite. They still recognize you by the accent, by a mannerism or a badly used idiomatic expression. That's where they get you, at the idiomatic expressions. It's like being on a witness relocation program: you start over, zip up the bag that was you, and throw it in the river or in the ocean like a corpse you are trying to get rid of.

Sometimes you are lucky and they never find the body, but other times the body washes ashore, and somebody recognizes something about the old you because maybe they are from the same bloody place you came from and they are better con artists than you are, or they saw you throwing a body over board when you left your guard down, your smiles turned to grimaces, and they report you, because there is a secret police hidden in almost everybody that walks down the street. And then it's all over.

You're done, you can't go back, and you can't stay where you are, you have to jump ship and go after the corpse you threw overboard, after the old you that is dead and rotting on some distant shore anyways.

By the time we arrive at Charles de Gaulle airport, I feel like a criminal on the run from the intensity of the multiple-choice self-examinations I have been subjecting myself to. Lack of sleep always does a number on me, but the children are relatively rested and excited they landed in Paris, their backpacks on and ready to go. My husband is smiling lovingly because he remembers the previous summer when just the two of us came to Paris for our first vacation ever. The journey I've been preparing for almost a year is just about to start, so I'd better make the most of it.

The two weeks of travel through France starting from Paris; passing through Bordeaux; the beaches and dunes on the southwest shores and the prehistoric caves with the first human drawing and sculptures; Provence and the city of Avignon with its wild theater festival drumming its boisterous spectacles all day and all night; the three-day train journey from Avignon, passing through Venice, changing trains towards Bucharest via Budapest; the two weeks on native soil recovering bits and pieces of my childhood and youth after sixteen years, have grafted themselves in my brain as a mad carousel of disjointed images and experiences seen and lived through curtains of tears, hysterical laughter, too much French wine, too much Romanian sour cherry brandy, too many pastries, old and new photographs, too many medieval forts.

It was all a mad blur of emotion color taste from which only a few scenes stick prominently in my mind. The children moved through Paris with the confidence of Westerners taking in sights and foods with curiosity and glee. An afternoon walk through the Jardins du Luxembourg watching the Parisian couples and children. A picture of my boys floating a toy boat on the pond in the middle of the gardens, focused on making it go, "Mama, all the French children speak French in France!"

Another picture of me and the children standing at the top of the Eiffel Tower against a fierce magenta and orange sunset, and afterwards a lunch at Café du Grand Zinc where my younger son discovered the delight of French onion soup, which the waiter took away before he had a chance to finish and after which he sobbed deliriously for fifteen minutes to the great distress of the entire staff of the restaurant.

The day we went to the Louvre was also the day I got robbed on the metro by a group of young men just as I stepped inside the train. The French police were charming and looked like movie stars. They complimented my French. I said, "Merci, j'enseigne le français"—"Thank you, I teach French." They complimented the children on their good looks and good behavior. They stared at my husband because he was American and older, and they didn't compliment him on anything.

They gave me the proper paperwork to recuperate my American Express checks while also calling me 'très jolie', which for a second made my head spin and my cheeks blush. Oh, those old-world delicious flirtations! At the Louvre, I made us all pass ahead of a line of two hundred people because I burst into sobs about having been robbed and the guards melted at my tears and the beautiful children.

An almost mystical image remains from our incursions inside the prehistoric caves, the sight of a delicate drawing of two animals that looked like the ancestors of deer, in faded red and black contours, kissing each other tongue to tongue, our group of four standing right underneath the lowering curve of the cave ceiling. A shiver, a ripple of the breath of all humanity reaching us from thirty thousand years ago! "No traces of violence are to be found in any of the paintings," the guide tells us. Inside the coolness of the cave, there is a fluttering of our souls in unison with one another, origins, the basics, oh and yes, Europe as the cradle of civilization. "Here, children, see your mother's continent, the first artworks by the first people!"

As we move on towards the south of France, closer to my place of origins, my senses are more alert and agitated. One day the children climb up an enormous sand dune that descends onto an endless expanse of golden beach by the Atlantic with topless women laying in the sun—the children rolling onto the beach in the shifting light in the distance almost like a hallucination.

I call my aunt in Romania from southern France to let her know we will be arriving at such and such a time in the Brasov station. "Yes, everything's fine, can't wait to see you, we are taking the train to Italy to Budapest to Brasov, crazy yes, we have sleeper compartments, see you very soon."

The night when we cross from southern France to northern Italy in the sleeper car is illuminated by a mad moon to make all lovers go crazy and all the wolves howl. As luck would have it, a French couple in the top row of bunk beds of the compartment must have been touched precisely by the lunar madness to the point of engaging in sexual activities and moaning right above my children's heads.

I yell at them in French to stop whatever they are doing. "Il y a des enfants ici!"—"There are children here"; and they go "ah, bof, pas grande chose"— "it's OK, no big deal." I pull down the blinds to cover the moon, and the children giggle like mad.

Memories of moonlit nights with my Romanian lover in the Carpathians flood my conscience. I doze off to the rhythm of the train wheels chugging like a monotonous lullaby. The train pulls into the Venice station at dawn, and the sound of Italian spoken on the loudspeakers and by the conductor passing through to let us know it's the end of the line taps on my memory, triggers images of my three Italian months in Rome, freshly escaped, hungry, greedy for adventure, at the edge of the big bad unknown, the uncertain future.

It's all about triggers now, as it gets closer and closer. I am the incarnation of the girl on the plane who escaped sixteen years ago. I am walking backwards through time, back to the very beginning of my refugee career, the con artist career. I wonder, have I done a good enough job? Have I made her proud, the girl on the plane, the girl on the train?

Venice lays at our feet lazy, stretching in the morning light, her reflection dancing in the waves of the Adriatic. We have one day and a night here, and then it's the final stretch. The day passes in a daze, in slow motion with images reflected in shards of colorful Venetian glass: the view of the canals from the hotel window in the early sun, such melancholy beauty like a dying princess.

The children are too tired. They don't really care about the melancholy beauty of Venice at this point. They just want to sleep. There is a Polaroid picture taken by one of the kids that morning of my husband and me standing in front of the window of the hotel with the view of Venice and its main canal in the background.

My husband is holding me next to him, tall, scrawny, his Clint Eastwood-ish face smiling towards me and his arm tightly around my shoulder while I look straight at the camera with a strained smile, tanned from the trip, my gaze touched by a shadow of more sadness to come, more separations after new reunions and encounters. He seems both familiar and a stranger, and my Provençal yellow swirling skirt is too much, too poufy, too yellow. There is a glowing beautiful sadness in the mismatch, and the Venetian steeples look too ornate to be real.

The few hours on the beach at Lido where I swim far away in the Adriatic while my husband and children are waving frantically at me from the shore to come back, end in a quarrel. I say, "it's a beautiful beach", but he says he's seen more beautiful beaches. "Fine, great, who cares, go to the more beautiful beaches, I'm staying here with the children."

Love is always a strain, marriage an even bigger strain. *Maybe you were not made for it,* I tell myself. Two children, two marriages, a professor husband, decades older than you who cares more about one of the kids than about the other. That's the family you are bringing back after sixteen years. What is everybody going to say and think?

You are going back where they know who you are, they know all the layers behind the con artist smiles, they know you since you were one day old. Who cares! I'm American now, and that's my package, that's the package I'm bringing back, alright, who said it was going to be perfect!

For the last leg of the journey back, we change trains again, to take the express international with sleeper wagons from Budapest to Bucharest, late at night with the arrival in Brasov the next morning. The Budapest station is crowded, and we spend the half an hour layover standing on the platform. The night is warm and slightly humid, and the moon at its complete orange fullness.

The shift from Western to Eastern Europe is obvious, exotic for my American husband and children, deeply familiar for me: Hungarian Gypsies gathered in bunches with large round sacks on their backs, women in flowery swirling skirts, men with straw hats and children running around. They are the only passengers not dropping with tiredness. The air smells of familiar trees in bloom, maybe elderberries or mulberries.

Everything is dustier and raw, the edges of the Balkans, and it all starts rubbing on my soul. An announcement in Hungarian on the loudspeakers and our train is shining its sharp headlights. In another minute it pulls into the station with a long screech. My reality shifts violently into the past.

A little girl on the train platform late at night with her aunt and uncle, in the next country down the road, saying goodbye to her parents who are waving at her from the train steps. A young woman sitting in the train compartment by the window years later, when she is the one saying goodbye, she is the one leaving and waving. The moon is wicked orange and full, an old song is trailing somewhere. The air smells of heartbreak, raw and definitive.

It's always the same girl, me and not me. She is going away, and I am returning. We are about to meet each other for one quick second in a flash as our trains pass by each other in the night at the edges of the Balkans. She is the girl I always see when I think back to my departure sixteen years ago, not me at the airport, but the girl sitting on the train by the window. She is my true heroine, the one who has stolen my heartbreak and my adventure.

This time our sleeper compartment is much nicer, just for the four of us, no sex-crazed French couple, fresh bedsheets and all. My parents left for Vienna in such a sleeper car once, in the other direction, forever, to meet me in Rome, but that was long ago, in another historical time. They had to take a sleeper car because those were the last tickets available that they purchased the day before the trip. They were on the run, trying to get out as fast as possible, and they had just enough money for sleeper tickets to Vienna. I plunge into a deep sleep in the lower bunk bed and I don't pull the blinds down, but let the moon splash its shameless light all over the windowpanes.

The next minute it's dawn. I'm fully awake, and I know I am on native land. I don't know why I know it, but I do, the way the fields stretch out in the sunrise, the shapes of the shabby houses, a crooked fence, a woman coming out with a babushka scarf on her head to look at the train passing. All the molecules in my body are sharply awake in this ritual of recognition. My soul shifts into its nook as if it has been off kilter, slightly out of its joints for all the sixteen years.

After that, it's all a blur of fractured motions, a derangement of the senses between memory and a familiar yet unfamiliar present. The border police ask to see our passports. My hair is on ends as I see the border police of sixteen years ago and I startle with a dread I had forgotten. It's all part of the ritual. You wanted it like you wanted water and nourishment, like your life depended on it, you crazy masochistic woman! Other normal people don't bother putting themselves through the agony of return. They are pleased with their good American lives and stay put in their nice American houses or go to Disney Land on vacation with their kids.

I yell at the border policeman who asks some question about my luggage. I know how they rummage luggage; I've seen it and lived it before. "You are all together?" he asks.

"No, we are strangers, but just thought we'd share a sleeper compartment. I got these kids along the way, when someone dropped them in my lap somewhere in Budapest." It flows out of me in Romanian rivulets of sarcasm. The customs police smiles, checks everybody's faces against the passport pictures, returns them all to me.

I'm the queen of American passports, a whole family of them. He tips the edge of his cap, thanks us, and wishes us a good trip. Don't you feel like a fool just now, Miss American Queen? Things have changed, remember, they shot Ceausescu on CNN ten years ago? Yea well, how am I supposed to know? It wasn't like that when I left. He's probably old secret police turned nice border police.

Splintered scenes have remained after the border control passed, arranged in no particular order. There is a photograph that my husband had the great presence of mind to take as I got off on the platform of the Brasov train station and met my family. I had waited standing in the train corridor for thirty full minutes staring at my landscape and thinking that though so familiar, I had never entered the city of my childhood, of glorious vacations and great love, from that direction, coming from the north of the country instead of from Bucharest, from the south.

When the train stopped, I almost fainted at the sound of the tune played on the loudspeakers before the spoken announcement, and my children had to help me get back up. Other passengers were returning too, and they seemed just fine, while my body was going through an emotional tsunami. Maybe I loved my country more than I had ever imagined, and the wound left by my brutal uprooting was forever gaping open.

In the photograph that my husband took, my cousin and I are standing in front of each other ready to embrace. Our faces are scrunched by impending tears, while my two sons with their backpacks neatly set on their backs are looking up at us with immense curiosity as if they were witnessing a major historical event, or the winning of the World Cup by their favorite team.

There is immense sadness and immense comedy amalgamated in that photograph: the years that had passed without me, the chasm of time and memory between youth and mature adulthood all frozen in one moment of devastating recognition mixed with the curiosity of the children caught in an unknown universe and witnessing the emotional meltdown of their mother from the distance of their foreignness, like a show.

One scene towers above all the others during the two tumultuous weeks of my stay. It towers above the agitated encounters with family and friends over abundant dinners like no others I had any memory of from before, above the walks along the paths I had walked with that lover who left me on the frigid February day in dreary communism, the sight of my children playing in Romanian with neighborhood children—a disorienting déjà vu—above the exhausting walks through a sweltering Bucharest which we visit at the end of our stay.

It towers above the moment of knocking at the door of our old apartment where I had lived for the first fifteen years of my life, the 'matchbox' apartment, when an old man opened the door barely ajar and said, "No, you can't come in, but wait a minute", and came back with a coloring book for the children that he slipped through the door with his stretched-out arm.

It towers above the sights of the stray dogs loitering and sleeping by the hundreds in the streets, children drugged on glue that people called 'aurolacii', sounding like the name of extraterrestrials. This scene happens at the very top of one of the highest peaks in the Carpathians where we go with my cousin for a day, her husband and her two young daughters, two and three. This scene defines and fixates forever the duplicity of belonging to two worlds at the same time. I have no pictures of the occasion and I don't need any. This time my tricky memory folded unto this day with voracity and is keeping it under its grip.

My children and husband are walking on the plateau wowing at the breathtaking layers of peaks, perfectly lined fir tree forests, with several cows and a small flock of sheep grazing on the alpine pastures. We are above the trees, at the level of the highest bald rocks. I am talking to my cousin and holding the tiny hands of my new nieces twice removed. My head is spinning a little from the altitude and the rarefied air. Fragrances, views, the feel of the soft pasture under my feet, the sharp cool air all embrace me like a cradle, in a settling of the soul.

I remember with a start that I was supposed to call my lawyer in America to check on the progress of the sale of my present house and the purchase of the sheriff's house. If he doesn't get the approval from me, he can't move on anything, even though he has power of attorney. The words power of attorney sound entirely ridiculous next to the grazing cows that we pass by on our hike.

I panic and tell my cousin that we might need to get back right away because I must call my lawyer, it's urgent.

She says, "Here, see if you can call from my cellphone." I don't yet have a cellphone in America but here is my cousin handing me hers, a voluminous but solid apparatus, and says, "You can call international on it." I am skeptical about the service at ten thousand feet altitude on a pasture among the Carpathian chains, but she says, "No, of course, it has service, here it's better because there, see the towers, it's all open."

After the revolution, Romanians legalized abortions and adopted modern technologies, cell phones, computers, Internet cafés. I am impressed and intrigued. I take my cousin's cell phone and call my lawyer in the small southern town where I live, and which now seems unreal and nonexistent, a figment of my imagination, while one of the cows next to me is mooing blissfully. He answers the phone, and I hear him perfectly well.

"Good thing you called," he says, "I just got the report from the house inspector, and it's very bad. The house has huge problems, the gutters, the roof, the windows. There is a lot of water damage, the electricity is old and needs to be replaced, and the plumbing too." He keeps on and on about the awful inspection report.

On the good side, there is a buyer for my house, and the lawyer got the sheriff's children to come down in price by ten thousand dollars because of the bad inspection report. "It's still a very valuable property," he says, "you can fix it up." My sons are calling to me from lower in the valley to come see something. Another cow next to me is producing a heartfelt moo, and my cousin starts laughing.

I remember the bay windows of the house, the morning light flooding through them, the perspective and depth you get at the entrance, the oak tree guarding the two acres of land many thousands of miles and several universes of culture and thought away. I need to tell him right away, he insists, the word got out and "there are a couple of other people who are very interested and would probably pounce on it and buy it in a heartbeat."

He repeats, "It is a valuable property, it is." I tighten up at the thought of the house being snatched away from me by some arrogant retired southern couple or even worse by one of my university colleagues. My heartbeats jump to a hundred and fifty per minute terrified of the people snatching my dream house from under my feet in an American heartbeat while my heart is here all

165

entangled in my Romanian bucolic landscape. I stare at the view and breathe in the brisk delicious air. The land at my feet, the chains of the Carpathians.

It's where my heartbeats are regular and my flesh and soul in tune with one another. But where is really my home? There are my children skipping around the rocks carefree speaking in English to one another, and for all practical reasons I have nothing here that ties me really. My work, my family are all over there. It was done and decided sixteen years ago, or rather I decided it then.

As I walk backwards listening to my lawyer, I step into a big pile of cow dung, soft and mushy. The cow next to me seems displeased with my encroaching so closely upon her intimate territory, and moos angrily this time. It appears as if she might charge at me. I step out of the manure with my shoes entirely ruined. My cousin is bending over with laughter and now so are all four children as they see me running away from the mad cow, my feet covered in dung.

My lawyer is urging me to give him an answer right away, from up there in the Shenandoah valley, another valley at the other end of the planet of this gorgeous valley right here with magnificent alpine pastures, symmetrical forests of fir trees and lots of friendly and unfriendly cows.

I keep running while still holding the phone and I take refuge behind one of the white rocks where my kids are looking at the alpine flora. The smell of cow manure drives them away laughing while my lawyer asks, "Should I go ahead with the house sale, it's the first and only buyer you've got."

I say, "Of course, sure, go ahead with the house sale." He says it's the best price I would ever get on the house, ten thousand grand more than I had initially bought it for. Not bad. At this point, I feel like I am inside that mafia movie again, dealing houses, guns, ten thousand grand this and ten thousand grand that. The peaks and chains of the Carpathians stretch all around me with dark brooding forests, snow caps, alpine pastures.

The shepherd guarding the flock of sheep completes the pastoral picture. He starts moving slowly in my direction and sees me. He waves and winks at me. Next, the lawyer asks, "Should I close on the sheriff's house?"

I say, "What do you think? It's still a beautiful house despite all the problems, isn't it?"

"It sure is, and even with the bad report, you are getting it at a great price. You wouldn't be able to get a house half this size for double the price if the sheriff's kids weren't so eager to get the money on their daddy's properties, and don't forget the land."

No, how could I forget the land? It's stretching endlessly ahead of me. I could be owning land right here where my body and soul are in sync with one another, and my flesh recognizes the fragrance of the earth. But if at eighteen it was already too late as the line in my favorite novel says, now at thirty-eight it's centuries too late.

I tell the lawyer to go ahead and complete the closing on the sheriff's house, sign the contract. He says he can even get home improvement loan approved and added to the main mortgage. I say, "Sure, go ahead, sounds great", and all the pieces are in place in the puzzle of my American life.

I hang up giddy and confused at the thought I just closed the deal on the estate in the Shenandoah valley with land and everything while my soul is pining for this land right here under my feet, cow manure and all. I have just thrusted roots deeper into American land while just getting reacquainted with the roots in my homeland under the devastating beauty of the fir tree forests and piercing clarity of the Carpathian skies. I have achieved a perfect schism of identity and belonging.

I turn around and the crazy cow that had followed me is right next to me staring intensely. My entire family, American husband and sons, my cousin with her daughters and husband are walking towards me as if to rescue me, not just from the mad cow but from the absurd paralysis of body and mind that takes over me as the gravity of two lands at two different corners of the world is pulling at me with opposing forces. My family can't stop laughing but they are nevertheless doing their best to save me from the tight corner between a rock and a mad cow where I had gotten myself.

The shepherd with the flock of sheep notices my predicament and smiles, comes over and boldly pushes the cow away making the bell around her neck ring sonorously. The sounds of the cow bell and the sheep bleating echo through the valleys around me and mix in with the children's laughter. The shepherd asks us for cigarettes. My cousin hands him her packet of Marlboro lights. He is delighted and so am I. He might have just saved my butt from a mad Romanian cow.

We get back into the city at dusk and pass through all the familiar streets, squares and alleys of my childhood sprinkled with strident mixtures of post-communist Balkan society and western economy: kiosks selling Rexona soaps,

Toblerone chocolate, Turkish sesame candy, Romanian versions of Playboy magazine together with brochures with prayers and orthodox Jesus images on the cover. There are sex shops, Italian shoe stores, and in the very middle of the main pedestrian area, reigning with its golden crown, a McDonald restaurant.

A boisterous colorful wedding party with a traditionally dressed bride and groom enter the McDonald's for what looks like their dance reception with accordionist, and fiddle and harmonica players. In the boisterous amalgam of street life, with their Balkan and Eastern realities, young women dressed like movie stars, hookers, beggars, a McDonald's traditional Romanian wedding, I see her again: the young woman of sixteen years ago, her last stroll through the city of her youth and great love.

It's 1983 and the stores are empty. The secret police everywhere. Not any part of her imagination can foresee how this will look in sixteen years, but the chains of the Carpathians and the rock next to which she had her first kiss will still be there in the distance, unmoved and indifferent. That, she is sure of. She is saying one last goodbye to everything in her tearful soul. She is secretive and fearful, and she can't tell anyone of her plans. She is on the verge of irreparable heartbreak but determined to get on the train and out of her country forever.

The Black Sea, 1983

The summer before I left for Italy in order to get to America—and I always go back to those last months like a ship that keeps returning to the same shore—I spent two glorious weeks at the beach with my best friend, her boyfriend, and my last Romanian boyfriend. We were in a village by the Black Sea called 2 Mai, or 2nd May, at the frontier with Bulgaria where all of Romania's population of bohemian intellectuals used to spend their summer vacations lodging at local peasants' houses and putting up with outhouses, outdoor showers, no hot water, in a word almost the same privations we were subjected to during the rest of the year by the Party imposed regulations, only this time willingly so, like it was the coolest thing to do.

The nude beaches were an added attraction to the scarcity or lack of amenities, as if a return to the most minimalist lifestyle, the unmediated closeness to the raw nature of sea and sand were the ultimate defiance against the prison of dictatorship.

That summer, I didn't care about the lack of amenities and wanted to experience the beaches one last time in the full glory of those bohemian rustic conditions. My parents and I had made our plans for the escape and submitted requests for our respective tourist visas and passports to Italy and France, all in total secretiveness. The only exception was my father's sister Mimi, who suffered from a bad heart condition, and we didn't want her to have a heart attack at the news we had disappeared beyond the Romanian borders, of course, in case our plans worked out.

Suspended in the wait for answers from the authorities, I needed one last leap into forgetfulness, a carefree vacation, and one last love affair with my country that I loved more than ever now that I was preparing to leave it. My friend carried the same unusual first name that I did, and we were often called blonde D and brunette D, with me being the blonde one.

We both attended the same section of English literature at the same university and competed in reading English novels that we borrowed from the library of the American Embassy and for which we were written up in the secret police files on account of having contacts with foreign authorities, librarians, and ideas.

Brunette D lived in a large apartment in the city center and threw boisterous dance parties, used modern birth control in the form of pills the likes of which I had never seen in my life, and was packing and sending pieces of furniture to Belgium where her mother had run away a year earlier. She was among the few in Bucharest and the only one I knew who was expecting to leave the country on a legal emigration visa for the reintegration of her family. But not even she knew I was preparing to leave too, at a moment's notice, were I to receive my passport.

I lived in a bubble of secrecy within the many other compartments of secrecy within the secrecy of our daily lives, a collection of Russian Matryoshka dolls of secret lives within secret lives, with one tiny indivisible hard core in the middle.

We reserved rooms in neighboring peasants' houses in the village by the Black Sea, only a short walk to the beaches, and we embarked on our vacation journey with great excitement. We had packed cans of foods that we were able to buy on the black market from foreign students before our departure: condensed milk—a real delicacy—sardines, and a special pâté we were crazy about.

After grieving the loss of my first love who left me for the Carpathian forests, I met my current boyfriend at the university, and we had been dating during our junior year. My boyfriend was also my neighbor in the brand-new building my parents and I had moved into, and a student at the School of Architecture.

He was everything that my first lover was not: loud, argumentative, red-haired, outspoken, and ironic about the communist madness in our daily lives. Except for his red hair and scientific leaning, he was very much a kindred spirit. My friend, Brunette D, had been dating the same young man since high school, and they were an enviable couple in our social circles: they were going steady, they were great dancers, and they were having safe sex, using western birth control pills.

I, on the other hand, was tormented by secretive defection plans, longings for lost love, fierce artistic ambitions to become a famous writer, living the life of the heroines I impersonated in the Attic Theater, paranoid about every step I heard echoing behind me in the street, and filled with an overall existential dissatisfaction with everything. I envied my beautiful brunette friend's self-assurance, her dance parties, her steady love affair, her open emigration plans to Belgium, and her birth control pills.

The sea was at its most brilliant emerald, its waters smooth, clear and cool, the beaches golden and endless and indeed inviting to nudity and to an overall primitive unleashing of the senses. Our rooms in the peasant houses were stuffy and hot but clean and fresh. The outhouses not so much. The outdoor water spigot was hidden behind a wobbly wooden structure that the hosts called 'the shower', cold and inconveniently situated in the very middle of the front yard so that while you were taking a freezing cold shower, you could also watch the other tourists having their lunches at the outdoor tables. But for those two weeks, never mind cold showers and outhouses, we had the time of our lives, one last time in the magical embrace of the Black Sea, its cooling sparkling waters and silky golden beaches.

I called my parents every other day to check whether the letter from the police passport headquarters had arrived with the answer about my passport request. Or theirs, for that matter, since they also submitted their papers only a month later than I had. We were all in a limbo before the big escape, wishing we got the tourist visas we were counting on, and grieving at the thought of leaving everything and everybody behind. I had taken time off from the theater work for the seaside vacation, though they were expecting me back to play Winnie a few more times.

The sea ruled my body and heart during those July days. We sunbathed in the nude on the endless expanses of the beach and swam in the nude in the deliciously cool waves of the Black Sea, forgetting that we lived under a communist dictatorship and that we were expecting passports and visas which if given, were going to take us away from those beaches and waves forever.

Out there in the village by the sea nothing seemed bad, and I often wondered why I was so intent on leaving, so determined to go on with my plan of going to America. I thought of Zoila Valdivieso and our chance encounter on a beach a few kilometers away from the ones we were now gracing with our irreverent nudity, almost a decade earlier. I wondered if I would have been

171

as intent on my departure had that encounter never happened. I remembered our afternoon chats when she encouraged me to think about leaving for America at some point in my life…And here I was exactly at that point.

The primitive living conditions at the peasants' houses, the relentless sun, the luscious sands and sea waters made us giddy and lustful, and deep down they made me more patriotic than ever, even though I abhorred the very word 'patriotism'. But there were no secret police agents in sight, no Communist Party headquarters, and as for the shortages of food and everything else, we turned them into a subject of jokes and laughter, indulging with voracity in the few luxuries we had with us: the cans of condensed milk, the sardines, the tea and instant coffee we had gotten from the foreign students, and the meals cooked by our hosts of locally caught sturgeons and other kinds of fish.

My boyfriend carried music tapes with Dire Straits and Woody Guthrie with him everywhere he went, and on some evenings, we danced in the small peasant courtyards, the salty sea air filling our lungs, the moon casting a delicate net of golden rays over everything, even over the rickety shower, the wobbly table and chairs, the small, thatched roof and stucco house, lighting our young faces. We were living it up for one last summer on the verge of beauty and heartbreak, desperation and reckless abandonment, fiercely greedy for happiness, with the moon and its golden bridge across the waves, across the greenish violet sea.

During those sunlit and moonlit salty days and nights, I hardly ever thought of my long-lost lover brooding in the Carpathians and indulged carefree in the relationship with my neighbor boyfriend. We were companions who had sex and fun. We had our smoldering moments that summer, shared wild laughs, and experienced the bittersweet romance of the relationship's ending.

But I thought almost incessantly of the totality of my life and my own self in the country I happened to be born in by no choice of my own, and how now under the shadow of a final and definitive impending separation, acquired a special glow, a layer of magic that touched almost everything in sight, every gesture I made, every word I uttered in the rhythms of my language. We were the irreverent intellectual youth of our country, speaking foreign languages, reading books from the library of the American Embassy, engaging in premarital sex and nude swimming, and enjoying luxuries acquired clandestinely from foreign students on the black market.

In the interstices between our wild swims, lazy walks on the warm sands, outdoor cold showers, evening dances on the beach or in the tiny courtyard to the music of Dire Straits, and our unleashed laughs late into the night, I felt twinges of regret and forebodings of longing, which made every moment all the more precious because of the imminence of loss. My dark-haired name sister-friend seemed more beautiful than ever during those days, and our gallant Romanian partners more spirited and fun than I had remembered either of them. In those tiny cracks through the makeshift house of our seaside happiness, I tried desperately to see far away into our future, far away from everything familiar onto lands that we were both dreaming of.

More than thirty years later, after all the tempests, even tragedies of our lives as immigrants, two of the four million Romanians in the worldwide diasporas, I am looking back at those last salty sunny days and am seeing us then look into the future which is today our present on different parts of the globe. I imagine us looking into a magic mirror revealing our futures and wondering whether we would have still thrown ourselves into what lay ahead.

The heartbreaks that came with our successes as a complete and inseparable package: my two divorces, the death of my father on a cold January morning, the death of her child killed by a reckless driver the same summer when princess Diana died, the multiple breakages of my family units and my many breakdowns, the end of her thirty-year marriage at a point when most couples settle into the comfort of 'growing old together' with their life-long partners, the death of my second husband and the realization of how much I had loved him come too late, our fulfilled and unfulfilled dreams, our ferocious ambitions and our love for our children.

Our glorious multicolored brokenness. I see us with great clarity: we are twenty-one years old, ambitious and hungry for life, for experience, for success. We are watching our future unfold inside the magic mirror, its dark and bright corridors, the shiny and golden times unmistakably woven with the painful and dark ones. I know we would have taken the whole package, irresistibly drawn to the shiny parts inside it, to the openness towards the world that our respective uprooting gave us in return: the travels, the houses, the books we wrote, the degrees we achieved, the families we raised on foreign lands which we shamelessly appropriated as us refugees tend to do.

My friend D and I recently met in Belgium after a fifteen-year hiatus in communication, and she took me to the beaches of the North Sea enveloped in the mellow hazy light that inspired the Flemish painters, a light that seems to hold in it bits of cold and bits of darkness, that seems far away and slightly unreal, and that begs to stay and be looked at because it is so short lived. Like our last summer at the beach in 1983.

Of course, we remembered and talked about our seaside adventure of thirty-three years earlier and on Europe's southern shores, the Balkan shores where the light is shameless and hot, unforgiving and dazzling. We were now the girls at the far end of the magic mirror, deep into the corridors of the future, in our middle-aged immigrant fury, nostalgias, and irreverent confidence.

I visited her at the elegant house she and her husband had proudly bought and decorated fifteen years earlier, soon after the death of their oldest son and the birth of another one, and which now was up for sale due to their impending divorce. Elegant high ceilings, archways, mirrors, fireplaces, a lovely inner garden, all touched by the sadness of separation and family breakage. But not all was sadness and breakage. There were also marks of hard-won successes, her books on film, the beautiful sons she raised. In the bookcase that she was getting ready to pack, a photograph stopped me in my steps: another movie still, historic.

In it my friend is wearing a shiny burgundy suit, radiant and smiling between the mythic Italian director Michelangelo Antonioni and the mythic French actress Maria Schneider, the star of *The Last Tango in Paris*, at an international film festival and colloquium in the nineties where she gave a presentation and interviewed Antonioni. Films had been her passion ever since I've known her, like theater has been my passion.

I suspect that in the magic mirror we might have looked into that summer at the beach as twenty-year-old women, both she and I must have seen somewhere in the distance amidst the many shadows moving in the hallways of the future, blurry but unmistakably bright, moments of glory and success that attracted us more than the dark ones scared us. Ferocious hunger and reckless courage are what make the con artist refugee a fascinating character and redeems them from the banality of regular con artistry.

On that trip, we also roamed the streets of Brussels, unaware of the curfew imposed because of the recent terrorist attacks and suspicion of new ones. We wondered why the streets of an usually vibrant city center were empty and why we were the only ones walking carefree and window shopping along the elegant boulevard with expensive designer stores. "Maybe there is a terrorist attack warning, I don't care," she said.

She had lost a child almost twenty years earlier, why should she care about a terrorist attack? I didn't care either. She was going through a divorce, I had gone through a couple of them, we had lived full tumultuous lives of immigrants, in between geographies, languages and cultures. We walked laughing along the empty streets of Brussels, in the cool rainy June evening after having seen an Almodóvar movie.

As young students in Bucharest, we sometimes went together to see foreign movies at the exclusive cinema for which she had a special pass. We were in Bucharest together, in the dark gray years of communism, and now in Brussels, in the dark times of terrorist attacks, after 9/11, after the Paris attacks. We laughed then, and we laughed now. We glided deep into the tunnels of time, history, memory, with bouncy steps. We had no fear.

The last days of our summer vacation at the Black Sea in 1983 came to an end, and we were sunburnt, giddy, exhausted from the sun, the swimming, the late nights under the moon, unwilling to return to our Bucharest existence. We met my parents for the last day, in the first city down the coast. They had also wanted to say goodbye to the sea, which my mother had always passionately loved. They were expectant and secretive, and I wondered if any news had arrived for me from the passport authorities. We didn't talk about it, but walked along the promenades, along the sea, lined up with beds of petunias and snap dragons.

My friend whispered just a few bits of news to my parents about her mother being in Belgium. We were all thinking of leaving, planning to leave, our double lives of potential future refugees were shimmering and quivering in the glowing purple sunsets at the Black Sea, with faint echoes of future goodbyes and farewells, as if the future spilled into the present and the present clung desperately one last time to our native landscapes and stolen happiness.

A month later, I was boarding the airplane to Fiumicino airport in Rome with my suitcase carrying the volume of short stories, family pictures, the winter coat that almost got me stopped at the border, the totality of my past with my Bucharest days and the Carpathians days and the Black Sea days, all neatly packed inside my heart.

The remaining month in Bucharest was a turbulent swirl of fear, anticipation, heartache, surveillance, tears, and theater. The day of my return from the seaside, I received the letter informing me that the passport had been approved. "We write to inform you that your request for a passport for a three-week trip to Italy and France has been approved. You will need the necessary visas…"

The specific mention of the three weeks struck me as ironic. I was in for my transatlantic adventure for all the weeks of my life, and yet I could still come back within the first three weeks if I found it unbearable. I could see Paris, Rome, Florence, come back, and start my last year at the university. I had a little window of escape from my own ambitions of escape.

In one last trip to the city of my first love in the Carpathians, I visited the places of my youth, carved them in my memory, caressed and cried over them: here is the valley we ran down in the rain one summer day; here is the peak with the overlook of the city where we had our first smoldering kiss; here are the side streets we walked on with the hurried restless steps of our tormented passion. I left diaries and packages of love letters tied with string in the pantry of my aunt and uncle's house, between jars of pickled tomatoes and peppers. I said goodbye childhood, goodbye youth, goodbye evenings in the fresh mountain air, goodbye a hundred times.

I got on the train back to Bucharest, played Winnie in the Attic theater one more time, packed, unpacked, repacked every single item for my forever suitcase. What to take, what to leave behind, take these five items of clothing and these two books, no, not this one, it's dangerous, takes these photos, leave everything else, parents, family, second boyfriend, friends, university classes, house, city, country, take the photos, take the short stories collection, take the stories. I walked surreptitiously, hurriedly for all my last-minute errands, yet trying to make every moment last and imprint it in my mind, looked behind me in the street and even waved goodbye at the Securitate guy always following me.

In the house, we whispered almost everything we said, even the ordinary domestic communication, "Is there any hot water today?", "Was there a line for bread?", "You are going to need a winter coat"—always the coat, imagining freezing winters alone in the unknown, in the streets of Rome or Chicago. I was going far away in a cold, cold world. We startled at the sound of the phone ringing.

One evening, as I was returning from the theater after rehearsal still inhabiting my feisty sassy character, I heard steps behind me, again the steps, always the steps, getting closer. The Bucharest boulevard I was walking along was almost empty. It was past midnight, and the steps were grinding their persistent little cruel knocks in my brain. I hurried up, and the steps hurried behind me. I slowed down, and the steps slowed down. I ran, and the steps multiplied in a rush. It could have been the Securitate, but it could have also been a rapist, a drunk murderer, a psycho killer like the one who used to kill nurses and waitresses in the seventies, who knows, maybe a new one had emerged who was killing actresses.

I stopped and turned around to face my stalker. Before I even had a chance to see his face, I started screaming at him and hurling every single insult and curse I could gather from my overheated brain. His thin scrawny face had an ironic smile, and after he took all the insults, he said in a nonchalant voice, "What's wrong with you, woman? Are you off your rocker?" I asked him why he was following me, and this time he laughed and said he had a right to walk in the same direction and told me to go home and sleep it off. "Go fuck yourself," he added.

I aggressively pushed the man out of my way although there was plenty of room for me to go around him on the sidewalk and told him to go to bloody hell and stop following innocent women at night.

I ran for a while in the night. I still had a twenty-minute walk home, and all the buses had stopped for the night. The streets were harrowingly deserted, like I was walking through a ghost town. I was seized by an unbearable fear and had a feeling I was never going to make it home, but that I was going to be killed before I reached the new building where we lived. It was a barely finished apartment bloc with parts of the walls still in progress, uncovered pipes, and rats gnawing at them that scurried by the elevator whenever they heard the metallic slam of the entrance door.

They were the newly built private properties that the government was now allowing people to purchase and move into before their completion. I ran in the middle of the road thinking it was better to be run over than caught by a secret police guy or a rapist. I wasn't sure in which category the man I had yelled at belonged, or whether he might indeed have just been a tired man walking behind me on the same sidewalk.

A white Dacia car was coming my way and I waved at it, hoping it would stop. I had never hitchhiked before, and midnight in the deserted Bucharest was not the ideal moment to be initiated in that experience. The car stopped in the middle of the road, and I asked if they were going in the direction of my address, which they were, a nicely dressed couple possibly returning from a dinner with friends. There were still people who had dinner parties and tried to enjoy their lives in my country.

The couple kindly drove me to the corner of my street, as if it was no big deal. Waves of gratitude washed over me. There were nice people in my country too. Not everybody was secret police, and you could even trust hitchhiking at midnight. I walked the half a block to my building in the desolate night of my native city with a sense of complete and irremediable loneliness, like I was the last person left on earth.

I remembered the running joke that the last person leaving the country should make sure to turn off the lights. Electricity was a precious commodity that the government always tried to save at the expense of our daily wellbeing. The street was dark, the hallway of my building barely lit by a sinister half-burned bare bulb, and this chiaroscuro invited a couple of rats to scurry past the elevator.

I knew why I wanted to leave forever and join Zoila Valdivieso in her colorful American haven, and I wasn't going to turn any of the lights off on my way out. Let them burn into eternity! There were no answers yet for my parents' requests for passports, but I moved swiftly to getting all my visas and speeding up my departure. I bought the airplane ticket to Rome. Suddenly, it was next week.

Seven, six, five, four days left, the countdown to the end of my Romanian life, the beginning of who knows what life. Running errands, making farewell love to my neighbor boyfriend, selling my American music records, engaging in random gestures and actions to fill the hours of those last days. Some hours were exhilarating, others unbearable with the agony of fear and heartbreak.

The night before my departure, my boyfriend and I went out with my friend brunette D and her boyfriend for one last time in my native city. This was our secret farewell. We went to the pizza place in the center. A pizza restaurant had opened to Bucharest for the first time ever, and the lines to get inside were interminable. But we were lucky that night, as we found a table for the four of us right away. We ordered three different pizzas—mushrooms, pepperoni, olives—incredulous at the temporary culinary abundance.

We devoured our pizzas like hungry wolves laughing like mad, reminiscing our seaside adventures of the previous month, whispering anti-communist jokes. Again, the worm of doubt and hesitation started gnawing at my conscience voraciously; why did I need to leave everything, everyone, all that, the fun, the new pizza on the boulevard? What was so bad about my life right then? There were new restaurants here and there, and I even had a newly tiled bathroom at home, for which my parents paid three months their salaries combined.

My boyfriend was hilarious and my best friend adorable and trustworthy. Except that she was going to be gone next year to join her mother in Belgium, and my boyfriend was going to finish up his architecture studies and be sent who knew where to work to supervise the building of some new apartment complex somewhere deep in the countryside. And I was probably going to be sent somewhere to the boonies of Romanian countryside as well, to teach some subject I had never even studied, like music or geography, to fifth graders despite my English literature diploma. The pizza was delicious though, and we couldn't stop laughing for some reason.

An uncanny levity enveloped us which even made us reckless and bold. So bold that we made an obscene gesture to the man sitting in the corner of the restaurant in one of the notorious Securitate leather jackets watching us and trying to take note of our riotous behavior and dialogue. We laughed off secret police and communist surveillance and stuffed ourselves with pepperoni pizza. Food was precious and a reason for joy anytime you found it in some degree of abundance.

After our pizza orgy, my boyfriend took us on a late-night tour of Bucharest in the brand-new Dacia car he had borrowed from his parents, screeching on the breaks, taking the corners in a swirl, stopping at the red lights only at the last minute. We laughed wildly over the Romanian songs on the radio. Who would have thought we lived under a brutal dictatorship? Nobody could stop us from laughing. The car screeched past our university and the famous statues, and we even laughed at the formidable statue of Michael the Brave, the famous king who united the three provinces into a greater Romania and killed many Turks, swishing his sword on his valiant bronze horse.

If only he could have swung his sword at the Securitate scurrying around like the rats in my building and killed as many of them as he did Turks, I wouldn't have had to tear myself away the next morning.

When I said goodbye to my friend and name sister, my heart startled, and I had no idea when or if I was ever going to see her again. I had no idea when or if I was going to see anybody and anything Romanian ever again. The night smelled of late summer, a bit humid after a recent rain, and chestnuts were falling from the trees and cracking on the sidewalk. I picked one up and felt its smooth glossy surface in my palm. I stroked its tiny crack, just like my heart at that moment, a tiny hairline crack that would only get deeper and wider with time.

I said goodbye in my mind to everything, Bucharest at night, my youth, and every part of me. That night I stayed at me boyfriend's apartment next door, and we made love with the passion of farewells and forevers. Maybe we would be fifty before we ever saw each other again, we laughed, we would be wrinkled and blasé. Would we even recognize each other?

Dawn caught us still awake, talking, laughing sadly. He was the only non-family person who knew what I was up to. A few times through the night, the fleeting thought passed through my head; what if my boyfriend was going to denounce me, and they were going to arrest me at the airport? Then I thought that was precisely why I needed to leave, to free myself of those rotten suspicions about everything and everybody. I wondered what my life was going to be like at fifty and if I was even going to be alive.

A Roma woman who had once read my palm had told me my lifeline was interrupted. But then it picked up again, she said as an afterthought. I laughed then, and I laughed to myself now. Yes, maybe I was going to die and be resurrected like the female and Romanian version of Lazarus. That was me alright. Was I going to have children, become a famous writer, person, become anything at all? I had no idea really, except that despite the flaming pain through my heart and every part of me, my will to carry through with my fleeing plan was unshaken.

I tiptoed inside my parents' apartment in the early morning, and they were both awake. My mother said, "You have to finish packing your suitcase!" Yes, the suitcase. I couldn't have cared less. I could have gone empty-handed. I was leaving my entire life, why did I even need a suitcase? "Because you'll be by yourself among strangers, you'll need some things." I was starting my last Romanian day, and the sun was shining over Bucharest with a mellow glow, like a consolation.

Farewells and New Beginnings

The new millennium started with the death of my father, only two days after I had said, "Goodbye, Dad, I'm waiting for you to come visit me at my new home in Virginia, remember? You came there a few months ago, now I have a big new house."

He said, "Yes, sure I'll come, tell your mother. I'm not going to last much longer, you know…You and your mother, the two loves of my life." He was sitting at the edge of his bed. He had gotten smaller, and his legs were dangling and didn't reach the floor, like a child's. I held him tightly for a few seconds. He was frail and thin.

I drove to Virginia with my husband and the two children to start my new semester. On the first day of classes, my mother called shrieking into the receiver that my father had died. That very morning. She found him dead in the morning. He had died in his sleep. Or as us Romanian say sometimes in our macabre humor, "he woke up dead."

We drove back to Chicago the next day and were welcomed by the frigid winds blowing over the city from the lake and my mother's tired face devastated by tears. The apartment sounded hollow, and my father's absence was heavy laden. Everything felt foreign. Even my father's special objects left on the night table just as he had left them the night before his death seemed foreign and out of place in an out of place apartment, in an out of place country.

I noticed a hand-crafted pipe, a golden cigarette lighter that he kept on his night table just because they were beautiful, as he had quit smoking long ago, his Mont Blanc gold-plated pen that he still used when writing articles about Romanian poets and his own poems of desperation about living in a foreign country.

All dressed up in his best navy-blue suit and carefully embalmed by the funeral home, my father looked like a waxen statue replica of himself. We were burying our first dead in American earth. I had traveled the full circle of existence, from the births of my children to burying my father, having taken a couple of crooked deviated paths in between. I owned a house with a big oak tree sprawling its roots far out into the American southern confederate earth and was now looking deep into the frozen earth of my father's grave in the cemetery of the Romanian monastery in Michigan, another simulacrum of my native country reality.

The monastery offered a bilingual English Romanian service. In America, you could die and be buried bilingually. The frigid January Michigan wind made it feel raw and real.

We had arrived on the coldest Chicago winter of the past century; my father had been hopeful and excited by our formidable adventure for a couple of months until he hit the ruthless reality of his irreparable foreignness in a city and country which felt to him like a huge mistake until the day he died. He died in winter on the very cusp of the new millennium in another merciless cold, like an undeserved vengeance. The earth opened and closed upon the coffin.

The children were struck by the finality of it all, and the little one refused to understand the meaning of leaving his grandfather all alone inside a box in the cold ground. That was when he started hollering, his face burning red despite the below zero temperature and the wind that made it feel below any measurable temperature. The older one cried softly and quietly, staring at the hole that was swallowing his grandfather.

After my father's death, I wanted to have another child. I went back to writing my book about tragic heroines in literature, murderous or suicidal women who broke all taboos of feminine gentleness, and I wanted to divorce my second husband, all in that order. The desire for another child was at odds with my desire for a divorce, of course, but I didn't care.

I wasn't made for marriage, but I was made for motherhood. I wasn't made for domesticity but for adventure. I was the bad woman frowned at by both traditional housewives and feminist working women. Too independent and sassy for the soccer moms, too flamboyant and motherly for most of the working women at my college.

In the small town still fighting over the right to public displays of confederate flags and at the revered university with a two-hundred-and-fifty-year tradition of male 'honor' and omnipotence, the Romanian professor with an accent, a loud laugh, bright lipstick, children, husbands, and rapid accumulations of published books was something of an irritating anomaly. Neither here nor there, unplaceable, unpalatable, an outrage.

For the liberal white women teaching at the university and speaking in unhesitating feminist slogans, this woman was equally an insult. She was too cuddly with her children, her colorful dresses were too tight, she was aloof, she didn't use the academic jargon, swore in public places, and used too many hyperboles while speaking out in faculty meetings. She was an outsider to all the sides. She fell in between the cracks and fully indulged in her free fall. It felt freeing and thrilling. It was the new phase of her American dream. The free fall phase, the living between the cracks phase.

She took hold of the girl on the platform who watches the train pull into the station, gets on the train, flees her country at the height of communist misery, waves goodbye to everything and everybody, leaves her great love without even saying goodbye. It was in the no man's land between belonging and non-belonging, between familiar and unfamiliar spaces, marital statuses, motherhood and work, with bluish mountain chains rushing by her, between the peaks of the Carpathians and the mellow chains of the Appalachians that she took hold of that elusive girl and her elusive story with more determination than ever to bring her journey to a glorious literary end.

The girl with the small suitcase carrying all her belongings and holding her purse with family photographs and no money tightly against her chest, saves her life. She writes her story madly, every chance she gets, between driving the children to their multiple sports and afternoon activities, cooking a healthier, revised diet, overseeing repairs to the old house, roofs, gutters, directing French plays, negotiating a friendly divorce.

She learned her lesson from the previous one. She is getting better at everything, including divorces. She is a better mother too. She feels it in the smoothness and levity of the weekend outings, vacations, weeknights with the children. Things are coming together while they are also falling apart again. She is more rested and surer of herself and is starting to accept her non-belonging, even makes a virtue of it, all while rooting herself deeper in her two acres of land with a prolific vegetable garden.

She drives a new turbo Mercedes in which she whizzes by the cow pastures and the stretches of confederate land. If only her father could see her ride in her golden Mercedes now. With some time passing, the girl who crosses the border illegally with her suitcase replaces the craving for another child. The

183

world is overpopulated anyways, and she is getting ready for her second divorce. One thing cracks, another thing emerges whole and strong like the oak tree in her back yard.

My second husband and I got a friendly, calm, and expedited divorce on Valentine's Day. It just happened so, and we only realized it when we signed the divorce papers and dated them. We smiled at each other. There were tears in his eyes, and he looked handsome in his tweed blazer. I knew I still loved him but couldn't stay married. Everything was too uneven, too lopsided. I might as well be a single mother officially than do all the single mother things and be officially married without any of the benefits of marriage, were there any to be found.

After we left the lawyer's office as freshly divorced exes, we went for drinks at one of the two local bars in town. Then we went to see the hit movie *Cold Mountain*. It felt like dating. The new freedom was sexy. We had done everything in the wrong order, child, marriage, divorce, dating, all jumbled up like the letters in a secret word you had to guess. It wasn't clear what the full word was yet, or whether it was ever going to be revealed, and I didn't care.

It turned out the film was shot in the region of the Romanian Carpathians where I had spent my summer and winter vacations, near Aunt Nina's house, and where my first love and I hiked and kissed and made love by the side of clear streams. It appeared that the area of North Carolina where the action of the film and the book took place, were apparently too developed to fit the setting of this civil war movie. The irony of that evening was priceless as I was seeing a movie with my Yankee ex-husband in the civil war town where I lived. A movie about a civil war story filmed amid my native mountains where Nicole Kidman was strolling and acting her tragic heroine part on the exact trails where I once hiked as a Romanian teenager with my sultry Romanian lover.

While everybody rolled their eyes at the sound of teenage boys or teenage anything, I loved mothering such boys. My sons' teen years were raucous and filled with irrepressible American energy, music, movies, cars, the kind I had only seen in a few movies when I was their age and now, I could live it through them. We did that in the wrong order too; they showed me the way to their America, and I created the safety net, the walls of love, healthy cooking, obligatory piano lessons in exchange for soccer and lacrosse, laughing with them laugh at me and my refugee Romanian ways, at my mispronounced or mismatched idiomatic expressions.

They were American boys raising a Romanian mom! This could be the title of a sitcom. I get our first cable TV service because my older son wins a small and weirdly shaped television with little flap doors, at the high school French bingo competition. I adopt all their new music tastes, Hanson, the Spice Girls, even alternative rock groups like AC/DC and Red-Hot Chili Peppers.

During the spring months, I burst with energy as if I were going through puberty too. I adopt the red buds and dogwoods in flower lined up against the clear contours of the Appalachians as my own, almost as if I truly belonged here, and to prove it I scream louder than any of the other mothers in the stands at my kids' soccer games, lacrosse games, tennis matches, "go, go, go, kick it, hit it, score, goal, point, we won, yay!"

I get an Alaskan husky dog that none of the three of us can control but he is too cute and beautiful to give away, until the day he bites an old lady in front of our house. And then we must give him away on an emergency basis. After two years of useless training, he runs out of the house one late night and goes crazy around the neighborhood.

My Russian friend and neighbor tries to help me by alluring him with sleeping pills wrapped in cream cheese. The Alaskan shepherd doesn't fall for it and runs like mad around the neighborhood until morning when I call the woman from the kennel to take him away.

By now, I see all my mother's paranoid predictions of him biting someone again and me becoming ruined for life with a million-dollar lawsuit as an actual possibility. In the end, it's my older son who catches him in the morning. It had been his dog, but somehow it hadn't worked out; too many activities, too little time, "the wrong dog for the wrong household," someone said, and I was only one working mother with two teenage sons and a wild herding dog.

A look of heartbreak and failure spreads on my son's face and large tears hang on his dark blonde eyelashes. My younger son is crying when the woman comes over in her truck. I make sure I tell her to give Moe to a good family in the countryside who can care for him and where he can run around freely. It strikes me we must be the bad family who couldn't deal with a beautiful large energetic dog.

I see my older son walk back into the house hunched over, his head hanging. He is tall and strong but still a child on the verge of adulthood, hanging between innocence and heartbreak. I say goodbye Moe and wave at him like he was another relative I'm letting go of. We go back into the house crying. It's as if we all lost a bit of our childhood this morning, and it feels like the biggest failure of the century, but it's a fresh century anyways. It takes Moe, the Alaskan husky, to show me again how far I still am from being an American. I am never going to be the relaxed American mom in jeans and sweatshirt playing with the family husky, roughing it, talking to him like he was her baby, "good dog, good dog, yea, you're a good dog, aren't you".

For an unknown reason, the day when we give away our husky dog, I get the idea that it is because of the lack of a man in the house that we couldn't keep it. My great feminist pride of getting rid of husbands to do it all on my own is now coming to haunt me, and my beloved sons are suffering for it. Studies and articles about the negative effects of single motherhood on children have been coming out like mushrooms, all written by white men whose wives take care of their children, so they can have the time to write such articles.

It's all a self-full-fucking-filling prophesy that us single working mothers keep getting caught in repeatedly. If we weren't single and if we weren't working and if we put up with all the crap that our husbands put us through, then our children would be in great shape, and we could also keep great shepherd dogs like Moe without having to give them away and break our children's hearts which will only mess them up even more later on when they can become subjects of research for articles on the negative effects of single motherhood.

My children's teenage and young adult years, high school, coming of age, girlfriends, sleepovers, mounds of beer cans filling corners of their rooms, tennis matches or lacrosse games in late spring and early fall, fast cars and late nights with loud music interspersed with suspicious silences and terrifying absences until the early hours of the morning—they all roar through me mercilessly, like a dizzying yet fascinating hurricane. An adolescence I never had.

The American adolescence of young people I had seen only in the movies. Now it belonged to my own flesh and blood children and swept through my century old house and the chaotic fragments of my life in irrepressible gusts. It rearranged everything, my own sense of self, of purpose, of priorities, my sense of belonging, my psyche, and the balance between my happy dreams and my worst nightmares.

A bitter taste of the darkness of America and its confused youth entered my life together with the energy and the vicariously lived excitement of parties, car rides, reckless pleasures of my rapidly growing sons. One minute I saw them walking luminous paths towards a bright American future filled with important diplomas, prizes, sophisticated work projects, and travels, and one minute I bent over in terror with gloomy images of their mug shot photos, as school dropouts, engaged in myriads of delinquent and criminal behaviors whose names I didn't even dare whisper to myself.

Their American friends' mothers seemed unfazed by the messiness of it all, barely worried by the long and often inexplicable absences, which I sometimes registered as disappearances and went as far as to call the local police, only to draw my children's mockery and exasperation, expressed in a barrage of American clichés. "Mom, you're being over-protective"; "I'm old enough"; "I'm not a baby, you're crazy!" The added clichés of other parents such as "you've got to let go"; "they have to learn on their own"; "kids are resilient"; and "they'll be back, don't worry!" made me want to vomit and slap the faces of those un-worrying parents and yell things like, *No, it's not OK, you dumb fuck. They might be dead in a ravine, high on drugs, drunk and alone in a corner!*

My anger at the hypocrisies of American life reached new heights during those times; this was a society in which everybody apparently loved and wanted children; an entire political party were doing their damnedest to decrease women's control over their own bodies and increase their chances of being trapped in an orgy of reproduction; everyone went ga goo over chubby babies in strollers and rowdy toddlers they saw in restaurants or fidgeting in grocery carts pushed by exhausted mothers amid gallons of hormone-filled milk, gala apples, and Jiffy peanut butter.

But once those cuddly little things grew out of their car seats and into moody teenagers with pimples and voracious appetites, everybody 'let go', rolled their eyes, complained, prescribed mood stabilizing medications, set up counseling meetings, sent them to camps, and breathed with relief whenever they were out of the house. At times I thought that maybe the communist unforgiving rantings against the 'depravation of the capitalist society of the Western world' had a point.

At other times I blamed myself for what smug un-divorced parents, devout Christians, and white male scholars of teen development called 'broken families'. That was what I had provided for my two precious, blond, blue-eyed, musical, multilingual, athletic, funny boys: one timid and brooding, the other spirited and talkative: 'a broken family!'

And it was only going to get even more broken, with two divorces, two fathers, one to the east, one to the mid-west of America, with me in the middle still trying to keep body and soul in sync with one another in glorious confederate land, and with the bit of wicked artistic ambitions left in between house chores, classes to teach, and exams to grade.

I was still clinging for dear life to the elusive girl on the train and laboring towards her birth. One day she was going to complete her adventurous journey and recount her full story. And then maybe it would have all been worth it. I would soar above the small provincial town that still seemed like a huge anomaly in the larger scheme of my life. My sons and I would move back to Chicago or to a bustling European city by the sea or both, divide the year between living in two places like I once saw the family of a famous French literary critic do.

I would find a sexy French professor who would generously act as a fun-loving stepfather and speak in deeply accented English about rock bands and European soccer players with my sons while winking mischievously and smiling lovingly at me as he is preparing a *salade niçoise* for us all in his summer house in Provence, and he would whisper to me, "Chérie, tu es magnifique!"

Then after dinner, we would make passionate French love with the full moon of Provence and lavender fragrances filling our room to excess. And my sons would walk onto their luminous path towards an international future, and we would all live glamorously between the hard bustle of Chicago and the sensuous sweetness of Provence. In this American/European version of my life, my husband number three would also be good friends with my two exes to give the children a sense of normalcy and continuity. A happy international modern family that negotiates and works everything out.

Instead, I got another dog, an abandoned puppy with an eating disorder and full of fleas, a golden Mercedes with turbo engine, and a neurotic chain-smoking French lover that I had met at a conference about the French writer, André Malraux. I now traveled to France every few months combining business with pleasure like a savvy hedonistic professional. Except that as soon as I arrived on French soil and met my self-important French lover who derided every bit of my research involving women writers or feminist studies, I started agonizing with worry about my sons, whom I usually left in the care of my mother or split between my mother and one of the fathers.

My life, my Romanian family, my American descendants, were spread across the world in a disorderly fashion. My older son named our new puppy Louie and learned how to drive in the golden Mercedes that he dented on both sides trying to get in and out of our driveway.

Our new puppy was a soulful neurotic needy creature that fit perfectly in our family wrought with neurosis and moral ambiguities of various kinds. I regretted I never got to drive my father around in the Mercedes, a 'very good car', whizzing through the misty Appalachians with its roaring turbo engine that got me three speeding tickets and one reckless driving ticket the first several months I owned it.

In my forties, I was living an American youth I had never had, while simultaneously trying my damnedest to be super-mother of the century and guard my sons from the very perils I myself was so drawn to: sex, booze, fast cars, a whirlwind existence of strong sensations and reckless choices. An American melody trailing on my car radio as I drove my energetic and now testosterone filled sons to their sports practices and games, would send me into a whirlwind of nostalgia for my pathetic Romanian youth, filled with hunger and fears, frustrations, food rations, and the secret police, yet sprinkled with moments of wrenching passions, losses, breathtaking views of the Carpathian Mountains, and sultry nights on the shores of the Black Sea.

Queen's *We are the champions* song on a record I found in a Bucharest bookstore weeks before my departure, represented what I had imagined then that America would be like. I had danced to Queen's song with my Romanian boyfriend in the glimmers of a late summer sunset seen from the balcony of our brand new privately-owned neighboring apartments in Bucharest. Gloria Gainer's *I will survive* that my high school classmate Daniela, who got pregnant and almost died of an illegal abortion, used to sing in front of the class to our absolute awe, was now broadcast on 'oldies' or 'classic rock' stations as I sat in my turbo Mercedes in the parking lot of my children's high school that happened to be a neighbor to both the local jail and the Seventh Day Adventist Church of Christ.

My children didn't care about Queen or the *I Will Survive* song. They were the real America of the twenty-first century, and the millennials generation, while I still carried in me trickles of an imaginary America filtered through communist restrictions and black-market purchases during a youth that in memory, seemed at times as unreal as my sitting in the parking lot of a high school next to a county jail and a Jesus cult church or watching a weird game of high school boys hitting each other with long sticks against a rural landscape of bluish mountains.

The Appalachians, the oldest mountains on the planet, corroded by millions of years of rains and wind, once inhabited by Monacan Indians and coyotes! Were these even my children? Who were they? Moments of gasping foreignness from everything and everyone including my own self took my breath away like a sudden vertigo. Tears of inexplicable yearnings filled my eyes at the most ridiculous and inappropriate moments such as welcoming my strapping boy of an American son at the gate of the stadium where his team had won another game of lacrosse in the regional competition.

My chain-smoking French lover broke up with me in an email message, which, although upsetting because it was by email, nevertheless gave me a feeling of relief. I didn't have to defend the importance of my scholarly work anymore, be wrought with guilt for my occasional absences from home, and deal with the debilitating jet lags. There was only one thing I missed about him, and it was the motorcycle rides across Paris at all hours of the day, the entire mystique of riding a motorcycle along the Seine as I was holding him and shouting French love words or funny sentences in the whipping Parisian wind.

I returned to my American second ex-husband like one who returns to a welcoming home, realizing I had yearned for him all along. We shared a luminous child conceived in delinquent mad turbulent passion, an undying love of French poetry and Tolstoy's *Anna Karenina*, an obsession with swimming, and an ineffable bond between our souls. Nothing was ever asked or mentioned between us about what I might have been doing and with whom I might have been doing anything whatsoever on my Parisian commutes. He was older and mellower, and I was older and more ferociously alive than ever.

My boys were moving through their adolescent years in waves and seesaws of quiet confusion, impatient exuberance, school assignments. I could no longer help them with homework unless they were studying English literature or French, complaining about unreasonable teachers with whom I had loud and belligerent arguments in the principal's office. My shrill accented voice sliced through the windowless hallways of the middle school or the county high school that my sons were attending, with all the jarring stridency of its foreignness. As it did on the playing fields whenever I cheered them on or during the self-important faculty meetings at my university.

Sometimes it seemed to resonate throughout the entire town against my will, with a force and will of its own, in ridiculous ripples of shrill vowels and clunky consonants. It once burst in the stuffy sweaty space of the office of some director of the local community sports organization when I went to complain about my younger son being left out of the more advanced soccer team.

Stocky pasty white men kept repeating, "Ma'am, calm down please," to which I breathlessly retorted, "Stop fucking calling me Ma'am. I'm not your fucking Ma'am!" The room became deathly quiet, and I burst out of it as turbulently as I had come in.

My voice sliced mercilessly through the southern drawl of church-going white Christians, of the good and nice people who judged my clothes, my mothering, my talking Romanian to my children as if that were the ultimate outward sign of my inner depravity.

A few years earlier, when the children were younger and wanted me around all the time, the main church dominating the most central intersection of our tiny town burned down, because of the mistake of one of the workers doing repairs on the roof. As I was driving down Main Street on a hot June afternoon to pick up my younger son from summer art camp, a formidable fire like the flames of Armageddon rose to the sky. My first thought went to my children. Were they safe and away from the fire? How do I get to both at once?

I revved the blue Nissan Sentra I owned then like mad on the side streets, remembered that my older son was on his summer month vacation with his father, thanked God for divorce and custody settlements, and that the camp for my younger son was two streets away, in a brick building. He was waiting for me in front of the building, his golden hair luminous in the afternoon sun. He was joyous and laughing as always, proud of his new art project.

"Mama, did you see the fire? The church is burning." Coming from his mouth in his sweet voice and perfectly pronounced Romanian words "arde biserica"—"the church is burning"—it sounded like a line from an old folk song. "Nobody is hurt," he informed me.

People stared at us as they always did, and our Romanian little secret cocoon of words somehow seemed even more incongruous and out of place because of the burning church. For a few seconds, I experienced a wicked satisfaction at the burning of the church, the white church dominating the city and the morality of its good citizens, and I burst into laughter, giving my son a tight hug and laughing into his hair. As he always did, he registered my mood and resonated with it like a bell, with deep, chunky giggles.

We went to the ice cream store on the next block and had our favorite, him plain chocolate, me lemon sorbet with coffee ice-cream. By the time we drove back home, the entire tower of the church had collapsed in demented wreaths of flames. I was fighting against my wicked satisfaction, the rift between the town and myself suddenly appearing abysmal and irreconcilable.

Years later, as my children were both petulant teens and I was faced with yet another foreign universe, that of the American high school culture, I sometimes calmed down from an unproductive argument with a teacher or school official by tapping for a quick second into that old vengeful satisfaction at the burning church and relishing in it. At the same time as I was doing it, I expected the town to punish me again with its solid Christian values.

Maybe I was the new Heather Prynne, only worse, because I was also a refugee, twice divorcee, I had a history of abortion and a huge scarlet stigma was pulsing on my forehead, on my chest, on my back. Any way I turned, the whole world could see the pulsing letters of my 'sins' and pagan foreign ways, not to mention the sin of being more successful at my work than most of my male colleagues who apparently had been surprised themselves at their own instantaneous unmerited tenures and promotions, whenever these promotions had been bestowed upon them in years past.

In the flames of the burning church, the girl on the train appeared magnificent. I had to save her and bring her out unscathed. She was saving my life just as I was saving hers. We were cooling each other off from the flames of our own little private hells. Slowly she formed her own destiny just as I was struggling with mine. The America of the small southern town I was still living in after ten, twelve, fifteen years was not getting any friendlier or more comprehensible. On the contrary.

Friendships with American women were thin and transitory, often disappointing to the point of heartbreak. I would have brief infatuations thinking I finally found my American sister. I confessed my life story to them leaving out some of the more shocking details like the double and triple adultery bit. I introduced them to my ex-husband/friend/father of my second child/ambiguous partner whom they usually measured in quick critical furtive glances from head to toes as a curiosity, not knowing what to make of our relationship, of his obvious old age, disheveled looks with a stack of scribbled note cards always stuck in his shirt pocket, of his odd habits such as reading the *Odyssey* as he was leaning against his red Nissan Sentra in a parking lot or during one of our son's tennis matches.

They didn't know what to make of our family, of my red dresses and the red lipstick I always wore, of the way I kissed and greeted my boys in Romanian even though they were now reaching or exceeding my height. Then a wall would set in between us, then an exhaustion and a boredom. I was too tired to reciprocate the dinners at my house, barely having enough energy to cook dinners for our own family.

Eventually, another friendship with one of the mothers of my children's friends or with a new colleague at the university would dissolve and be reduced to an occasional exchange when we ran into each other in the grocery store after work, as we were checking prices on the organic Boston lettuce or Roma tomatoes. I felt relief.

I had more time to devote to my girl who was now caught in the complications of her passionate love with a Romanian boy in the town in the Carpathians. She was starting to have suspicions about her lover, that he might be collaborating with the secret police, and she was preparing her escape, what would it be? The train, of course, she had to leave on the train, her entire destiny was going to be determined by that definitive gesture of her last farewell from the train window, her tears streaming down her face as the train departs and her face stuck to the windowpane, all the familiar landscapes rushing by her.

In his last two years of high school, my older son started a rock band with some of his friends and played in the shed in our backyard, to my great delight and the exasperation of our neighbors except for my loyal Russian friend. My younger son was taking piano lessons and every time his father and I had an argument, he went to the piano and played furiously to cover the din of our bickering.

During those years, our house and neighborhood resonated with my children's music, domestic bickering, laughter, our big messy lives. Spring and early summer weekends had a Tom Sawyer-ish lull and rhythm for a couple of years. It was mid-2000, and an exhilarating freedom swept through me in my forties coupled with my sons' young adult irrepressible energies.

The mischievous teenage boys playing rock in my backyard, The Who, Free Bird, hard rock rhythms thrusting through the walls and windows, Mozart's Rondo alla Turca galloping its trills from the inside. The boys' romping up and down the staircases of my old house gave me wild rushes as if it were my adolescence too. I took sandwiches and fruit to their band in the shed, brought them all in for my improvised dinners. Invariably though, every afternoon, about an hour into their practice, a police officer would show up at my door to tell me I was breaking the noise ordinance.

Every time, I argued with him and told him, "They aren't doing any harm. They are young. It's four in the afternoon on a Saturday. Would you rather they be doing drugs?"

And every time, invariably, the policeman would say, "Ma'am, it's the law."

I would say "What law? Show me!"

He would repeat, "Ma'am, it's the law! The neighbors are complaining. They either quiet down, or I'll give you a fine."

It turned out it was one of our neighbors, an old Hungarian man with his old American wife living two houses down from us, who called the police on us every time. She dusted the grass on her front lawn with a duster. This is how much she loved her front lawn and her afternoon quiet. I thought, of course, he was calling the police on us because he probably knew I was Romanian and was taking revenge on ancestral territorial feuds between our two nations: Romanians claimed northern Transylvania as their own and so did the Hungarians.

Americans and westerners in general, if they could even locate either one of our countries on the map, always took the side of the Hungarians and didn't want to hear or know about the Roman ruins found in different parts of northern Transylvania, the Hungarian or bilingual schools and churches strewn across that part of the country, even though they all said they were discriminated against, and always referred to Bucharest as Budapest. It wasn't only once that I told an American that I was from Bucharest to hear back that Budapest was a beautiful city.

My Hungarian neighbor with his well-dusted blades of grass awoke in me the last traces of nationalist pride I possessed. I considered him a clear enemy of my household and of my children's artistic development. I encouraged the rogue band playing in my shed with my son as the bass player to express themselves freely, one lazy afternoon after another. The police tired out and stopped coming to my door, but the tiny Hungarian man didn't, and one glorious afternoon as I was getting ready to go to the city pool for a swim, he beat his fist against my glass entrance door with a vengeance.

My ex-husband was happening to be visiting at that time, and he got to the door first as I was coming down the main staircase. He opened the door and the neighbor barged in pushing him away like he was entering his own house. My ex-husband pushed him right back, yelling "Hey, hey, what do you want?"

I suppose nothing intimidated my Hungarian neighbor because he pushed right past him, yelling my name, pronounced perfectly even with the sound of the cedilla on the A in my last name, which no American was ever able to pronounce. In trying to get to him faster, full of the fury I felt for being aggressed in my own house, I stepped over the last three steps on my way downstairs and instantaneously felt a shooting pain in my foot, realizing I had probably sprained or broken my ankle.

In the mixture of anger, pain, and confusion, I didn't follow any of his agitated perorations, and being sure he had come to complain personally about my son's band and their loud music, I yelled at him, "Shut up! Who are you, the secret police or something?" The pain in my ankle was unbearable as was the presence of the aggressive neighbor and the sight of his nose hairs and red face.

My younger son rushed in to see what was going on and stood in the doorway of the living room, staring bemused at the scene. His father must have noticed my misstep on the staircase and the grimace of pain on my face because he touched my arm gently after which he turned to the man and spoke to him in a firm tone like he was a child, "Leave her alone. She's a hard-working mother. Stop calling the police every time the boys are playing music, will you? It's good for them to play music. It makes the street more cheerful.

What's wrong with you?" The man was taken aback and hesitated for a few seconds, looking almost like he was going to turn around and leave.

Instead of responding to anything that was just uttered to him, my Hungarian neighbor pulled out a crumbled sheet of paper from his shirt pocket, stretched it out, and said, "Will you sign this please? It's a neighborhood petition about the streetlights. We need more streetlights on our street."

I held on to the banister to release my hurt ankle from the pressure and said to him, "I'll sign it only if you promise to stop calling the police every time you hear these kids play their music. What's wrong with you, were you never young?"

The man suddenly displayed a pained look on his face, "It's not me, it's my wife. She can't stand loud noises. She suffers from a chronic illness."

"That's too bad," I said, relentless, "tell her to use earplugs. If you want me to sign the bloody petition, you'll have to promise you'll never call the goddamn police again."

The man looked defeated and sighed but still didn't make the promise. Instead, he said, "I was never secret police, never, my family suffer from secret police in Hungary." Undoubtedly, communication was a tricky endeavor with that neighbor of mine. I felt sorry for him and his grass dusting wife with a chronic condition.

A memory of the man who appeared at the door of my old Bucharest apartment and handed an old coloring book to my children through the half open door instead of letting us in to visit the apartment, surged in my mind. The Hungarian man reminded me of the crotchety scared Romanian man during my first return visit, he reminded me of old Europe and its fastidious old men with memories of pre-communist times, with memories of war times and of post war times, half ceremonious half impetuous, with lives stretching across large historical periods, monarchies, wars, dictatorships.

Only that the one standing in front of me with his pathetic petition about the streetlights lived in small-town America in a house with a picket fence and perfectly dusted lawn. Nobody on this street cared about the feuds between our countries; nobody cared about our countries at all in the small town we lived. And yet even here, we had a tiny goddamn melting pot considering the size of the town: a Romanian living in an old sheriff's house, the first woman owner in its one hundred and forty years of existence, a Hungarian in the small house with the picket fence, my Russian friend who was hated by the confederate group in town because of her letters to the editor condemning displays of their stupid flags and who lived across the street in the bright yellow house.

Our memories stretched thousands of miles beyond those fences and streetlights, to an area known only by us, the Carpathians, the Black Sea, the Urals, the Danube, wide pastures roamed by shepherds and their flocks, old cities with five-hundred-year-old Byzantine churches. And there we were now within the circle of the Appalachians and the syncopated rhythms of southern speech, each cocooned in our homes and personal solitudes.

It wasn't communities, it was the conglomeration of solitudes of all ethnicities that made the spice of America. The pain in my ankle was making me half delirious as the seconds passed, and I wanted to get rid of the small Hungarian man and lie down in my spacious bedroom with a view of the maple tree tops.

I remembered that on our first morning in that house, my then husband, the man standing right next to me who was now trying to protect me from the neighbor's intrusion, had said, "Waking up here is like being born again." I also remembered that the first thought I had when I saw the inside of the house when the sheriff's ninety-year-old 'ditty' as the family called her, opened the door, was, *I want to die in this house.*

I had finally caught roots that entangled and wrapped themselves around the big old oak tree in the back, the maples in the front, the magnolia on the side, the dogwoods on each side, the buck-eyed chestnut at the back window, the crab-apple trees in the back yard. I was doomed, it would be heartbreak to ever leave the house, the town, the area.

Just when I was about to sign the petition, a car with flashing lights pulled right in front of the house. It was no other but the sheriff's car. The band in the shed was playing a version of Lynyrd Skynyrd's *Free Bird*, preparing for the talent show at school. The Hungarian neighbor was pushing a pen into my hand to sign the petition for more street lighting.

I thought the sheriff's car was there for trouble with some other neighbor, maybe the transients living in the rental house down the street. But no, there was the sheriff himself with his big sheriff hat coming right up the front stairs of my house. He shook the knocker on the front door just as I finished signing the petition. I limped to the door to open it, and there was the county sheriff looking stern and no nonsense like he was going to arrest someone. I thought for sure it was the music. But it wasn't.

It turned out that my angelic younger son, who wrote poetry and played Mozart on the piano, and his best friend decided to use my clunky cell phone to make prank calls, and it so happened that one of the calls reached the sheriff's office. That wasn't the worst part though, but the fact that my son's best friend asked the sheriff, who answered the phone, the million-dollar question—"Would you like to suck my hairy balls?"

This is what the sheriff described to us in the sternest possible manner. In the meantime, our little Dachshund Louie rushed to the door and started barking passionately at the sheriff. My prankster son and his friend came to the door to face the sheriff bravely. The Hungarian neighbor watched the scene with unflinching calm, happily holding his signed petition to increase the electrical input on our street.

My ex-husband produced a loud laugh at the sound of the boys' misdemeanor. I wasn't sure which of the two was stronger: my searing ankle pain or my desperate desire to also burst into irrepressible laughter at the sound of the sheriff pronouncing the misdemeanor and his self-important threatening seriousness. My son's friend on the other hand started bawling like mad, afraid of what his father was going to say and afraid that the sheriff was going to arrest him.

Neither my son nor his friend was old enough to have fully developed 'hairy balls', and the sheriff's fury seemed overblown. Between Louie's shrill and relentless barks, the sound of 'Free Bird' soaring from the shed in the backyard, the boy's unleashed crying, the effort I was making to abstain from laughing on the one hand and not to keel over from the ankle pain on the other hand, the sight of the street, of the beautiful and ornate front porch on which the sheriff was standing with one hand at his belt as if ready to pull out his gun and shoot, the sight of the majestic banister to my staircase, the crystal chandelier hanging above my head—all that seemed to turn round and round in an unstoppable carousel.

I was standing on the threshold of my house that had once belonged to the most famous and powerful sheriff in town, the present sheriff was standing on my front porch chastising my child and his friend for their obscene prank call, the maple branches in front of the house swayed in the afternoon summer breeze as if admonishing us all, or maybe just laughing at the scene. I had no reference to anything like that in my past.

I was caught between the ghost of the old, venerated sheriff and the Aryan young sheriff bouncing all too confidently from one foot to the other! Finally, this was a scene that didn't carry me to childhood or teenage scenes and landscapes and people in my past and whose layered madness, confusion, absurdity, and display of law and order existed in and of itself fully in the present.

Maybe I was crossing a threshold of pain, joy, and memory in this small town where I had been living for the entire life of my prankster son. Maybe the Free Bird of my older son's band was carrying me beyond the shackles of my past all while the house, the maple trees, the ornate porch and banister, my teenage sons were all grounding and rooting me.

Something in me changed in those moments and freed me from the agonizing neurosis of comparisons between the old world I was coming from and the new world I had resettled in more than two decades earlier. The European feeling of superiority that every immigrant I met, suffered from. The disdain towards 'the lack of history' of 'manners', of 'good tomatoes' that my compatriots with the only exception of my mother always expressed towards Americans and their country.

The mental burden and habit of always finding parallelisms between the European and American landscapes, food, manners, places, people, trees, birds, streets. Everything that I loved and hated about America was gathered in that moment on the threshold of my southern colonial house. I hated the very fact it was 'colonial' which meant at one time in its history it did not allow Black people to purchase it, that slave ownership had once existed on those very premises, that the university I taught at had been built with slave labor and shamelessly carried the name of the 'great' Confederate general.

I hated the smug whiteness of the sheriff and the whole good Christian bit, all wrapped in a lot of overblown sternness. I could have bet my entire paid portion of the house I was standing on that the stocky sheriff on my front porch who was preaching about the dangerous and inappropriate nature of the boys' prank, considered himself just such a good Christian even as he might have been judging everything about me at that time: my tight dress, my accent, my inattentive mothering that allowed for such misbehavior, my ironic smile instead of an obedient look, the fact that I worked and raised children all at the same time.

And everything I loved about America was right there, too; the wildness of it all, the rock and roll coming from the shed, the feeling of power that the ownership of the house gave me, and the feeling of freedom that my rootlessness also gave me, the fact that it didn't matter one bit that I was Romanian and the man with the petition and noise disturbance complaints was Hungarian and nobody gave a damn about the ancestral feuds between our countries.

The fact he could submit a petition signed by local citizens to city council to improve lighting on our street, and he wasn't going to be arrested for it. And the tall rugged scrawny old man who had fathered my child, standing next to me, half amused by the incident, half worried about my ankle—I loved him too, for who he was and for all the ways he embodied that American wildness, proud solitude, irreverence to almost every bloody norm of settled behavior and lifestyle.

In the meantime, the father of my son's friend showed up to pick up his son, and he looked utterly shocked by the crowd and commotion he saw on my front porch, with county sheriff and all. The sheriff was happy to oblige and to recount the entire event to the father all over again, the prank call, the lewd request by his son, the danger of making prank calls to the sheriff. The boy got a second wind of energy and restarted his howling. His father started scolding him vehemently.

The sheriff was still holding my phone, which I reclaimed right back, promising I was going to be more careful about where and in whose possession I was going to leave it. In the meanwhile, the boys in the shed concluded their practice and the four valiant rock and roll stars were coming down the side of the house, laughing and horse playing. They saw the flashing sheriff car before they saw the sheriff on my porch and my older angelic-looking son yelled, "Fuck man, what the fuck is the sheriff's car doing here?"

I was praying to all the spirits of the Native Americans that had once inhabited those lands before their genocidal decimation by white people like this sheriff right here, that no beer cans were to be found in the shed and that the sheriff wasn't going to get the idea to check on that. The sheriff heard the comments and stared at me as if to say, "Quite some mother you are, teaching your children such language."

That was when I came out of my own stupor and fascination with the scene and said, "Thank you, Sir, Mister Sheriff, sorry for the inconvenience, you have my word this will never happen again." Then I turned to all the young people on the premises and said, "Children, go inside!" I said a firm goodbye to the Hungarian neighbor with a tone that meant "I've had enough of you, please get the hell out of here".

I was 'femme sole' owner of my house indeed, as the contract on it read and indeed sole femme in that crowd of boys and men of all ages, many times 'sinner' in that town of confederates, standing next to my septuagenarian Yankee ex-husband, pioneer of sorts and having started a fresh generation of men on American soil.

After everybody left or went inside, the neighborhood resumed its quiet lazy summer afternoon lull. The pileated woodpecker that inhabited one of the trees surrounding the house announced its presence with its precise tick tock measuring the precarious yet precious seconds of our passage on earth. It was my favorite bird sound, and my children knew it by its Romanian name as well, *ciocănitoarea*. Whether pecking against my maple tree or against a Romanian birch tree in the Carpathian forests, the pecking sounded all the same.

I contained both of those realms inside me, and the woodpecker sounds on both continents coexisted in my conscience not just as memory and experience, but as the very reality of my flesh and blood existence, stubbornly encased in my body and soul.

That evening I ended up in the emergency room because of my right ankle strain, and a spider bite I hadn't noticed on my left foot, which had swollen to an alarming degree. My ankle was sprained, and the spider bite had reached a dangerous level of infection. It could have infected my blood and given me septicemia, the emergency doctor proclaimed.

Lucky, lucky me, always flirting with one disaster or another. I was barely able to walk with both feet wrapped in bandages and looking like a pathetic invalid. Twisted and poisoned limbs were not a good beginning to my summer, particularly since the children and I had travel plans back to Romania in a month. Treading on both adoptive and native lands appeared to be a challenge. I was going to be limping my way through that hot summer, searching for roots, attempting to grow new ones, letting go of old ones. Or not really letting go.

Earlier that year in April, when the dogwoods and the red buds were quivering their way into full bloom, I opened my email to the most astonishing letter of the century. A long, long, soulful and detailed letter from the man who had shaped my entire notion of love and marked my youth in irreversible ways. It had been a quarter of a century, we had crossed major existential thresholds, had become spouses, parents, professionals, and I a traveler to faraway lands, an exile, twice divorcee, a citizen of the United States, a citizen of a small American town and property owner of a respectable estate and piece of land from the old southern confederacy.

I was now part of a radically different history and landscape while he was still living in the same town of Brasov. It all came back with a vengeance in my corner office sitting in front of my computer: the memory of cool summer mornings, fragrant nights under the magical moon of the Carpathians, fragrances of pine tree and *regina noptii,* queen of the night flower, the languid whistling of the trains pulling into the nearby railway station or leaving toward far away destinations that I always yearned for. My youth, my love.

All unraveled and unearthed in a letter reaching me from the depths of time, in cyberspace, through a system of communication that twenty-five years ago would have appeared as fantastical as the episodes from *Planet of the Giants* we used to watch on our tiny black and white TV.

He had taken an engineering job in the depths of the Romanian countryside soon after my departure. He thought about me night after night watching the moon, reliving our love, regretting it, watching the moon again, living in a rural area in the middle of the Romanian nowhere with outhouse and water from a well. The secret police had followed and interrogated him after my departure, wishing to know if he had helped me escape. Then he met his future wife.

He mentioned that event as a quick parenthesis with no specific details, and yes, he would like to see me when I returned to the country. I spent the entire day at my office rereading the letter, trying to imagine his facial expressions as he wrote certain phrases, remembering tiny details of his face, the way he often filtered his looks through his dark lashes staring at something unfathomable in time or space, his laughter, his sadness, the way he placed his hands on my face, cupped the back of my head in his hands, his kisses. I sat and sobbed in my office on the campus of my university in the southern town where I was living in the United States of America, not sure whether it was the loss of country, of love, of youth, of native language that hurt the most.

I sat in my office until dusk fell over the ridges of the blue mountains, the old Appalachians whose contours I could see from my office window on the third floor of my university building. Layers of bluish mountainous ridges covered in pines and maples and sycamores, red buds and dogwoods, they were beautiful and foreign to a degree that caused me another heartache. I was a patchwork of heartaches, a quilt of heartbreaks in all shades of red, from the brightest cruelest red, like fresh blood squirting out of slashed flesh, to the darker shades, to the rosy shades of timid cuts, to the burgundy of scars and closed wounds, against the blue ridges of the Appalachians, on the same earth and yet so foreign.

Foreignness hurt like hell, and there was no remedy for it other than delight in it, embrace it, wallow in it, cuddle it like it was your own baby lost on the immensity of the planet. You made it your own and sang a bilingual lullaby to your own goddamn loneliness and foreignness.

When I entered my grand historic house that evening of the historic letter, my sons were having a dinner prepared by my ex-husband. He sat at the table proud of his dinner, a collection of foods poured out directly from cans and jars into bowls and plates, including a jar of beet-juice that he presented to the children as borscht and at which they were both staring with suspicious eyes, not really daring to taste it.

I was suspended between layers of foreignness and heartbreak cracks, and the beet juice matched my patchwork of bleeding wounds while also making me burst into laughter at my children's desperation in front of the makeshift dinner. They were not foreign, they were the one reality that was the very opposite of foreign, my roots, my America, my world, in whatever country we might have found ourselves; they were still going to be my flesh and blood children.

I said, "I'm going to make a mamaliga with eggs and cheese," the classic Romanian meal or side to meals, comfort food made of corn mush.

"This isn't very good, Mama," said my younger son in Romanian, referring to the outrageous bowl of beet juice presented to him as borscht soup. My older son agreed and took advantage of the moment when his ex-stepfather wasn't looking to spit the spoonful he had taken back into the bowl.

I laughed in my head at the notion of the ex-stepfather, I laughed at the whole damn scene, at myself and my refugee ongoing melodrama, because that's what us Romanians do best, laugh at our misery, cry at our joys. We even have a Laughing Cemetery, now a hot tourist spot in the north of the country and a UNESCO protected site. A blues song started playing on the radio in the kitchen, sultry, dark, bittersweet, telling a story of heartbreak and mistreatment, of loneliness and lost love, as most blues songs tend to do.

It cheered me up and it filled me with all the melancholy of the world all at the same time. It reminded me how much I loved America, like a wild and sexy lover, that America of the broken-hearted and the lonely, of the endless highways with trucks and cars incessantly whizzing into the great American night. The adventure I had always dreamed of when I was preparing to leave my then communist country, in the end landed me in the place I had least expected—rural deep America, the south, the small town cradled in a curl of the Appalachians.

With adventure came freedom, with freedom came loneliness. If you got fucked one way or another, you might as well embrace it. As I was stirring the cornmeal mush in my luxurious kitchen listening to the sexy melancholy blues song, to my children's chatter, to my ex-husband's comments, I knew I would have done it all over again and again and again if given the chance to rewind my past and start over. Leave my country, that is.

I was a mistress of many masters, of many countries; two husbands and a few lovers, I wanted it all, in packages of contradictions and paradoxes, the adventure and the safety, the freedom and the roots, the loneliness and the family, Blues, Rock 'n' Roll, Chopin, Europe, Romania, France, America, the world.

That night, I announced to my children we were going back to Romania in the summer via London, why not? Although they didn't show a huge amount of excitement, having been several summers in a row already, the news of London made them perk up and forget the less than satisfying dinner served to them. The Romanian polenta made things a bit better, as hardy comfort meals tend to fill the belly and appease the soul for a short while.

The summer evening with my son's phone pranks that brought the county sheriff to my door, with my twisted ankle and poisonous spider bite, we all sat in my spacious backyard watching the fireflies sparkle in the long stretch of grass and the surrounding bushes, listening to an Edith Piaf record. I brought outside the boom box that my ex-husband had gotten fifteen years earlier to fill our passionate love sessions in Chicago hotels with Chopin's nocturnes or the sentimental songs of Edith Piaf like the one we were listening to right now in the big American summer night adorned with fireflies and sprinkled with the fragrances of honeysuckle.

Everything had a history and every object and bit of space I had surrounded myself with, contained layers of my past, of the countries I had left, imagined, traveled to, made my home in or yearned for. My sons made fun of my two bandaged ankles and said I was going to travel in a litter pulled by servants like an Indian princess.

Nobody knew I was also preparing for my epic encounter with my first love on my journey later that summer. I held my secret and cradled it like a fragile baby staring at the dizzying dance of the fireflies. *Non, je ne regrette rien*, sang Edith Piaf as *Free Bird* still resonated in my memory of earlier that day. A day like a year that stretched across the arc of my cultural and geographic promiscuity with all the thrills and agonies of an incorrigibly double life.

The Trickery of Success

One April towards the end of the 2000s, on the exact day of my father's birthday, I received an email message from my literary agent whom I had found in an encyclopedia-sized book of literary agents the year before, that had me gasp, hold my breath, and burst into sobs—all in that order. After sixty-four rejections from literary publishers over the course of the previous year, my first novel that emerged from years of tours and detours, searches, creative agonies and ecstasies was not only accepted but 'bought' by a major publishing house for a sum larger than my entire annual salary at that point in my life.

The language of the big trade publishing world was new to me, and the fact that somebody was going to pay a five-digit figure for my book manuscript was unbelievable. In the typical manner of the catastrophic thinking of my people, added to the super calamitous thinking of my own family, with the joy came the fear that a tragedy was lurking in the near future in order to balance out the enormity of such an unthinkable success. The power of the two opposing forces battling each other inside my brain kept me in a state of paralysis in front of my computer.

Scared by my sobs, my sons rushed into the room to see what had happened. They laughed mischievously at the news and mocked my crying. "Wow mom, that's really cool, it's awesome," they said almost in unison after which they went on about their business, music, or homework assignments.

Mine was a classic 'rags to riches' story, I thought to myself after I calmed down. The girl on the train had pursued and completed her journey and her voice must have touched the chords of an important editor in a New York high rise. Except for my immediate family, I kept the news secret from all friends and colleagues until near the publication date the following year. All the Romanian superstitions came to life in my otherwise supposedly atheistic brain while I was also inwardly gloating.

Over the next months, publishers from all over the world were throwing tens of thousands of dollars, euros, and British pounds to publish my novel in widely spoken or small circulation languages, from French and German to Dutch, to Hebrew and Lithuanian. Two British publishers competed over my book in an auction, and I gave it to the one that also paid me to write my next novel.

For sure, my writing career was set, and it could only keep ascending for as long as I had stories to tell and novels to contain those stories. If only my father were still alive to see me now, if only my aunt Mimi who died alone in her Bucharest apartment during our first summer in Chicago could see me now. I was vindicating my father's unpublished poetry books, my aunt's un-produced plays, all the writers and dreamers in my family.

I was the first Romanian in America with such meteoric novelistic success, not to mention the two acres of land that I owned behind my historic house. I was also vindicating my own miseries created by my relationships with university colleagues who had been mean and hostile, had put me down or treated me as invisible, had spoken behind my back, had stuck their noses into my private life only to punish me for it in the workplace, and had tormented me with myriads of hostilities before my tenure.

Maybe now finally, I could leave my teaching job at the small southern university and teach at a prestigious university in a big city away from the stupid confederacy. Still, I held my glorious secret like a precious baby, both vulnerable and delicious, protecting it from evil spirits, jealousies and envy, walking the streets of my town with a new bounce in my step and a mischievous smile.

My older son was finishing high school and my younger one middle school, moving through stages, rites of passage, puberty, first girlfriends, preparations for college for one and for high school for the other. It was a chaotic and whimsical spring, with heavy rains and flash floods, outbursts of wicked sun, stridently pink and magenta dogwoods, and red buds in bloom. On top of the news of publication I also received an international fellowship to teach in Romania, at the university located in my mother's native town, deep in the heart of Transylvania.

I was at the top of my game for sure, yet the accumulation of success brought with it incomprehensible fears and restlessness. My sons were restless too in their burgeoning bodies and confused teenage spirits, and as usual, I absorbed all their anxieties and ecstasies, their highs and lows, while also attending all their games, recitals, concerts. I tried to breathe in unison with them hoping my breath will keep them safe and protected.

From the first installment of my advances, I paid off all my debts writing huge four and five-digit checks like I had never done in my life, feeling like I finally matched in income the majesty of the house I was living in, which some people in town were still resentful I owned because they had wanted it for themselves. Or that was my perception, based partly on rumors, partly on comments made directly to me by these kind people.

One afternoon that spring after returning from one of my younger son's games and stopping for a bite to eat in a neighboring town, the friends who were accompanying us received a message on their cell phones that a high schooler, possibly two, had drowned in the river at a dangerous junction near the dam where the waters were furious because of the recent rains. I knew by name and face both kids mentioned. In a small town, everybody knows everybody's children.

These were kids I had seen at piano recitals, band concerts, end of school years celebrations, games, hanging out on the benches in the little park in the center of town. I had seen them grow from toddlers to awkward looking pre-teens to apathetic or hyperactive teens. The mood at the table of an Indian restaurant in a mall by the side of an interstate became gloomy. I had one child with me while the other was still in town, possibly at Lacrosse practice, or playing music with his friends, or just hanging out.

The area around the river junction where the two youth might have drowned was a popular spot where kids and teens practiced their various sports, bathed in the river, or listened to music blasting from their pickup trucks. It had once been a lock, a point of passage for the flat boats going down the river with merchandise in the previous century, maybe even a point through which one or two slaves from the tobacco plantations might have tried to escape. Good for them! Heavy southern histories simmered under every stone, at every corner, at every bent of the river in that town and county that was now my home.

No plantation owners had been in any of my lineage, and I had enough of my own European histories of fascism and communism to contend with. I used to love waiting for my kids at that point of the river, watching groups of middle-schoolers and high-schoolers laugh, playfully push each other around, smoke secretively—being young in America—something I had never been and had always voraciously wanted to have been.

As we were delving into our Indian curries and nan bread that afternoon, the father of my son's friend, the same one who had invited the sheriff to my doorstep a couple of years earlier with his naughty phone calls, sent a text message about the status of the search for the two boys. One had survived, while the other was swallowed by the furious waters. After many panicked attempts, I was able to reach my older son who told me he happened to be at the famous spot by the river with his friends.

His biology teacher and another musician friend of his were the ones who had saved one of the two boys but lost the other one. The waters were too swollen. The boy got entangled in algae and was carried by the current down the river towards the dam. They couldn't find his body. I cringed and bent over at the image of the young boy entangled in algae, trapped and drowned at the bottom of the muddy flooding river waters. My son was drowned in sadness. He knew the boy, red-headed, a talented pianist and consummate swimmer and scuba diver.

Upon our return to town that evening, the bridge across the river was filled with townspeople looking over the rails as if searching for the lost child, and police cars, ambulances, fire trucks were blocking the entire area. An ominous gloom enveloped the town over the following days, as teams of rescuers and professional divers from neighboring cities had come to find the body of the lost boy.

I stayed as close as I could to my sons, dreading, like all the other parents in town, what it would be like to find ourselves in the shoes of the lost boy's parents. A tragedy in a small town took on an entirely different rhythm and shape than in a big city. Life, death, birth, all the rights of passage acquired a wrenching poignancy and stridency. They hit you in the gut whether you wanted it or not, because it all happened right next to you and because you knew everybody.

The news of the many international deals for my novel flooding my email inbox seemed almost offensive at that time, irrelevant and unimportant. The last line from the play *Oedipus Rex* kept ringing in my head during those days, "Do not consider yourself a happy man until you have lived your last day on earth." I translated it into, "Do not get arrogant and too sure of your success, and do not gloat because misery can strike at any time".

The refugee that I was knew better how to deal with difficulties and obstacles than with success and happiness. That refugee girl was going to be forever mistrustful of the stability of happiness. And the tragedies that were looming over the little town where I had ended up, were the very proof of that. Even though I held idealized images and fantasies of what it would have been like to grow up in America, I felt that everything bad was happening now precisely because of America. The recklessness of it, the fixation on the independence of children before they were fully cooked human beings, the carelessness of the parents, the cars, the booze, the obsessive athleticism, the bad temptations of drugs, porn, guns.

I had horrific fantasies of my children being swept away by the mad currents of all that like the red-haired boy being swept away by the current of the swollen river. The spring before, a girl who had babysat for my children had been killed in a car accident driving with her boyfriend from the prom. They were sixteen-year-old children. And still that same spring, a month later, a high school boy shot himself in the head with his father's gun. So much for how safe and nice a place to raise your children our town was! It all felt dark and wickedly unsafe to me.

With each one of those accidents, a barrage of sickening clichés would start circulating about 'the town coming together' and 'praying for the family'. Vigils and romanticized gatherings of the high school friends and classmates were held in one of the pretty natural spots around town. It all seemed fake and misguided. I would have wanted to see dark mourning and loud wailing across town, a long cortège of wailers with no words.

As the town was filling up with rich white retirees settling into expensive mansions to spend their old age in the quaintness of the town and move between the proliferating banks and churches in their luscious sedans, stocky and severe looking cops kept multiplying and making sure no teenagers were 'loitering' at street corners or on the park benches to spoil the pristine look of the town. It wasn't clear where other than their parents' basements were those kids supposed to spend their free time when they weren't running and hitting a ball on the playing field. I started hating the entire notion of the 'nice community' and 'the nice town'.

I was hoping that my writing success was going to allow me to take my teenage boys away from that provincial setting, sell my coveted property for a mega sum, and move back to my first American city: the rowdy, windy,

210

bustling Chicago amid all the pollution, traffic and noise. For sure now that I was a rising star in the big trade publishing world, I should have more career choices, be hired by a bigger university in a real city.

And yet, I was becoming more entrenched in the town with every new spring and every new graduation, high-school prom, sports season, summer camps, first dogwoods in bloom, then lilies in bloom, then irises bursting in their mauve glory. The plant cycles enmeshed with our lives, the lives of the Romanian speaking family in the big sheriff's house. I had witnessed the tragedies of the town, cried for its prematurely lost youth, rejoiced or cringed at band concerts and Christmas parades.

Every street and corner of the town quivered with memories of my children at different stages of their lives. And as I became more entrenched in our American small town, I was also spreading my tentacles across the ocean back into my native land in my insatiable voraciousness for home, land, the totality of me.

I was preparing for my six months away with extraordinary anticipation. My children were rooting me in American soil with every step, yet precisely because of that, I needed more than ever to search for the childhood and young adulthood I had left behind one September day in 1983. It always came back, hopelessly—the day of my departure, the last goodbyes, the suitcase, the heartache, the airport, the customs officers, the suitcase again, the airplane to Fiumicino Rome, the arrival in Rome ready to forget everything and begin everything.

The girl on the train had luckily come to life during that first decade of the new millennium and was now on her own, ready to go out into the world and unfold her story of love, escape, train rides, heartbreak, new beginnings, America, and to return after twenty years. Her story was complete, but I was not. Her story was making me a lot of money but was not making me whole. My life of doubles, of returns and back-and-forth journeys between native and adoptive lands was only starting.

That spring and summer of my big breakthrough in the American literary scene, of the tragedies in my hometown, of preparations for my older son's going away to college, and of my own preparations for a temporary simultaneous existential re-rooting/uprooting, life unfolded in a rollercoaster of unprecedented thrills and anxieties. Publishers from across the world were enticing me with book deals and contracts, with thousands of dollars that were wired into my bank accounts and plans for glamorous book tours, interviews, choices of book covers.

They 'loved' my story. They all said that 'the voice is so unique', the style 'so lyrical, so poetic'. They all marveled at how 'amazing' it was that I wrote in English so well. The line about my good English always sounded more like an insult than a compliment. I was the non-native speaker, the one speaking English as a second language. Among the many editors who had earlier rejected my manuscript, there were often those who praised the mastery of my English 'despite' my non-native status and yet wrote their rejection letters in worn-out clichés that to my non-native ear sounded rather simplistic and repetitive coming from a native speaker with an editing job at a major American publishing house.

I remembered one of my graduate school professors in Chicago who once told me I was never going to be able to teach English literature in an American university because of my foreign accent, so I should consider pursuing my degree in Romance languages instead of comparative literature which had been my desire. I was wickedly thinking now that if I ever saw her, I would say to her something like, *how many international presses are paying thousands and tens of thousands of dollars to obtain translation rights to your insipid books of literary theory?*

I didn't allow myself such gloating pleasures too often though both out of ancestral beliefs of impending catastrophe and out of very contemporary anxieties about splitting my already thinly spread family in two: one son going to college in America, the other accompanying me to Romania. In between the two stretched the unfathomable chasm of ocean waves and continents.

The following months galloped at a dizzying rhythm, punctuated by more heartaches and thrills. Taking my older son to college, getting him settled, and leaving him in his tiny college dorm room, his brother bursting into tears and saying 'it's the end of an era', just days before we were leaving on a six-month adventure back to the country I had run away from at full speed twenty-five years earlier—it all came with a sour taste of freshly cut wounds, like the taste of blood in your mouth after a hard fall or a hit.

A deep rattling confusion was taking hold of my entire being and a sense of breakage, of crumbling homes like the sound of broken glass years earlier when my younger son kicked his soccer ball full force through the front door.

Shattered glass, it all sounded and felt like shattered glass in my heart and in the new reality I was plunging into.

All throughout departure preparations, my new editor from the big New York press would send me copious editorial notes about how I should revise, rewrite, cut this part here and this part over there, this one is too jarring, this other one is too slow, too lyrical, not lyrical enough, too detailed, not detailed enough. What year exactly did this character take this trip, what color of eyes did this character's friend have? There was always too little of something, too much of something else.

I should have known it all came at a price: the money, the sudden low-grade fame in the larger scheme of fame, the breakthrough of a lifetime for me. The proverbial selling of your soul to the devil. Selling a bit of yourself and of the very writing that brought you where you were, in exchange for what? Money? My work, my story, my voice became the property of the publisher, and I had to play by those rules of commodification if I wanted the success. And boy did I want the success. Why else had I left everything and everyone a quarter of a century earlier if not for that kind of success?

A basic truth became clear during the months prior and post publication of my first novel; I could have had marriages, divorces, children, even a post revolution house in my native land, but the writing success was the overriding reason for the brutal choice I had made as a young woman. The much idealized yet not to be taken for granted freedom of speech, freedom of expression, blah, blah, blah. I had left with the unpublished volume of short stories titled *Yes but Life* in the mythic suitcase, with one thought towering above all others, *I will become an important writer one day, an artist!*

I was now damn close to that initial dream, yet the question of true freedom of expression became tricky, without a clear-cut answer. It was a larger cell with movable walls, a larger cage, but still a cage. One form of censorship took the place of another. An imaginary Reader was always invoked for every chunk of writing I was asked to take out or transform, "this chapter is confusing for the reader", "you have to make this clearer for the reader", "the reader will have a hard time with this passage".

I didn't know who that Reader was and didn't care a bit about them. If such a Reader existed, they were a profoundly confused Reader to start with, one who needed to be spoon-fed and held by the hand at every step of the plot of my highly priced novel. One who couldn't think for themselves, couldn't imagine what was not said from what was being said, who had trouble following the meandering paths of memory, who needed to be entertained at every step, for whom my Romanian heroine was an exotic ethnic distraction like Vietnamese food, embroidered Mexican blouses, or Thai massages.

At times I wanted to give it all up and say *fuck this, I don't want to take out this part here and this other passage here just to satisfy some dumb imaginary reader consumer.* I wanted to stop the entire process. And then what? To give it all up for an ambition and a whim? At other times, I sat at my computer for hours and diligently worked my way through the maze of markings and notations, trying to convince myself that the line being fed to me by my editors, agents, assistants to editors, that they were all wanting me to polish the book into 'the best that it could be' was true.

Everybody knew better than the writer what that meant, even though the writer had spent many years already doing just that: working to make the book 'the best that it could be', molding her story this way and that way, following the girl on the train obsessively on all her early morning escapades to her forbidden lover, following her as she leaves the country that she loves forever in an empty train compartment, no, in a compartment with several other people, following her as she leaves on the train to Trieste, no as she hitchhikes from Belgrade to Trieste in a yellow Fiat driven by an Italian businessman.

Everybody knew better about the book than the author herself who, besides having written and nursed it with the meticulous care you would have for a beloved child, had also read and studied entire lines of national literatures, the French, the British, the Italian, the American, the classics, the neo-classics, the moderns, the post-moderns, the stream of consciousness writers, the traditional linear narrative writers, the 'écriture féminine' with circular and spiraling narrative writers.

This author had pored over manuscript pages of famous French writers, deciphering their handwritten notations and revisions on typed yellowed pages, compared them with the published originals and noted they were almost entirely similar, the manuscripts and the published versions that is. It appeared that no Gallimard editors demanded of André Malraux or Albert Camus to take out whole chunks of their novels or rewrite entire passages. Yet she never dared allude to her literary knowledge in any of the communications with the prestigious editor from the prestigious press, for who was this unknown Romanian author but a refugee writing in English as a second language?

This, she timidly mentioned a couple of times when the occasion arose: so were some big writers, the likes of Vladimir Nabokov, Joseph Conrad, Jack Kerouac to name just a few, forsaking their native Russian or Polish or French to write in various brands of British or American English. But launching into such commentaries only made this author appear 'too academic', which was a bad thing to be in the American trade publishing world.

Not that I always found myself at ease in the academic world I had been part of for a couple of decades and some, and not that I hadn't often found the glaring pretentiousness of that world annoying as hell at times, but this was a different type of pretense that seemed just as pernicious. The pretense of having no pretense, of posing as the surprise writer emerging out of the blue, out of the difficulties of immigrant life with no literary role models, a colorful mushroom sprung out of nothing in a brush covered forest. There was also the other revered model of writer cuddled and molded by the famous Iowa creative writing school or their equivalents.

Any way you turned, your book and your person had to be labeled, catalogued, prepared for consumption with all the right frills and packaging. The more sensational, the better. I had urges to illustrate the great revelation I had once had on the plane during my first return to native soil, that refugees had to be perfect con artists. I crawled under barbed wire across the Romanian border towards freedom, I floated inside an inner tube across the Danube River, I escaped hidden in a vegetable box in the back of a truck driving to Yugoslavia smelling of onions and rhubarb, and I gave myself in to the customs police upon my arrival out of the veggie box.

There were all 'true stories' of ways in which some of my compatriots had left Romania during those dark hungry scary eighties, but they were not mine. Had I hitchhiked from Belgrade to Trieste like my heroine? Had I left by train? By boat, what? No none of that. I had left on a plane with a tourist visa to Rome. My heroine had been a lot more adventurous than me. There was such a thing as a writer's imagination, I wanted to say smugly, irritated by the compulsive need for the 'the real story'.

I now admired Emily Dickinson more than ever, how she lived secluded in her house in Amherst, Massachusetts, with a minimal social life, away from crowds and blitz of any kind, and said everything there is to say about life, love, death, loss, despair, joy, and beauty in her perfect poems. She had never become 'an author', but she had remained just a poet, and I loved her for it.

But then again, she was born and raised in one of the most intellectually sophisticated towns and environments in America, never uprooted, disrupted, transplanted from native soil into foreign soils across an entire ocean. It all came down to the refugee thing again and again.

Sometimes, I resorted to tricks I had learned during my young years in Romanian schools. Who said living under a communist dictatorship didn't have its lifelong benefits? A passage I cut here, reappeared later in the book as a memory, condensed and shortened. Details I was asked to add or develop ballooned into new images or episodes. Images I was asked to replace reappeared under different guises, a game of hide and seek with words against the big corporate machine of publishing with its hundreds of editors and assistants to editors and publicists and assistants to publicists all working on a top floor of a 99-floor New York high-rise inside cubicles and offices looking out onto the Empire State Building or the Hudson River or some other mythic New York landmark.

After the publication of the book, it wasn't all stifling and irritating though. There was glamour, money, paid trips to New York, fancy lunches to such and such special restaurant with some famous Greek owner and chef, times when I truly admired my editor, her savvy mind and eloquence, and the way she had gotten to the very top of that huge publishing corporation. I hoped she would publish all my future novels that were already bubbling inside my overstimulated brain.

In those moments, I was bursting with love and affection for my editor, my press, the entire staff working on the publication of my book all the way to the concierge at the bottom floor who always asked for and kept my picture ID whenever I visited the press. I gushed with gratefulness to everybody who was paying attention to the refugee me and to my novel beyond any of my wildest dreams of publishing success. A refugee's gratitude to anyone lending them a hand to hop from one shore to the next!

And then there were the times when a deep hollow emptiness settled inside me and when the persona, I was expected to represent loomed alien and fake and hovered above me ironically as I was picking at a famous Greek salad. I looked 'so Romanian', I was told, which I had no idea what it meant, and the strain of trying to fit some image of the author that wrote the story of the girl who grows up in Bucharest, falls in love with a man in the picturesque city at the foot of the Carpathians, leaves lover country and family on a train to

Belgrade, extended my psyche like a weak elastic band and threw me into unnecessary revelations of personal details about my life, which I sorely regretted the next minute.

The persistent question always remained, "What was real, autobiographical in the novel?" I didn't know anymore, and I didn't care. It wasn't important, I tried to explain. But yes, it was. Had I myself lived through all that was in the novel? "Readers are interested in the person of the author." Again, the famous Reader looming above us: the avid consumer of books by ethnic authors who needed everything in the story to be spelled out. I was caught in a game of fluffy falsities that looked and tasted delicious, cotton candy for a starved soul that left you even more starved after gorging on it.

The book tours over the following few years were a whirlwind of new countries, photo shoots and intrusive interviews in which I was asked repeatedly how autobiographical my novel was and how bad had it been to grow up in communist Romania. I played along until I couldn't stand hearing myself utter the same lines, the same boohoo story about how I escaped my dictatorship ridden country, started from nothing in Chicago, 'missed my country', worked so many jobs while finishing up my university studies, on and on.

So, I would start embroidering around my so-called story, searching for shocking paradoxes like "everything and nothing is autobiographical" in my novel. I sometimes wanted to invent inexistent chunks of my past, fictionalize myself until nobody, not even I knew anymore where autobiography ended and where fiction started. All and nothing indeed. I had escaped my country hidden in the toilet of a train going to Belgrade, after which I lived in a refugee camp in Trieste and arrived alone and starving in America on the good will of a charitable sponsor I had met at the Romanian seaside in the seventies.

I could go on and on inventing my so-called story. In an interview on French television, I said something like this, "My novel is as autobiographical as Vincent van Gogh's sunflowers or chair." The famous French radio interviewer moved on to the next question, dismissive of my whimsical answer.

The best interview ever was in Amsterdam because it was not about my autobiography or my novel, but about cars, which was so bad that it became good. It was an interview coupled with a photo shoot to market the newest brand of the Romanian-made car, Dacia. A Romanian American author driving a Dacia, coming out of the newest Dacia model, sitting on the hood of the new Dacia Logan in a futuristic park in Amsterdam or at the wheel of the sexy and affordable car. A Romanian author driving a Romanian car in Amsterdam.

I embraced the stereotype and the simplistic coupling, as if anything Romanian went with anything else Romanian, an author with a perfume brand, an athletic shoe brand, an ice-cream flavor, a hot-dog type, it didn't matter, as long as it had even remotely come from Romania. I rejoiced in the photo shoot like a movie star on location. At least nobody obsessed about the autobiographical elements in the novel.

Passersby stared curiously as the photographer of the famous Dutch car magazine was taking shots of me in a variety of curious poses on top of, near, or inside the glossy blue car. My younger son who was accompanying me everywhere, approved of me and smiled at my glamorous love affair with the Romanian car in Amsterdam, concluding "that's really cool, Mama."

Success was like a treacherous lover, thrilling and terrifying. And it always left you dissatisfied, like a big-time *coitus interruptus*, often vacuous, at other times offering addictive and fleeting satisfactions. This was a luxury you had dreamed of, never thought you would afford and suddenly there you were staying at a five-star hotel all paid by the publisher, overlooking one of the most picturesque canals in the city, where other writers much more famous than you had been lodged in the past.

You were asked to sign a copy of your book for the hotel to add to their collection of signed copies of authors, and you imagined a future where the autographed copy of your novel and a picture of you holding your book become a treasure that the hotel will proudly show to other tourists—here stayed the Romanian American author in September 2009—like you see pictures of Frank Sinatra or Dean Martin on the walls of semi famous restaurants.

Aren't you lucky to have eaten an arugula salad in the same place where great Hollywood stars swished by in the sixties or seventies? It stopped being about the work you put into making the book, and it started being about something frivolous, painfully transient, and pleasurable like the high of a drug. You were caught in it and couldn't stop, wanted more of the high, craved more desperately for the attention, the amenities, all the surface things that gave you temporary pleasures until the surface became the essence, and it was all you wanted.

After the rush was gone, you felt vacuous, embarrassed, drenched in inexplicable sadness. You had to hold on to who you were, to the part in you that had written and imagined out of the sheer joy, agony and necessity of it, not because of the high it gave your ego when you were signing your copy of the book for the staff of the five-star hotel or the fun you had sitting cross legged on the hood of the Romanian-made Dacia car against a wall of stylized Dutch graffiti.

But first came the Romanian six-month sojourn, and the book tours rumbled into my life the following years, as if I were starting over all over again only from a place of glamour and success. Arriving in Northern Transylvania with a son starting his first year in high school, four suitcases, and a lot of apprehensions was something of a comic mini drama. Although we had gone to Romania frequently in past years, arriving for half a year on a scholar's teaching fellowship was a different story.

The official driver that picked us up from the airport in Bucharest and took us to the hotel where we were supposed to stay for a few days raved against his own compatriots for an entire forty-five minutes, calling Romanians every insult under the stars, from retards to imbeciles to charlatans and always returning to imbeciles, as his preferred insult. Good entry into my country!

I had left it a quarter of a century ago for very clear reasons, and men like our temporary driver were among those reasons. Moving through my native Bucharest after decades of absence was always like being inside of a Luis Bunuel movie, gliding through someone else's dream of a dream. Familiar streets become unfamiliar, doors didn't open, dead end streets I had thought were entries onto a boulevard, always something unfinished, a conversation interrupted mid-sentence, a road that melted into an unknown passageway.

I was happy when I escaped from the maze of familiar unfamiliar streets, rundown buildings, a bank in a high rise where an eighteenth-century church might have been. I was happy when my son and I got on the train to the destination where we were going to spend half a year of our lives. We were northern Transylvania bound, to my mother's birth city, from where her family had to flee during the war traveling on cattle trains when the entire region had been taken over by Hungary because of the Vienna pact in 1940. At the end of the war, the region was returned to Romania, but my mother's family were already settled in Brasov, the city at the foot of some of the most dazzling Carpathian crests. The city of the setting of my first novel.

As our train pulls into the station, I am filled with my mother's wartime memories as if they were mine. A bay window from where she was staring at the courtyard, a linden or a walnut tree on which she climbed every day and made adventurous tree houses with her sister. A summer during the war when she became delirious from a tetanus infection in the house on the other side of the mountain, in a village with an ancient fort where their family had taken refuge from the bombings by American fighter planes.

This city of my mother's birth breathes with ancestral memories though it is new to me and am yet to discover it, being a foreigner in my own birth country. The candy-colored baroque buildings of the opera house, the national theater, the palace of justice, they soothe most anxieties I might have had about living here for half a year. This is my journey to a utopian Romania that I have never known but only dreamed of.

Over the following months, I recklessly re-root myself in it with the gusto of a famished exhausted weary traveler. My son follows in his mother's reckless steps and makes friends, falls in love, learns the slang, studies hard to excel in the school I enrolled him in, just as if he were going to live here for good. These are also the months of my growing success, delicious, dizzying, and addictive.

The manuscript of my novel with copy edits written in red pencil by my editor is being sent to me by international express mail, no money spared. Plans for a photo shoot by a famous photographer who had photographed Samuel Beckett and Simone de Beauvoir are made, and we take weekend journeys across my birth country staying at the fanciest hotels that most natives cannot afford.

We take taxis everywhere, many taxis, with taxi drivers who befriend me and take us on tours to nearby sites and cities, or just around our host city as if they were family friends. Until one of them who treats me so much 'like family' only to scam me of no less than several thousand dollars. Ani is the only woman taxi driver in town who happens to stop one rainy afternoon when I flag her at the corner of a busy intersection as I am carrying my heavy backpack filled with my laptop computer and books and a grocery bag in each hand.

Ani's children are working themselves to death in London and not managing, so she said. Ani has bad teeth, a cheating boyfriend, her taxi is a rattling Dacia car. Ani spills all her miseries into my ears and melts my vulnerable Romanian American refugee heart so that I start giving her higher and higher tips until the tips turn to monetary gifts or expensive taxi trips to far away towns for which I would have paid a third of the amount were I to have traveled by train.

The Ani story of con artistry burns me to this day not because of the several thousand dollars, though that's not negligible either particularly when three thousand dollars is still an average yearly pension in Romania, but because of the colossal suspense of common sense that my brain decided to fall into, because I had been conned so shrewdly and obviously. Me, who had thought of myself as the con artist refugee of the century.

There was raw excitement mixed in with wrenching melancholy to those days in the unknown but strangely familiar city. A taste of ancestry and times gone by, of traces of family stories lingering at street corners from the times of my mother's childhood on the cusp of World War II. There were thrilling and troublesome incongruities about my life journey and about where I was at that point in my life in relation to where my mother had once been three quarters of a century earlier.

The taxi drivers connected me and my son to the city in colorful and sometimes adventurous ways. We took three or four taxis a day, we made friends with the drivers and called or texted them to pick us up at such and such an hour and at such and such a place, to take my son to soccer practice, to drive him to a school activity at 7 am in the morning.

They became friends, babysitters, story tellers. Some drove the wrong way on one-way streets, some drove with nails in their tires and asked us to wait while they fixed their tires, others showed us pictures of their grown emigrated children smiling on some manicured lawn in an American suburb, others volunteered long speeches on the sociopolitical situation of the country at that point in history, others asked curious questions about our situation as Americans living in Romania for half a year.

But Ani was different. She was a bundle of tragic and funny stories that constantly evolved and that she shared with me as if I was a family member. A weakness, a loose link in my psyche needed that shared vulnerability, a misplaced sense of guilt because of my present economic abundance and professional success via-à-vis the misery of poverty surrounding me. I needed to make a big show of philanthropic generosity.

For a while, she took us everywhere, we wanted to go on weekends, long trips to other cities in the region. "Why take the train," she said, "when I can take you there?" I paid her generously as we 'settled on a price', and she always waited for us and smoked in front of the car even when it got cold and it snowed.

Then she started complaining about her boyfriend who was cheating on her with his ex-wife, then about her son and daughter-in-law working themselves to death in England where they had gone as migrant workers to make money but for some reason were making no money. They had a small baby and lived in a tiny basement apartment, and the daughter in law worked as a seamstress sewing for rich people in London. Who in that day and age sewed and embroidered for rich people in a basement apartment like in a Charles Dickens novel? I wondered, but in the end, I believed her story.

She was a good storyteller, and I was always a fool for a good story. Then she complained about her teeth: she had really bad teeth, abscesses, loose teeth. One day she came to pick us up with her head wrapped up around her chin as if holding her teeth from falling out, barely able to talk. With each of her calamities I pulled out money from my bank accounts, three hundred, five hundred, a thousand dollars, and the sums grew with each one of her new stories of misery, one after another, tirelessly, sometimes overlapping one another.

I was the "savior" of tragic taxi drivers in Romania, the least I could do, as I trotted around my mother's native city in my designer's red boots and fur trimmed black coat or in my red coat to match the boots. That winter of my rising success on the American literary scene, I was both the savior and the victim of beggars, taxi drivers, and con artists in Romania.

I had underestimated my people's con artistry in a big way. Ani managed to extort several thousand dollars from me as huge snows covered the entire country, from northern Transylvania to Bucharest. And I let her.

When Ani didn't drive us, we took trains that squeezed their way on the frozen tracks up the hills in the heart of Transylvania and that seemed to be swallowed into nothingness once night fell. My son and I were in constant movement through the snows, in taxi cars and trains, in a perpetual odyssey through what was not even my own past. We had reached something primitive and necessary in our journey. Roads covered in snow in the night.

A con artist taxi driver with falling teeth swindling me for big sums of money and me allowing it to happen, old women selling turnips and withered chrysanthemums in the street next to newly sprawled designer stores and malls, the new capitalism on old communist ruins, and me spreading wealth around from my novel earnings.

The night before our departure and return to the states, a fierce blizzard was raging through the city where I had rooted myself over the six months of my fellowship, on top of the broken roots of my mother and her family. A sepia photograph of my mother at four, holding her mother's hand in 1940 on a street in that same city followed me everywhere I went: my mother is wearing a coat with fur trim at the collar and sleeves and my grandmother a long-tapered winter coat with a luscious fur collar.

The summer of that year, they were going to travel south on cattle trains out of the city as war refugees after northern Transylvania was going to be taken by the Hungarian Horthy's government. But in that picture taken in February of 1940, my mother and grandmother looked serious and content in their fur trimmed coats, standing on one of the streets where I was trotting now with my own American son, everything in bright colors with the sepia photograph underneath.

I often felt I had gone to that city because of the sepia photograph taken the year of the Vienna dictate, as if to mend the family roots, to place my own colored image next to their black and white image at the beginning of World War II. If they hadn't had to leave the area that summer, my mother would not have met my father years later, and I would not have existed. If I hadn't left Romania as a refugee in the fall of 1983 with my volume of short stories illegally tucked underneath the suspicious fur coat, I would not have had the son whose hand I was holding now in those same streets as in the sepia photograph.

Our entire family existence had been shaped in the cracks between torn roots, in the sweeping movements of runaway refugees. My sojourn in that city was maybe an impossible mending of broken roots. At the end of the war the city and the region were returned to Romania like a misplaced object. Only too late, my family had already settled in Brasov, only to be displaced from their magnificent house with bay windows at the end of the war by Russian soldiers who simply barged in and made the house their own turning it into communist party offices.

The day before our departure and return to America, the fierce blizzard raging through the region smashed the glass of the apartment building's entrance door. The strident metallic sound of the crash cut brutally through the silence of the building. Ani called again for more money. I went again to the cash station and got some more hundreds, maybe another thousand, knowing full well I was being swindled, that she was never going to return a dime to me, that her fictitious tragic migrant children and seamstress daughter in law were going to collect my money and put it towards who-knows-what shady business, or maybe just collect it to live on it for a while, who cared.

I was breaking my heart all over again, leaving after returning, uprooting myself after the months of sweet re-rooting, of sweet existence among the pastel-colored baroque buildings of that old city in northern Transylvania. Crash, broken glass and the fierce blizzard sweeping the staircase through the smashed door, it was all coming to a screeching halt, my epic return, my journey into the past, and my love affair with an idealized country of my origins.

The return to my less than utopian adoptive country lasted forever. We spent an entire evening and night of layover in Frankfurt in frigid February weather with mounds of snow in the streets of the fairy tale decorated German city. All Central and Eastern Europe was covered in heavy snows that February of my return from the return, and I was delaying and drawing out every little second of contact with the earth of the old world.

I dreaded the moment of my landing at the Washington Dulles airport with the fake smiles and harsh welcomes of American customs officers. My son and I had a two-hour-long dinner in a Frankfurt restaurant that looked like Hansel and Gretel's house, with a heavily mustachioed waiter who flirted with me like mad and where I was verbally assaulted by a group of Canadian football players. Everything North American seemed vile, violent, and hopelessly insipid at that point in my trajectory back to where my de facto home really was, with my big house and its voluminous land, my job, my older son, my mother, my father's grave, my success, and my salaries that were paying for my European adventures.

America was the land where you made a career and money. Europe was where you enjoyed life. My post-communist native country was where my heart felt in one piece and all the grimaces and agonies of my immigrant soul took a break.

We wrote down everything we had done and seen in the Transylvanian city with cobblestoned side streets and taxi drivers with complicated stories and fiery temperaments. The six months of living in my native country at the peak of my American success unfolded like hallucinatory slide projections, a silent movie with me and my son as protagonists. Some of the slides showed an American-looking blonde woman in a red coat gliding through the afternoon crowds returning from work carrying a huge backpack, hailing a taxi at a street corner, always hailing a taxi, a shining blonde teenage boy of small stature always at her side or walking swiftly ahead of her.

Here was a slide of the two of them attending an avant-garde theater show, here they were crowded in a trolleybus because the boy preferred public transportation to taxis; here she was giving an interview to a radio station; here they were both on a talk show on national TV, their faces transported into the living-rooms of family and friends who twenty-five years earlier were watching the communist dictator waving his hand at a starving population.

A few taxi drivers even recognized the two of them from the TV, "you are the writer from America, I saw you on TV"; slide after colorful slide until the plane landed with a thud on American earth where suddenly, everything appeared colorless.

But here is where you made your success, your money, and your children. It's your home whether you like it or not and on the way to your big colonial house, driving in a friend's car, all you hear is the screech of the glass door crashing with the gust of wind on the cusp of your departure from the Romanian apartment building. Heavy snowflakes and frigid winds sweeping through the hallway of the building where you had spent your glorious half a year, the kind your father who died on an equally frigid January day in Chicago yearning for his country, had only dreamed of but never experienced since the end of the war.

You miss that snow sweeping through the entry way. Huge tears are flowing on your cheeks all the way home just like you describe the girl on the train when she leaves her home twenty-five years earlier. You find your estate in the tiny Virginia town completely bare, all the bare trees in your backyard look even barer than bare trees should look in the winter, like skeletons against the lead gray February sky with no snow.

You almost don't recognize your street, and your own home decorated with Romanian rugs and artifacts to remind you exactly of where you left forty-eight hours earlier, is a grimacing simulacrum. You cry for a month every morning like a ritual, and you wake up soaked in tears, all the tears you should have cried the very first time you left twenty-five years ago.

And your son tries to comfort you, "It's all right, Mama, it's good here too, don't cry," although he too is wrapped in sadness like in a cocoon and he tries to break the sadness by furiously hitting the soccer ball against the shed, against the big oak tree reigning over your two acres of land. You are squished in between the upside-down chaotic roll of departures, returns, separations, reunions, you no longer know which is which, in what order, whether the returns contain separations and the departures contain reunions and where you really belong if anywhere.

Maybe you have been jolted so much this way and that way that there is no more belonging for you anywhere. You just roll wherever the wind takes you, impossible to take root in any soil. And maybe it's just as well and you should rejoice in this bitter freedom instead of soaking pillow after pillow in your overly sentimental tears.

From the gray and blurry winter following my return to Virginia that winter, a frigid February day in Washington DC stands out like an ironic reminder of the thrill and fragility of success, the core of bitterness in the very middle of its sweetness. It's when a famous photographer hired by the prestigious press takes a couple of hundred headshots of you to have the perfect picture for the back cover of your forthcoming novel.

He shows you his portfolio of black and white head-shots of famous authors like Jean Paul Sartre and Simone de Beauvoir and Samuel Beckett, and you can't believe your eyes that the same writers you have been studying or teaching for your entire adult life once posed for this same crotchety old man who is leafing with trembling hands through his impressive portfolio in the café of the Amtrak train station where he decided to meet you.

Then he spends an hour taking overly posed shots of you in the building of the main post office in Washington DC, behind a marble column, in front of a marble column, on the side of a fucking marble column, until you start feeling like a decorated marble column yourself, in your velvet dark red dress. You wear red despite the strong advice from your editor to not wear red. It's not cool and pretentious enough, too strident, too you, and not enough like the other New York writers posing in a white shirt against a tree or sitting at their writing desk dressed in black and dreamily holding their head in their palm as if they are thinking up a new novel just then or as if they don't really care.

The famous photographer ultimately tells you to change into the black dress you brought just in case, and he also tells you he doesn't like the ankle boots you had brought from Romania. He moves you to a famous catholic cathedral in Washington for the next two hours of the photo shoot where he tells you to take off your winter coat in the frigid temperature and from then on, it's a delirium of forced poses between formidable granite columns and blistering cold.

Your teeth are clattering in your mouth like loose change, and the only heat you feel is coming from your angry eyes. Passersby, tourists, and practicing Catholics alike stare at you during your photo shoot.

At some point in the cold, you start feeling glamorous and miserable in equal combination—"now come towards me", "now turn your head", "oh here, sit here on the steps", "now look up"—he orders you this way and that way. Only the tears burning in your eyes are warm. The sound of the crashing glass in the building of your past Romanian apartment in your mother's city of birth the day of your departure slashes through your memory almost with tenderness. You miss that fierce blizzard and everything around it and in it, even the toothless Ani who cleansed you of several thousand dollars.

You miss the sound of your native tongue on the lips of peasants selling turnips in the market. You've turned into an angry icicle by now, and you curse the majestic Catholic Church with gusto in your mind as you turn this way and that way. In between the granite Gothic columns, your smiles are daggers but for one moment you think of the Nobel prize winner idol of your studies and theater practice whose play about a woman singing her happiness as she is buried in a mound of earth, saved your life in your last year of communism, the great, the morose, and the always despondent looking Samuel Beckett.

The thought that this same maniac of a photographer might have once tormented him too on the steps of Sacré Cœur makes you laugh or at least grimace in half of a spontaneous smile. You think to yourself you are important after all. You taste a bitter drop of success on your lips purple from the cold. You rejoice in your agony. One day when you are dead and cold as these granite steps here, you might be famous too but who will care then.

Of the one hundred and seventy-five poses taken on the February day in Washington DC, the one in which you thought of Samuel Beckett and produced a tiny smile ended up on the paperback edition of your book. In fact, you weren't smiling at all, you just thought you were. You look over your shoulder straight at the camera in defiance and with a twinge of irony.

You are the hell of an actress and a survivor if you could produce irony on a blustery February day between marble and granite columns in your thin black blazer bought in a boutique in northern Romania. Irony of ironies, for the hardcover version of your book, your editor chooses one of the photos in the post office, standing against a marble column, wearing your red velvet top, a little victory. You won the red of the picture on the back of your smashing first novel that was sold in a dozen countries.

You are looking sideways in a three-quarter profile and are carrying something of a disdainful smile, the picture is all touched up, you almost don't recognize yourself, so perfect you look. The famous photographer never thought of touching up Beckett's wrinkled rough face like a map of old age, wrinkles look good on men they say. Your face though is smoothed out and perfect, and you look like a forties' movie star. It's your picture of success, a contrived, touched up you, against a majestic marble column.

A woman once told me on a book tour, in a bookstore where only five people had come to my event and they included my two sons, "I've read everything I could find about you on the Internet, and I think you and your life are much more interesting than all of your books together." I wanted my book to be more interesting than me and my life, more suspenseful, more sellable!

I didn't want to sell my life but my book. In fact, it sickened me that it was all about selling. I didn't want to sell anything. I wanted to soar in an incandescent swirl and leave a singed mark on the walls of literary history. My two sons were looking at me with big smiles of admiration. Their births, their growing up, their highs and lows, the life I had shared with each one of their fathers, the dark days of single motherhood, the bright days of motherhood, the flamboyant sometimes reckless choices of lovers, the abortion, the kidney stones, the nights in emergency rooms, sledding with my sons on frigid nights under the full moon of the little town we lived in, that was my life, it was fucking autobiographical, and it wasn't for sale.

The picture of me in the burgundy velvet top against a majestic marble column in the Washington post office stared at me with irony from the back cover of my book. I stared at the woman who went on and on about my life being so interesting on internet sites, and I told her I had worked hard for my book and I didn't care to talk about my life, did she have any questions about the book? Reality TV, reality TV, it was all about the so-called real, about a reality caught on tape and edited by a sensationalist reporter who got a slot on prime-time television and was desperate to keep it.

And if my life sold, with all its sensationalized bits of immigrant hardships and dictatorship terrors, then apparently so would the book, and the press would get back its big advance and make a profit. It all hung in the profits. I had skipped most of my Marxist philosophy classes in high school and college and had never actually read more than three pages of Karl Marx's *The Capital*, but I started to feel that some of what I had heard about it made sense, the voracious greed for profits at the expense of all else, whether you were a writer, a photographer, a welder, or a tennis player. The transformation of the human being into an object for sale.

At that book reading with the woman who was taken with the bits of my biography sprinkled on internet sites, I had the distinct feeling that it was all going to be short-lived, the success that is, and that I was being conned into its deceptive coils, in a worse way than I had been conned by the pathetic Ani the taxi driver. I was the one getting the money for now and they were getting slivers of my soul.

Success was a steel heart after all; it only bent with the wind of profits, and in the lack of profits, it stood relentless, gray, and unmoved. You could smash your little naturally blonde Romanian head against it creating the masterpiece of the ages, and it didn't matter. If you failed to make money and if you lost your exotic touch, you were nothing. Today's exotic soon became yesterday's generic ethnic cliché. You were exoticized out of existence until editors lost interest in your stories.

You developed crazy fantasies of taking on new personas and maybe writing about over-the-top subjects like Afghani transgender sex workers for example, were there any to be found. Your editor told you to try your hand at young adult fiction, or Romanian contemporary realities, only you had no stories about those realities, nor were you inclined to start writing stories of dissatisfied American teenagers growing up unloved by millionaire parents in a rich suburb.

You were stubborn about your stories, and the next one came out of the shores of the Black Sea, from your burning disheveled summers washed by the irreverent waves of that wild sea. You held on to the stories you needed to write and didn't relent to the pressure. Your new heroine swims across the Bosporus to get to the other side of the dictatorship, and you follow her to Istanbul. You take the journey there in real life to research for the new novel.

You go with your ex-husband and walk through pungent spice bazaars, dazzlingly colored silk bazaars, and sparkling jewelry bazaars like the ones you remembered your father telling you about when you were seven years old, and he went on a bus tour to Istanbul and brought you back a pair of filigree gold earrings.

A couple of years later after the Istanbul trip with your ex-husband, your fervent novelist imagination takes you to the post Balkan Wars bazaars of Sarajevo, more spices, more shimmering orange and purple silks mixed in with almond glazed deserts. You are drawn to the pumping wild hearts of the Balkans this way and that way and walk through the bazaars with your cortege of female characters even though your American editor of the famous press rejects your second novel of the heroine who swims across the Bosporus one Fourth of July when you are traveling in England with your blonde son as your companion. You persist in starting your third one and almost don't care about the rejection of the second.

What matters is that you keep writing. You know all about the rejections and miseries suffered by the great writers of literary history, some of whom only became well known and appreciated postmortem, so the presses got to keep and gobble up all the profits while the writer was sleeping the sleep of eternity in a uselessly but beautifully adorned grave in a famous cemetery. So far, the British publishers still love you and publish your second novel for which you had already gotten a big advance.

You are living on advance money like a real writer, and the rejection from the United States press doesn't hit you too hard as you are riding the wave of the continued British success. You even give an interview on BBC radio. You console yourself that you are appreciated in the country of Shakespeare and Thomas Hardy, and your second novel published in two editions makes number forty-one in some bestseller lists. It lays on the front tables of airport bookstores and is even on the tables of the bookstore in Paddington Station in London where you arrived from the airport once when you first took the children to London the summer of the sheriff's visit to your house.

Thousands of travelers pass by it and see it every day. You buy your own book in that very bookstore before boarding the train to Dover where you spend the day with your son drinking in the light, the wind, the white of the cliffs, and the fierce blue of the sea surrounding them.

You feel like the East European postmodern embodiment of Catherine from your favorite British novel, *Wuthering Heights*, recklessly passionate, blonde hair blowing in the savage winds. And you still have no idea what 'wuthering' really means, but for you it will always mean crazy, windy, recklessly passionate. Standing at the very edge of a cliff in the savage wind and not caring. You are relentless in your creative madness, you are 'wuthering', unstoppable in your drive to write one story after another, profits or no profits.

You fly to Sarajevo from London to learn about the war of the nineties and to talk to survivors of the siege. It's the second decade of the new millennium and you are thirsty for tragic stories; you fill the huge gap in your gut with other people's stories of war and devastation. While some people get a massage when they are down and desperate, you drown yourself in stories of genocide, dictatorships and tragic losses. They teach you about survival and give you hope about the fierceness of the human spirit.

You and Samuel Beckett were looked at through the same lens of the heavy formidable camera of the American photographer who kept photographing you in the Washington cold February day for hours. You have what to be proud of. You have tasted bits of success, bittersweet droplets of its dangerous potions. You left your country for this. You put your first manuscript in your Romanian suitcase next to a ridiculously big old-fashioned fur coat and stepped out into the world recklessly breaking your heart in un-mendable pieces. You climbed up many wuthering heights and tumbled down as many wuthering lows.

And when your third novel sells to another famous publisher for a six-digit figure, you are convinced it's time for your true wuthering heights. Your heroines, the two war survivors from the Balkans, one blonde one brunette, like the blonde D and the brunette D that my best Romanian friend and I once were, have filled all your living spaces for several years. They woke up with you on frigid February days in your Virginia home as you were agonizing over the mononucleosis of your younger child in his last year of high school ready to fly off to college, the hardships of the older one taking life by its horns after college, having moved to the dizzying Rockies of Colorado, the new frontier.

You think you may have exhausted the number of pieces that your heart can break into, and the years have passed like restless flocks of swallows flying off the chimneys of Romanian villages. You live in big, compounded metaphors that overlap your many realities, at least the metaphors bring things together, they are the only unifying thread in the organized chaos that is your life.

The heroines from Sarajevo swirled through your life before dawn during the last years of your children's teenage and early adult years. They grew up, side by side with them. It's no longer that you become your heroines, it's that they take possession of you in unprecedented ways. These girls are fierce and fearless, harsh and edgy, not like your sweeter Romanian girls making love in the Carpathians or on the beaches of the Black Sea. One writes stories of war from a bomb shelter, while the other stands in antiwar demonstrations in Paris at the start of the Iraq war hand in hand with a Tunisian lover.

The world has erupted into new wars since your children were small chubby and innocent angels in the nineties. And your own world keeps erupting into its smaller wars of failed long-distance love affairs, the umpteenth separation from your second ex-husband whom you still love but whom you can't stand any more, the atrocious jealousies of your colleagues who want to squish you under departmental intrigues and overloads of elementary French language courses, *je suis*, *tu es*, *nous sommes*.

You're sick of tenses and verbs, of the reaffirmation of existence through the irregular French verbs. They are eating your brains out like voracious rodents. You crave for the clarity of dawn and the birds' songs; it's why you salute the sun with the voices of your sultry Balkan heroines on the edge between violent death and survival.

When the book appears in bookstores in its glamorous cover with a new headshot portrait of you on the back cover that was not taken by the famous photographer because he is dead by now, but by a student in the art department, nobody asks you if the book is autobiographical anymore, but why it isn't. How come you wrote about characters from Bosnia and Serbia when you are Romanian? Why the Bosnian War, and why now?

You are always borderline in the wrong, marginally delinquent via-à-vis the big American publishing world, and not just American, Western European too. You are Romanian, and you write about Serbian and Bosnian realities! How dare you? You must be Serbian to write about Serbia, Bosnian to write about Bosnia, French to write about France, and apparently French editors

232

can't stand books about Paris written by non-Parisian and particularly by non-French writers.

It is the end of the imagination, and you can only write about the corner of the world you were born and grew up into. And when that corner loses its exotic touch, and the three minutes of attention span of that indomitable Reader you have been told you are writing for, are up, then forget about getting any attention for your writing. You never seem to get it fully right, too exotic, not exotic enough, too Balkan, not Balkan enough, too European, not European enough, never American enough. You are in limbo. You try not to care, but you do.

Your dream of being a writer is what pushed you over the border of your country into the abyss. You have swished by the highest peaks of success, famous presses, big advances, glamorous book tours, yet something doesn't seem to stick and hold you there for more than the equivalent of a few milliseconds in publishing success time. It's the profits, again and again; it all hangs in the profits, the sales, which everybody tells you are 'disappointing', like you failed again and again.

Sometimes you find your latest novel tucked in between many other forgotten or recently published books on the shelves of a big bookstore in New York or Chicago, and you go to the bookstore staff inquiring about the sales on that book. They tell you that two copies sold. You ask why isn't this book on the front table with other new arrivals? They look at you ironically as if asking *why are you bothering us, don't you see all these other more important, more sellable books*, Hillary Clinton's new memoir, David Baldacci's newest thriller, John Grisham's newest mega bestseller?

You know there is something in you that doesn't want to sell. You know you don't want to be exotic because you don't even know what that means. You want your book to shine and send shimmering rays from its secret nook where it seems to almost have been purposefully placed for oblivion and not for remembrance. You want it to be sacred and shiny from where it sits tucked in between two other books that you don't care about, in a battle for life and death, for eternity versus oblivion. Which one will survive?

It will have to be you because you ran away from everything with a small suitcase that carried a volume of short stories in it and your forever broken heart was the price for your book sitting there quietly and already forgotten in between Phillip Roth and Edgar Allan Poe. They can afford to be tucked away in a corner because their name is already forged forever in the holy book of literary history with shiny burning letters, and yours is not.

Your name, with its jagged combination of open vowels and liquid consonants, is on the very cusp between a wannabe exotic name and an irritating hard-to-pronounce foreign name. It's not exotic, it's foreign and it's not foreign enough to be erotic or fascinating. It's just a square east European name like a square wooden chair with a horizontal cedilla on the first *a* sound, which you dropped from day one of your arrival at the brutal JFK airport in 1983.

A cedilla like an overturned umbrella which gives your real name a Slavic softness, but it was shaved off the top of your name in all legal documents and in the thousands of mispronunciations and misspellings it has undergone ever since. You are even tempted to change your name and make it hipper, give it a Polish ending, a good cedilla that will stick, a *tz* sound or end it in an aspirated *h* sound, make it Middle Eastern or North African.

In a society where most of the power is in the hands of very few, those of us filling concentric circles around the center are by various degrees pitted against each other and caught in a ferocious fight for a front seat or even a lousy seat at the much desired table of success. One seat gets freed up, a hundred fight over it and one alone gets those precarious fifteen minutes of attention while the other ninety-nine get back in the fight over the next free seat. In the end we are all hungry and are left staring jealously at the small crowd feasting around the table with the unshaken confidence of the entitled.

You wanted to write about transgender Afghani sex workers, but who will buy that book with a name like yours? Too much cultural appropriation. They will kill you in academic circles. You can only write about the bloody corner of the world you came from and that was already obsolete ten years ago when the story of the girl riding the train through the Carpathians came out in a flurry of foreign sales and deals.

You see your name between Philip Roth and Edgar Allan Poe in a famous New York bookstore and you know you are falling through the cracks. You went up, up to the top of a jagged rock and then slipped. The economic crisis didn't help you, it's still following you eight years later, and you find out that your most recent editor who looked at you straight in your blue Romanian eyes over a Greek salad in a fancy restaurant on fifth Avenue soon after she bought your newest novel for a six digit advance and told you that she wants to be your editor for life, you find out that she just postponed the publication of the paperback edition and that she's leaving the press in search of new ventures.

You guess the press didn't feel like dealing with the paperback production of a book with inadequate sales and managed by a leaving editor, so they might as well drop the whole thing, as you are nowhere close to the success of Nick Sparks who is a fellow writer of the same publisher.

Just after you had a smashing photograph taken for the paperback cover, this time by a local young photographer, against a peeling wooden wall to make it rugged postmodern, you find out that the hardcover low sales are now canceling out your paperback. So, you stare at your name between Poe and Roth and as you get all teary-eyed, you see yourself fall between the cracks, among endless rows of bookshelves as high as the Empire State Building a few blocks away.

You are falling in perfect standing position as if you were going to fall right on your feet like a cat in her seventh life. Two more and you're done, so you'd better survive this fall. And you're falling faster and faster between the cracks of world literature, between the P's and the R's, Pushkin, Pincheon, Pound, Plath, you focus on the P's on one side more, trying to catch on to one of them, you somehow think the P's are more solid, the R's are slippery.

You catch on to Plath for a second, your beloved Sylvia Plath. You have a special place in your heart for her. You get drunk on her words and cry out loud for the loneliness despair hopelessness you imagine she must have felt on the February morning when she killed herself after making sandwiches for her two sleeping children.

Then you pass by some of the R's all in a cluster; Rabelais, Reza, Ronsard, Rostand, you realize they are all French or Francophone. You studied and taught them, and you don't mind it at all passing by them, falling by their voluminous poetry, prose and drama volumes. You remember that a student of yours found the French translation of your novel right next to the works of Rabelais in a French bookstore in Paris, and that was a boost to your ego for sure. You try to hold on to Yasmina Reza for a quick second, as you taught her works too. She comes right after your name.

You are between Rabelais and Reza in the R section in the imaginary world literature library in between whose cracks you are having a formidable free fall. The R's are quite rare, so are the women, and you are an R woman writer and a foreigner, and that makes you super rare. Maybe that should be your pitch, your selling point that would draw the attention of the *New York Times* literary critics that apparently can 'make you or break you', or so you've heard.

And maybe the anonymous critic from one of the major trade journals who writes in simple sentences like a middle-schooler and used the word 'overwrought' whenever referring to your writing style for each one of your novels, would finally give your writing the light of day as they say. Or maybe he gets fired for his own middle school style of a hundred-word vocabulary. The women writers with R is where you belong.

Sylvia Plath is almost an R, but she would be 'overwrought' too by the anonymous critic's standards, the New York standards, the Iowa school of creative writing standards. You are in with the 'overwrought' girls.

You remember how your first editor begged you to give up the idea of putting your name spelled the fully Romanian way with the overturned umbrella cedilla over the *a*. "It would look too foreign," she said as she was worried it would drive away readers. Because a thousand readers for sure would stop in front of your book with your name on it, be interested in the book, be drawn to the title, the description of the plot, the writing style, the enthusiastic endorsement by some mega bestselling writers, but at the last minute they would see the cedilla diacritic on top of the *a* in your last name, and they would put the book back on the table, on the shelf between Philip Roth and Edgar Allan Poe and say to themselves or to the friend accompanying them, "Shit man, I ain't buying a book by someone with that kind of fucking cedilla in their name. That's way too foreign for me. I think I'll go for this novel by David Baldacci. After all, he's got no fucking cedilla."

You also pass by Salmon Rushdie. You keep quoting some lines by him, something deep he said about the life of an exile, every time you give an important talk or book signing event. There was once a price on his head because he upset some groups of crazy Islamists, that pushed up his sales like mad while he was hiding somewhere in London. Or maybe that was all made up precisely to give him the mega publicity. Maybe you should also do something radical to upset a Fascist group, the Pope, the CIA, to have a price on your head, and then become a mega best seller.

You are about to hit ground zero, the rock bottom of your fall between the colossal rows of literary history in the famous bookstore of New York City where literary fame is made and unmade. But before you do, you hear a tiny voice addressing you, "May I help you find anything?" It's one of the salesclerks, a young woman in her twenties who speaks in a thin high-pitched voice like she is five years old, the way so many American young women do. Despite the all black attire, so New York, and five sets of piercings and tattoos, she still wants to sound like a little girl.

You recover quickly from your hard fall and hitting rock bottom. You've used up your eighth life but it's OK, you've still got one more, you'll make the most of this one and you'll make it last as long as the other eight. So, you say, "I'm looking for a book by..." And you utter your name with the Romanian pronunciation with the cedilla of the upside-down umbrella on the *a* and she looks at the row in front of you and points to your book and says, "here it is," in her tiny puzzled little girl voice as if she just won a Barbie doll competition.

"Oh, how foolish of me," you say, "it was right in front of me," and you pick it up from the shelf and pretend to look at it and read the cover like you don't know what it's about and you wait for the little Goth girl to disappear.

You debate with yourself whether you should buy the book and show the store that your book is selling and they need to order another one, or whether you should put it across facing the aisle full frontal like some of the prominent new arrival books have been placed. Some even have a little note saying they are one of the bookstore's salesclerks' choice, like 'Katie's choice of the month', 'Muriel's choice of the month'.

You realize you don't have the cash in your wallet, and you'd have to pay by credit card, and then they'll see you're buying your own book, so your choice is made for you. You wait for the high-pitched voice Goth girl to disappear. You look around like you are a thief trying to find the moment to run away with a book without paying for it.

You even look around to see if any video cameras are directed your way, and you place your book facing full frontal across Philip Roth and Edgar Allan Poe and Salmon Rushdie's Midnight's Children and Salinger's Catcher in the Rye; your book covers a lot of famous writers. Then you pick up Isabel Allende's latest novel, The Japanese Lover, and take it to the cashier to pay for it. She should have won the Nobel Prize before some of the other male Latin writers who did, you think as you are handing over your credit card to the cashier girl with an even more high-pitched voice than the previous one like she's about to take off to the high heavens on her voice and pierce through the ornate ceilings. You see that her name tag says Muriel, and you smile at her, the most generous smile of your day.

You leave the famous New York bookstore in the late September dampness with Isabel Allende's book, and with an incomprehensible sense of joy and accomplishment like you were just nominated for the Nobel prize yourself. At least your name and your book are out there tucked among the greatest of world literature, cedilla or no cedilla. You go back to your Toyota minivan parked in a two-hour spot on a side street with its loud red 'Virginia is for lovers' sticker as frantic New Yorkers are making signs from their cars asking if you are leaving your parking place.

Whoever said New Yorkers don't drive? Another New York fib! You make a definitive sign of *no* as you rummage through your messy trunk out of which you've been living for a week, you pull out an armful of hardcover copies of your most recent novel that isn't being published in paperback as of yet.

You still have an hour left on the parking meter in the West Village, and you start walking down the beautiful New York street holding your pack of recently published hardcover novels. You wonder what to do with them. You are tempted to hand them out to people in the street but feel awkward about it. That would just look pathetic. You look at the beautiful little wrought iron fences framing the trunks of thick maple and oak trees with perky marigolds and pansies planted around them like miniature gardens and you get a crazy idea that surges from the depths of your being with childhood memories of yellow marigolds and pink dahlias.

You start placing your novel, one book at a time, in the little gardens in front of the imposing Brownstone buildings. You are placing them gently on the humid earth in between marigolds and the fallen yellow and russet leaves of the trees, as if you were planting seeds and bulbs to grow for next spring, as if you were placing them for a nap into the humid eternity of the New York soil, the hard, hostile New York soil, stubbornly pushing your roots into it whether it wants you or not.

Once your arms are freed from all your volumes that were put to rest, to seed, or to rot next to the roots of New York trees, you walk briskly in the September humid air, you pass by the grandiose public library where only this last spring you attended the one hundredth anniversary glamorous party of the press that published your first novel. You remember the formidable glamour with champagne and silver trays filled with meatballs you couldn't eat and the crowds of New Yorkers who all knew each other and greeted each other loudly kissing the air.

You were walking through the crowds encased in your foreigner aloofness loneliness not knowing a soul, until you saw your first editor who lovingly edited your first novel and got stuck on the cedilla on your name. She was dressed up in a sequined pant suit shining like the moon. She looked straight at you and acted happy to see you. Maybe she was, you'll never know.

In your inexhaustible refugee hopefulness gullibility naïveté, you chose to believe she really was happy to see you. She said "We'll always have *Train to Trieste*," like "we'll always have Paris." A spark of joy lit up inside you when you heard that. That spark died the next second as she turned around and started talking to Garfunkel from Simon and Garfunkel who had just published his memoir with her press.

He was truly red-haired, turning white, small and aging. You had bought their records on the black market while a student at the University of Bucharest and listened to their music during your last summer at the beach with your best friend, brunette D.

You felt worlds apart from that crowd, clunky in your cowboy boots that didn't match at all your Italian crushed velvet little black dress. You should have been wearing light pointy sparkly shoes to take off towards the colossal crystal chandeliers of the public library and amaze everyone with your levitation skills learned in the Grotowski acting classes in Romania, a whole lifetime and a planet ago. But the biggest startle was when Tony Morrison herself appeared to give the closing speech of the evening, and that was when your entire system lit up inside and out like a Christmas tree and you felt in the presence of greatness.

You never liked celebrity cults, but you felt a special vibe, like a wave of the soul moving through the crowd from where she was. You were lucky after all. You were one of the authors gathered there. Your name and book title were forever printed inside the elegantly bound book with all the publications over its one hundred years of existence, and there was this goddess writer in the fullness of her ripe age right in front of you who had arrived in Chicago as a wretched furious refugee in the coldest winter of the last century thirty three years earlier, with your pathetic suitcase, your communist Mary Poppins Suitcase with all its shameless dreams, illegal objects and documents, and with your legal I94 political refugee visa. One thing at least was fully legal.

But when you leave the fancy reception at the end of the night and are getting your coat at the coat room, they can't find your umbrella that you had bought on the way there in a New York souvenir shop, a clear round deep umbrella with I love NY written on it. You say you gave it to them, and you show them your ticket. They say *we're sorry, but we don't have it, maybe someone took it* and you say, "Well, if someone took it you should get me another umbrella just the same."

They say *here you can take this one*, and they show you an enormous black umbrella with a wooden handle that makes you think of the umbrellas that mafia families in the movies carry at funerals. In that moment, it all becomes about the umbrella that those New York young people wearing earbuds and listening to their streaming music, have misplaced or given to someone else by mistake. Now it is all about you walking in the rain in your cowboy boots and crushed velvet dress, with your "I made it but not quite" refugee walk and mentality, your "I don't belong anywhere" feeling and your confused always lost in space gaze at the spaces around you.

You started crying over your stupid umbrella as Garfunkel from Simon and Garfunkel and Patty Smith whose memoir had also just been published by your former editor are milling around with champagne glasses right there a few feet away. You made it that far and then you didn't. You slid down that slippery slope of success like you were your own mudslide and the entire earth of your existence were opening and closing in on you and swallowing you in its voracious hunger.

On your way back from the grandiose public library walking with heavy steps in the stubborn rain and carrying the clunky huge umbrella that replaced the round clear umbrella lost in the coat room, you passed by a young homeless woman sitting against the wall of one of the magnificent New York buildings with thick marble columns. She was shyly begging. You went past her by a few steps and something in her eyes, because you often look the homeless in the eyes, made you go back, retract on your steps and you started talking to her. You wanted to do something but felt that giving her a dollar would be an insult.

You wanted to know how a young smart-looking woman in America gets to live on the street begging. She had the worn-out unhealthy face and hair of those who live in the street, but she told you her story. She didn't even ask for money. Her husband was beating her, and her parents didn't welcome her home, so she was looking for jobs. She was hungry and wanted you to buy her a ham and cheese sandwich, *what else, what else* you asked her, *nothing else,* she said, *just the sandwich. You look nice*, she said, you didn't know what to say, and you gave her encouragement, some money.

You went into the café next door and bought a big baguette ham and cheese sandwich, but nothing sufficed. You felt ashamed of your success neurosis, how you worried about not being famous enough. What a joke that was. One day you were going to make a theater troupe with homeless young people like your friend Norma in Los Angeles.

One day you were going to have the resources to take people like the homeless girl under the columns of a magnificent New York building off the street and into a sheltered life, like a life with a shelter, a roof above her head and not as charity but as just that: theater with the homeless people who will no longer be homeless. You stayed for a while and watched her eat, kept her company as people in fancy coats and shoes were coming out of the public library celebration.

As you watched the face of the homeless girl hungrily eating her baguette sandwich, you remembered with a painful pang in your chest the deaths by overdose of drugs of two of your son's best friends earlier that spring, one after the other, beautiful soulful boys, gone just like that in their early twenties, in the street, alone in their American cities. You knew them well. You had spent time driving them around, feeding them. One played the guitar and wore a Tom Sawyer kind of straw hat in the summer, the other loved nature and hiking.

You once took a wild trip in a Jeep with your son and this friend in the wilderness of the Colorado Rockies. You couldn't understand that kind of society where things like that happened, where the youth of the country, "the future of the country" as the shameless cliché went, were abandoned and despised, and left to die in the street and psychologists and social workers vomited a whole bunch of useless clichés about how *it was up to them. They needed to want to recover*, but how do you recover when nobody cared for you?

You felt nauseated by the crowds of people talking loudly and laughing in the New York humid night as if the world belonged to them. You felt it again: that maybe you had immigrated to the wrong country. You thought of your father who used to quote Lenin's words about America being in the end destroyed by drugs, violence, and pornography. You hated the idea of agreeing with Lenin, one of the biggest yet most brilliant criminals of the previous century.

You walked slowly to the metro and a beautiful melody being played on a violin resounded throughout the metro corridors, a sentimental French tune. It always came down to Europe, the old world. It was an Edith Piaf song, played by a young woman wearing a long dark green velvet coat, and you smiled at her as you passed by her as if in recognition, but she was focused on the violin though. You didn't give her any money.

In the metro, you watched an Indian woman feed her young daughter from a cake or a sandwich inside a brown bag, mouthful by mouthful, while the girl ate heartily, and the mother smiled happily with each bite. And again, you went back to your thirty-year-old circular thinking, that no, you had done well, you would do it again, immigrate to America that is, where else would you go? Your native country is still a mess, pretty as it might be and a recent member of the European Union.

France would be nice and very romantic, but you would always be a foreigner there, and who would give you a job teaching French literature among the native French? Sweden had endless winters with short days and people committed suicide from depression caused by lack of light, for all the high standard of living and gender equality. Spain had huge unemployment and people with PhDs lived with their parents for all its luscious cities and passionate dances.

Italy was too chaotic and disorganized for all its magnificent churches and fountains. Germany had a healthy economy, but you didn't know the language. America had chosen you long ago when you met Zoila Valdivieso on a beach by the Black Sea and you had birthed children and grew roots into that soil. It was your home, harsh, and cruel and disjointed, but your home.

Now, on this September day of that same year of the party at the New York Public Library, as you are getting close to where you had parked your car, you are possessed by the impulse to run back to where you put your books to rest in the little gardens by a row of stately Brownstone houses. You run, run, run, towards the street, like your life depended on it.

You forget the street name and the way back because you live in an eternal spatial confusion, and as you turn the corner towards the street where you think you might have done that ridiculous deed, you see a man in raggedy clothes and a big beard standing on the sidewalk and looking through your book. He could be borderline homeless but you're not sure, but he could also be a bohemian artist or a punk. So many homeless in New York next to all the magnificent Brownstone houses!

He is looking through your book. You want to turn around, but he sees you and recognizes you from the picture on the cover and he says, *Hey you're this writer, you dropped your book on the sidewalk.*

You can have it, you say.

Really, will you sign it for me? he says, and you are happy to oblige.

You happily sign the book he found on the street, and you say, *I hope you enjoy it*, and he says *I'm sure I will, I love books.*

And now, as you pass again by the Public library back to your car for the second time, and you are freed of your newly published novels that are feeding the New York soil, though one is in the possession of a semi homeless New Yorker, and you are back to your car with Virginia license plates and the 'Virginia is for lovers' sticker, you breathe in deeply the humid September air, and you feel inexplicably happy.

It's a happiness that is more like a powerful wave of life energy, a tsunami of the heart that carries with it magical colors and pearls as much as carcasses and trash, all mixed up in an indomitable wave that carries you towards a shore. You are both the tsunami and the shore. Indomitable is a word you learned in tenth grade from your English textbook in the Romanian high school. It's a hard and unforgiving word, yet round and complete. You love words and that's why you're a writer, for the words more than for the stories.

Love, Death, and Chicago – All Over Again

There are parts of my immigrant story that I hardly ever talk about, because they seem incongruous with the rotundity of my core story, because they seem like a corner, you would rather cut, and they don't appear aesthetic or suspenseful enough. However, they are crucial in the making of my life and in its actual realization. One such part is my first, my initial, my exploratory visit to Chicago before I left Romania for good in the fall of 1983.

Most Romanians even don't understand it, and most Americans I know would be bored by it. Therefore, I tell the faster, more dramatic version: how I decided to leave for Chicago in America via Italy in my third year at the University of Bucharest, soon after the secret police man asked me to join his ranks of informers in exchange for some 'minor services for the country and Party'.

Luckily, I got a passport and a visa and left on that hot September day with a suitcase and a lot of determination. *Amazing*, they all say, *so courageous on your part. It must have been so hard*, people also say. That always gives me a great sense of discomfort, of sadness and even failure, as if had I decided to survive the dictatorship and never left and endured the various deprivations and hardships like the rest of my family who remained behind did, would not have been courageous.

The part I never mention is that the year before my definitive escape, I visited Zoila Valdivieso in Chicago on a tourist visa for a two-month summer vacation. I went there, saw the city, liked its pulse and energy, traveled with her to Alabama and Florida to meet both her adoptive Baptist millionaire family and her Cuban Catholic fun and rowdy family, visited my mother's best friend since childhood in Denver, Colorado on the Greyhound Bus, went with her and her Puerto Rican husband to Las Vegas for a five day gambling and gorging on cheap foods vacation, crossed the desert in their BMW, went back to Chicago, and made up my mind that I was going to return with my parents the following year. Just like that.

I was so confident in my special star, that I planned mine and my parents' escape in Zoila's suburban Chicago apartment, went back to Romania, and then went ahead with the plan to ask for passports and visas to Italy so that she can sponsor all of us to come to Chicago for good.

I found her unchanged when we met at the airport in her colorful summer clothes, although almost a decade older. She was talkative and joyous as I had remembered her, with the same irrepressible full laughter that flowed out of her in delightful giggles. She took me to Carson's Pirie & Scott to buy new clothes to replace my plain Romanian clothes, cosmetics for my acne ridden complexion, sandals for my calloused feet used to the coarse Romanian shoes I had been wearing.

She also took me to the Hispanic Chicago neighborhood to meet one of her brothers and her sister in law at the jewelry store they owned, drove along the brilliant Lake Shore Drive and on all the labyrinthine Chicago highways with great smoothness in a huge Oldsmobile that she was going to donate to us when my parents and I would arrive the following year in December for our definitive sojourn, all while talking about everything and nothing.

She was laughing and telling me about her family, her work at the suburban high school where she taught Spanish, remembering in every detail, episodes from her visit to Romania and always bursting into rivulets of laughter at the memories. She remembered all the funny episodes. She missed my parents, my aunt and uncle and talked about them as if they were family.

I moved through every day in a blur oscillating between the fascination that the cubist sight of the city lined up along Lake Michigan produced in me, the discomfort that the humid July heat gave me, gorging greedily on the colorful foods she served me, smoking menthol Merit cigarettes secretly at her bathroom window, and wondering all throughout my waking hours how it would be to live there in that city.

I didn't particularly like the suburb where she lived which seemed deserted with only big cars driving around, no people in the streets, as everybody moved from car to enclosed air-conditioned spaces to car to air-conditioned spaces in a continuous robotic kind of traffic. It made me think of the TV series we religiously watched on our small black and white television sets in Romania,

Lost in Space and *Planet of the Giants*. Everything was shiny, big, and deserted. Or so it seemed, as the people all gathered inside and spared no time walking in the street.

The city center though roared with traffic and swarmed with people of all colors like I had never seen before. Zoila took me to different areas of town that she called neighborhoods, which seemed like small cities in themselves and differed from one another: in this one, you found Swedish cakes, in this other one, Mexican churros, over here, the best Chicago hot dogs, and over here in this other neighborhood, the best Indian food. Everything was judged in terms of food. I gorged on all of them every chance I got.

I found the long journeys across the American land from Chicago to Alabama to Florida magnificent. I couldn't have enough of those long expanses, Zoila's smooth driving through them, her continuous chirping about big and small things in life, family, the world, God, fashion, cars. I tried to imagine a life for myself in every place we stopped. I smoked my secret Merit cigarettes in all the gas station bathrooms, as I was embarrassed to smoke in front of her.

The small, quiet town in Alabama where her adoptive millionaire Baptist parents whom she called Mama and Papa Simmons lived was not a place I would have chosen to live in. Everybody I met seemed programmed to talk and act the same, laugh at the same kind of jokes or lines, and overall exhibit a level of politeness that sounded like the English dialogues on some of the VCR tapes we watched in school to learn English.

When VCR tapes appeared, our language teachers used to take us to the language lab and make us watch and then repeat after the actors in the little skits. *Would you like some coffee? Yes, please, no thank you. Would you please pass the salt? Oh, she is from Romania, darling, did you hear that? How interesting! Let's say grace. Dear God, thank you for this food and for the visit of our guest from Romania, and for all your blessings. Pass the salad please. What language do they speak in Romania? Your English is so good, better than mine, ha, ha, ha. Would you like some more casserole? No, thank you, goodnight. I love you. I love you too.* Quickly, go to the bathroom for a menthol Merit!

My jaws hurt every night from all the English and all the smiling I had to do. I wanted to say swear words in the bathroom and become a devil worshiper. But Zoila floated through every situation with her delightful laughter, her colorful clothes, her sweetness and nonjudgmental acceptance of everything, only scrunching her nose a bit when she didn't like something.

Papa and Mama Simmons also owned a lake house that was situated exactly as the name sounded, that is on a lake, standing on wooden poles and with a long staircase that spiraled down to a deck from where you could jump in the water to swim or from where you could fish. We went in Papa Simmons's boat all around the lake throughout a labyrinth of trees that looked like giant weeping willows, a landscape which seemed hallucinatory to me, particularly since my eyes and nose were always watery from the humidity and the abundant vegetation. The bizarre remoteness of the landscape that blended in with the artificiality of conversations weighed on my body and soul.

I was happy when we left Alabama as Mama and Papa Simmons waved at us goodbye from their front porch, and Zoila and I took off towards Florida, where her Cuban blood family lived. She played oldies music from the fifties and sixties, all the way on the drive with the windows open across southern flat lands and endless highways.

I sometimes sang along to all the songs I knew from my Romanian youth, from records and tapes obtained with great difficulty from friends or on the black market, from dance parties in tiny Bucharest apartments of high school or college friends. During those parties, the songs were disembodied melodies in the absence of the landscape, the people, the culture, and they brought with them a tantalizing air of Western unleashed freedom and joy that we mythologized or invented. Now they blended organically with the landscape and everything else, and the effect on my psyche was inebriating. I imagined a life of traveling across American landscapes with the radio blasting, the windows open, my hair blown by the hot summer wind.

Jacksonville, Florida, and Zoila's Cuban family were many times more real and exciting than the adoptive Alabama portion of her life: loud, warm, argumentative, filled with foods with pungent smells and the constant mixture of Spanish and English in indiscriminate combinations and order. Their houses were colorful and replete with decorations and adornments, wall hangings, tapestries, beautiful rugs, pots of exotic plants. Spanish melodies floated through those houses. They all offered to show me around the city, take me to the beach, take me shopping, and feed me fried plantains and yucca.

The English rolled off their tongues with deep Spanish accents, rolled Rs and B sounds aspirated into Vs, and vice versa, all the Vs into feathery Bs, an

247

airy kind of English, sexy and delicate that I could have listened to all day long. Zoila's twin brother who exuded the smoothest charm I had ever encountered also smoked which made me rejoice as I could smoke with him in the back yard of their house among the flowering azaleas, bougainvillea, and cacti.

It all felt like a family I must have had in another life, a familiar exotic that made me feel at home, and my soul replenished after the plastic politeness of the rich Alabama families. I understood why Zoila was the way she was, and what really made her tick and click, her almost inexplicable joy of life and love of the world. Although I had a hard time tolerating the humid heat that felt like liquid glue on my skin, the sight of the Atlantic Ocean for the first time in my life made me gasp in awe.

I ran to it and threw myself into its wild waves with voracious lust. It felt like a primal cleansing, so much stronger, bigger, and more spectacular than my Black Sea. I wanted to shed all my Communist shackles, smooth out and replenish my body exhausted from a lifetime spent with cravings and deprivations, weighed down by anxieties and desperation, my feet calloused by bad shoes, my hair and skin irritated by rough soaps, my heart exhausted by raw yearnings and heartbreaks.

By the time Zoila and I were back in her suburban luxurious apartment near Chicago, I had made up my mind that I wanted to make the leap and leave Romania. But not quite yet. I had to plan it, so my parents could be involved too. I just couldn't tolerate the thought of the shock and grief that they would suffer, were I to stay and not return from that trip. Then intervened my mother's best childhood friend who lived in Colorado with her Puerto Rican husband, the adventurer who left Romania on a whim in the late sixties and had become something of a legendary figure in our family.

When I called her from Zoila's apartment, she said she thought I should stay right then, or I would never be able to leave the country again once I returned, was I an idiot, or what? She sent me a round-trip ticket on the Greyhound bus to go visit her in Colorado. Zoila was excited for me and talked to my mother's friend on the phone about my trip. She shouldn't worry, she was going to drop me off and pick me up at the Greyhound station, and I was going to be fine, she said, since, in her words, I was a "mature smart young woman."

The bus trip, which I started with some level of adventurous spirit and excitement, and which turned out to take one full day and one full night, ended up being a small ordeal. The Alabama and Florida humidity must have perversely sneaked inside my body unused with such climate, for within a few hours I was shaking with chills, dizzy from excruciating sinus pain and my menstrual period that had graced me two weeks earlier, most likely as a result of the shock my body was going through in a new climate, with new foods, new everything. I had no idea where to find and how to ask for the menstrual cotton I was used to in Romania and that was obtained at the end of long hours of queuing at a pharmacy.

When the bus made a dinner stop in Omaha Nebraska and the driver gave us an hour and a half before we had to re-board the bus, I went directly to the drugstore of the bus station and looked for aspirin for my fever and sinus pain and something for my period. I had no idea what to look for and what to ask for. The cashier asked me if she could help me, and I said I was looking for aspirin.

She got me a large bottle of Bayer aspirin, and at the same moment when I picked up the aspirin bottle, a jet of menstrual blood burst out of me, and my beige linen pants that Zoila had gotten for me at Carson's Pirie & Scott soon after I arrived in Chicago turned bright red.

The cashier, a sweet-looking Black middle-aged woman, took one look at me and picked a small blue box with Tampax written in bold white letters on it and handed it to me. She then took me ahead of everybody else at the cash register and whispered, "The bathrooms are right around the corner, honey!"

I gave my last dollars for the aspirin and the box of Tampax and wished for a quick and painless death to forget I was at the head of a long line of people who stared at me, with my bloody pants, sweaty armpits and a face the color of a boiling lobster. I rushed to the bathroom and locked myself in one of the stalls where I first read every word on the instructions of the box of tampons, the likes of which I had never seen in my life, became terrified that I was for sure going to die a painful death from the toxic shock syndrome that the page with directions warned against, put the tampon in anyways following the instructions, cried in the stall for a few minutes thinking I was never going to make it to Colorado to see my mother's friend, but was going to die in the Greyhound bus station in Omaha, Nebraska, either from my head exploding or from the toxic shock syndrome given by the menstrual tampon.

I was also wondering why in God's creation anybody would manufacture an item that you were supposed to insert inside the most intimate part of your body and that could give you an awful sounding lethal syndrome. A woman asked me from the neighboring stall *are you all right, honey,* but I didn't answer. I took off my bloody pants and wrapped my pink jacket around my waist like a skirt.

I came out of the stall, washed my pants in the sink, dried them in front of the hand drier, put them back on, swallowed two aspirins with water from the sink, and left the bathroom in a hurry as the woman behind me said, "you'll be alright, honey". I thought it strange that everybody on that trip called me 'honey', and in the hour that was left of our dinnertime, decided to take a stroll around Omaha, Nebraska.

I started walking away from the bus stop in the direction of the tall buildings, the high rises, like the one I had seen in Chicago. The streets were deserted like after a disaster or as if nobody lived there. I persisted and kept walking, got nearer to the high rises, went down one street, then another, then saw a whole bunch of people waiting for the bus in a bus stop and rejoiced at the sight, people did live there after all.

It was getting dark, the setting sun erupted in a blinding flash right before disappearing behind one of the high rises. There were Black people going home from work. A sense of utter desolation and loss overcame me as I wondered where everybody lived, why were the streets deserted when the high rises around me could house thousands of people yet they seemed to all be empty. What was America all about?

Tears must have been coming down my startled face because one of the women in the bus stop asked me, "What's wrong, honey, do you need help?" I didn't know what to say, I made a sign with my head that, *no, I was fine* and whispered a meek "thank you", fearing I was going to explode into a flood of tears and sobs. Then she came closer and told me, "You shouldn't be here at this time of night, go home, honey!" I had no idea what law prevented me from being there at that time of night, and the expression *go home* at that juncture in my life sounded outlandish.

The bus came and everybody got on it, leaving the entire street deserted again. I looked at my watch and saw in horror that the hour had passed, and I was certainly not at the Greyhound station. I started running at the highest speed I was capable of. I had never been a good runner, but somehow I felt I had wings and ran and cried, thinking for sure the bus had left without me and I was going to be lost forever in Omaha, Nebraska, wandering the deserted streets until I was going to be arrested and then forcefully sent back to Romania in handcuffs directly in the arms of the secret police because by the time I would have gotten out of prison, my visa would have expired.

Never the sight of a bus produced such joy when I saw my Greyhound bus at the same place where I had gotten off an hour and a half earlier, with the bus driver impatiently waiting outside in front of the door and looking at his watch, the people on the bus staring through their windows at me running like a mad woman, my face streaked with tears, my pants wet in parts, my jacket crookedly tied around my waist, and me panting loudly.

My mother's friend waited for me with her Puerto Rican husband who to me looked like a darker version of Rhett Butler from *Gone with the Wind.* They both seemed ecstatic to see me and kept asking if I *was doing all right* and *did I have a good trip,* all the way to their BMW car in a nearby parking lot. My mother's friend looked indeed beautiful and modern, in jeans and a checkered shirt, her proverbial green eyes luminous and smiling though her face was marked by deeper wrinkles than I was expecting.

"I haven't seen you since you were seven years old," she said. "She is a beautiful girl, isn't she?" She added as if I wasn't there. She spoke to me in Romanian, while he spoke in English with a Spanish accent like Zoila's family.

I became even more disoriented, if that was even possible, given I had not heard or spoken one word of my native language in a month. By the time I got to their home on a hilly street lined with tall pine trees, I recounted my traveling adventures, snippets of my parents' lives back in Romania, the journey through the American South with Zoila, in broken bits and pieces, translating myself from Romanian to English, to their great amusement.

The air was finally breathable and dry, though reified because of the high altitude of the Rocky Mountains, like the air in the Carpathians near my family in Brasov. A sharp nostalgia crossed me and was mixed with the excitement of being in the mythic Rockies, which from the sight of them looked like the double in size of my Carpathians, hovering like petrified giants over the highway.

The West, the Wild West, I was moving from fantasy to fantasy, from Al Capone's Chicago to Scarlett O'Hara's torrid and racist South to John Wayne's rugged wild frontier territories. Yet I was also reaching out for slivers of memory of my childhood and home, now that the encounter with my mother's friend opened that closed chamber. The occasional visit of a strikingly beautiful brunette with gorgeous eyes and an infectious laughter who dropped unexpectedly by our tiny match box apartment in Bucharest bringing with her always an air of freshness and irrepressible liveliness, appeared in a blur.

Then one day, the news that she was gone, that she had escaped from a seaside town in Yugoslavia to Trieste. No one knew how she did it, but they knew she had settled in Paris and was doing fine. Then years later, we heard that she had gone to America, first San Francisco, then Colorado, and she was doing even finer in those remote territories. Her mother and sister visited us often and related to us the news they had from their monthly phone conversations with her over an intensely tapped telephone line. She had spent her winter vacation skiing in Aspen, her summer vacation gambling in Las Vegas, her birthday on a ship in Vancouver watching whales.

She entered the book of legendary escapes and disappearances of Romanians and now I was starting my own little legend while entering hers. The Romanians abroad, the Diasporas, the 'condemned' by the State and Party back on Romania. I wasn't yet among those 'condemned' since I wasn't part of any diasporas yet. I actually worried that the secret police who worked abroad on behalf of the Romanian government was going to find out I was staying with a political refugee, track me down, and bring me back in handcuffs. Always the same fear, sleeping or awake, the same nightmare of wicked men following me everywhere.

Once I entered their pine-smelling log cabin type house with large ceilings and a glorious sunroof, my fears dissipated. They took me to their family doctor who discovered a serious sinus infection and a deviated septum after which they took me to a Mexican restaurant with huge sombreros hanging everywhere, where we ate delicious burritos and fried ice cream that was brought to the table in flames.

I was so amazed by both the look and the taste of the fried ice cream that I asked if I could have another one, which again produced great hilarity among the two of them. I was bursting through my pants, tipsy from the margarita, and queasy from the ice cream and the antibiotics when we left the restaurant but filled with a new and wicked sense of adventure. The closeness to my mother's legendary friend seeped into my medicated, inebriated psyche like a dangerous yet thrilling potion. What if, what if, what if I stayed? Should it be Colorado or Chicago? I had no idea.

I had no time to give any more thought to any defection plans because the next morning very early we left for Las Vegas, another American Mecca, and drove for many hours across an endless desert, orangey red and rocky, arid and sprinkled with enormous cacti that looked like prehistoric creatures. The road became hallucinatory. I was thirsty all the time and overcome by an inescapable sleepiness.

The tiny gas stations suddenly emerging in the middle of the orange desert at enormous distances from one another, the continuous chatter in the car between my mother's friend and her husband and sometimes addressed to me, the country Western music on the radio alternating with sentimental Mexican music, it all became an ongoing surreal film that I seemed to also be part of.

I was sliding into a strange state of in between dozing and wakefulness where I was mechanically answering, contributing to the conversation, though not through a will of my own. I must have produced nonsensical statements because at some point, they were both laughing wholeheartedly. There were snowcapped mountains in the distance or so it seemed, and it felt like I was going home, that the Carpathians were at the end of the desert, but then the mountains disappeared and a brutal realization of the enormity of the distance between where I was and where my home was, opened up like a dizzying void inside my head.

After the thirst, I was devoured by hunger, and neither the bottled water nor the sweet and gooey snacks bought at the gas stations satisfied me. I asked about coyotes and hyenas, weren't we going to be attacked by them if night fell and we were still on the road? And how could John Wayne cross those expanses of dessert on his horse carrying guns and treasures on his saddle? That seemed to produce more hilarity, after which I must have fallen into a deep sleep because when I woke up it was dark, and we were riding along brightly lit avenues lined with hotels, casinos and prostitutes.

At least so I thought of the women strolling along with skirts that barely covered their asses and boobs that popped out of their tight blouses, for I had never seen an actual bona fide prostitute in my communist country. Not that there were not women who had sex for money, but they didn't walk around the city streets parading their butts and boobs to cars and passersby.

When we got out of the car in front of our motel, the heat struck me with violence, making me gasp for air. The heat was palpable, and it seemed to rise out of the earth like tongues of fire. I thought I was going to faint and when my guides saw the paleness I must have displayed rushed me into the air-conditioned room of the motel raving about the breakfast we were going to have the next day, for only one dollar, all you can eat pancakes or waffles with strawberries.

It sounded like a food fairy tale, the land of all you can eat strawberries. The rest of the trip to Las Vegas unfolded in a dizzying carousel of gorging on all you can eat and all you can drink buffets, slot machines and waitresses walking around with free drinks and dressed like the prostitutes in the street, or maybe the prostitutes were dressed like the waitresses, an exotic musical show with female dancers in richly plumed costumes who became topless on stage, walking through the furnace of the streets late at night and then starting all over the next morning with huge plates of pancakes smothered in whipped cream and strawberries.

A black and white picture taken in front of a slot machine with the three of us smiling at the professional casino photographer was left of that excursion, and ironically made it back to the United States in my purse among a handful of family photographs that I stuffed in my purse for my final escape-departure the following year. In it I look pudgy from the all you can eat and drink experiences, my dress with too many ruffles, my hair too big and a languid sadness in my eyes from the glittery emptiness of it all.

I was happy to be back in Chicago, which now felt familiar and welcoming, brilliant and gritty at once, combination that attracted me a hundred times more than the glitter of Las Vegas and it's all you can eat strawberry pancakes, the formidable Rockies, the eerie marshes of Alabama or the endless beaches of Jacksonville. All of that seemed made for vacations, Chicago was made for living.

After the depravity of Las Vegas, Zoila's maiden apartment all in blue and pink upholstery, flowery wallpaper and fresh flowers in a crystal vase was such a solace. It was time for me to start preparing for my return and the heavy discussion of the future, an eventual plan of escape to Western Europe followed by immigration to the States lingered from our dinner to our breakfast to our lunch meals.

It was daunting and overwhelming, and it all hung on me and my decision: all our family's future. My mother's friend kept calling to check what my decision would be, will I stay or will I go, could I afford to let go of such an opportunity in the off chance I might be able to leave again? Could I cause

254

such heartbreak back home and even more importantly, was I really ready for that step?

It turned out I wasn't. I must have been so entirely preoccupied by an escape plan in the future, that my memory is a perfect pure black hole of oblivion when it comes to my trip back to Bucharest from Chicago.

Sometimes it feels like the year in between that return and our definitive escape via Italy, the following year was a dream, a short parenthesis that held in it the reports I had to write about my trip for the secret police officer who visited and harassed me repeatedly following my return from Chicago, our heated planning discussions in the living room of our brand new apartment, my mother's excitement about having had the bathrooms tiled coupled with a mild regret that just when we had a nicer apartment with tiled bathrooms we were going to leave everything, the leaps into the dreamy world of the theater in the Attic with my wild Winnie flurries of poetic passion, and the summer right before my departure, with the weeks of nude swimming, dancing to the music of Dire Straits or Simon and Garfunkel, and gorging on canned condensed milk in the peasants' house at the Black Sea.

After that Romanian parenthesis, Chicago started as if for the first time, because now it was definitive, and the vacation of the previous year almost didn't count. It started with the brutally cold winter of our arrival, the brutally hot summer of my superfluous wedding plans with the Midwestern poet and the death of my father's sister back in Romania and all the subsequent summers and winters that followed, my schooling, first child, marriage, Lake Shore Drive and Lake Michigan with their various shades of green and blue reigning over everything in all the seasons.

Then came the deep brackets of my life in the cradle of the Appalachians, university career, books, second child, second marriage, single motherhood, tumultuous returns to the native land, European travels, and Chicago vacations in smaller and multiple parentheses. Always, the return to Chicago, a stubborn return to the 'real thing', to the first American me!

In my thirty-third American summer, Chicago called again with the urgency of love and death: my second husband and father of my second son was dying and calling for me. In late July, my son let me know calmly that his father had interrupted his cancer treatment of his own will and was now in hospice care in his Chicago apartment. Hospice, a concept still so foreign to me as I am eternally stuck in the Romanian way of dealing with death, in its brutal and always unexpected arrival without preparations and without sanitizing, had a sinister ring in my ear.

We were driving back from the airport, as he had just returned from a trip to Peru. He gave me the news looking straight ahead at the road and his calm extended briefly over my own usually frantic psyche. We let it go, and talked about other things, as if they were more important than his father's impending death. Climbing the Machu Pichu, the adventures of the three-day trip to the top of the mythic mountain with the Peruvian guide and insufficient water!

I was trying to navigate the labyrinth of highways between the airport and the city as I invariably get lost at Chantilly and take that exit, as if the French sounding name would catapult me between French lace and whipped cream. Instead, it's always just Fairfax, Virginia, the important civil war site. Why the French names, I always wonder afterwards as I'm desperately trying to get back on the correct highway, from exit ramp to exit ramp, torn by an irreparable sense of foreignness.

Hospice, hospice, the word returned to the front of my conscience starting to nag at me. I took the wrong exit again as I was trying to correct my mistake. *How much time, how long till the end?* I'm not sure if I asked those words out loud in the air conditioned yet stuffy space of the car, or just in my mind. My son seemed to have heard my thoughts even if I hadn't asked the question out loud. *It's still a while, you know*, I wasn't sure at all what that meant, a month, three, how many?

I hadn't seen him since the spring, when he came to my book launch in a Chicago bookstore, looking like a ghost in his best red shirt and brown tweed blazer, barely walking yet still remarkably distinguished, his hair barely gray with rebellious strands falling over his high forehead. He looked at me with the old and unextinguished love. Then he disappeared soon after the reading, while I was talking to people and trying to sell my book.

I had a sharp pang of longing and irremediable loss, like it was the last time I would see him. I looked around and rushed outside in the unforgiving Chicago cold even in April and the taxi he had called was driving away. The year before, I had broken my promise that I would go to Chicago for Thanksgiving. He had sounded sad about the cancellation of my trip yet resigned and understanding. I was too tired from work, the drive to Chicago was too long, and I needed to rest, I complained.

I should have learned to never postpone seeing and talking to a loved one who is near the end. After all, I had absorbed from the womb my mother's grief for losing her mother before she had a chance to see her one more time, I should have known better. She had postponed the journey to see her because she was too pregnant, too tired, and too long of a train ride and that irreparable regret must have seeped from her womb through me. I was now 'guilty' of the same careless postponement. The living never learn. Driving through the frightful maze of northern Virginia trying to find the right highway with my luminous son next to me, the sinister word hospice ringing in my brain, I was drowning in sadness.

I hated northern Virginia with its shameless conglomeration of malls and skyscrapers more than ever, and I yearned for the blazing blues and greens of Lake Michigan and the colorful neighborhoods of Chicago, its grit, its energy with my great love dying in it. The only place in America that felt profoundly like home. Memories from the twenty-five years we had been part of each other's lives exploded like fireworks in my conscience: the tumultuous passionate illicit years, the trying to make a family years, the angry years of breakups and reconciliations and more breakups and more reconciliations, the dozens of swims in the waters of that lake that my father had hated with a passion and that we adored, the gentle friendship years of long talks over the phone when he was too ill to drive to Virginia and see us, like he had done for twenty years, a wild and proud commuter between the Midwest and the confederate South.

Just as well, he had said many times, he didn't want to die in confederate land, the New Englander that he was, with a Harvard graduate German father who had escaped Nazi Germany during the war and a fierce Midwestern mother raised in Illinois.

The first time he came to visit me in the Shenandoah Valley right after I had moved there for my new job and I was pregnant with our son, he was driving to his mother's funeral in Concord, Massachusetts, to the famous Sleepy Hollow Cemetery. He took a detour to visit me on a late summer afternoon under a torrential fierce rain. We met in the Walmart parking lot. I saw him first as he got out of the car not caring a bit about the torrential rain.

He looked regal in his one fancy black pin-striped suit he had bought for the funeral of his nephew dead in a plane crash possibly caused by the CIA a few years before I had met him. We went to a local motel for a couple of hours to make desperate love and to cry in each other's arms about our twisted fates of adulterers falling in love too late, too married, too far away from each other.

I had followed the work; he had stayed for the work, an enormous stretch of American land with many Appalachian ridges and cornfields between us. The little town I had moved to seemed strange and unreal, everybody too proper, too nice, and me sticking out in the midst of if with my accent, my shrillness, my European ways and clothes, my secrets that were going to be spilled into the wicked local courthouses the following years and into the hallways of my university by equally wicked colleagues.

Now our son was sitting next to me in our white Toyota minivan, returning from Peru and announcing to me the news of his father's impending end. Hospice, hospice, the hollow sound of it resonated again in the car as memories of our wild impossible story spilled into my brain mercilessly.

We must go see him as soon as we can, we must go to Chicago, I think I said or maybe I believed to have said it out loud. There was a missed heartbeat between my thoughts and my words, an intermittent break of consciousness. I managed to get us on the correct highway. The American spaces were still unfamiliar labyrinths in which I got lost again and again, yet through which I always found my way in the end.

We make it to Chicago only a week before his death, in the sweltering heat. The lake is blue green, impenetrable and yet refreshing as every summer since my first summer. We are all arriving from different parts of America. Who said death doesn't bring people together? Adult children from different marriages and me the 'beloved ex-wife', begrudged by some of those children, despised by the other exes.

Who cares now, in front of death the great equalizer? My son is the youngest of all his children, child of his old age, as I am the last love, 'the great one', as he used to say. He is waiting for me in his hospital hospice bed in his apartment on the south side of Chicago, in the Flamingo building where even Barack Obama once briefly lived in one of his many steps to glory.

On the way from Virginia to Chicago as I am driving across the West Virginia mountainous wilderness, the blue grass of Kentucky, the Indiana cornfields that he loved crossing on his trips to see us, in the car with my older son, I get a text from my younger son. He had arrived there a few hours before us from New York, and he writes, "Dad, can't wait to see you."

258

My non-native English tricks me again with its idiomatic expressions. In my grief and confusion, I take it literally, like *he can no longer wait for you to get here and he will die before your arrival.* The metaphoric layers of language escape me in the face of the most literal and definitive of all things that is death. I am seized by atrocious panic that I won't see him alive one more time. Can't death wait for a few hours until I cross all the goddamn states on the way to Chicago?

The past love, the fierce love I once felt for him comes alive like a torch lit by the very closeness of death. Love and death, which one is stronger, until death do us part, the deceitfulness of language particularly when it's not your native language, it all hits me at once, all the gaps between reality and language, past and present.

I call my son, sobbing and beg him to beg his father, "Please no, tell him to wait, to not die yet, I have to see him one more time."

"Calm down, Mom," he says. "He meant he is looking forward to seeing you, he is excited about seeing you soon, you know, it's an expression. He can't wait to see you." Yes, of course, foolish me.

My refugee self is confusing and tricking me even now at this moment of life and death, my life in translation is always getting in the way of the real, the untranslated and untranslatable reality. Yet there is something cruel and deceitful in the very expression itself *I can't wait to see you*, which I must have used thousands of times in the correct colloquial sense, the writer that I am. But when a dying person says *I can't wait to see you*, they might mean just that, *I may die before you get here.*

There is still time, calm down, mom, says my son again and again. And calm down I do indeed for the next several hours across the Indiana endless cornfields with their majestic windmills like gigantic birds rotating slowly against the cruel clear horizon, until the entrance into Chicago onto the Lake Shore Drive, with the view of the lake that this time looks insultingly blue.

I get it now why my father hated it. Nothing should be this blue when you are losing the battle for happiness and the battle for life. *I am losing the second most important man in my life*, I think as I speed on Lake Shore drive towards the Flamingo apartment building, my father being the first one, *the men so crucial to my formation as a woman, a professional, a person.* I get closer to the building and turn on the Mexican radio station that we sometimes used to listen to; everything here is singed and tattooed with memories of the most crucial episodes of my past.

It only lasts a week, a ferocious week of torrid Chicago days in the smell of death and of tumultuous nights filled with agonizing whispers. Both of my sons and I take turns staying with him and caring for him as if we were a family again. As if we were the family, we would have liked to be but were only able to be on brief stolen occasions. It turns out there is a stark cleanliness in the smell of approaching death, nothing is as imagined.

There is a palpable undefined heaviness in the air, yet life appears in all its shameless stridency, with its needs for food, for water, for air and light. We once argued on a Parisian metro about the existence and persistence of the soul after death. He said he didn't believe in it, I said I did.

I was wearing a summer bright red dress, and I was furious at him for not saying he believed in it. The Parisians on the metro stared severely at us. I was an atheist that believed in the soul, and he was an agnostic who didn't believe in the everlastingness of the soul. He smiles at the memory now, when neither of us believes in any of that any longer.

The Philippine women caring for him from hospice services tell me how eagerly he had waited for me. "You are the love of his life," they tell me. They all love him, as he is kind and still witty on these last days. How does one keep being kind and witty when so close to the end and particularly when you don't believe in the immortality of the soul? I wish I had been next to him earlier.

I wish I had kept all my past promises of visiting earlier, of sending him the audio version of my last novel when he could no longer see well enough to read it in its published version. Too late now, it doesn't matter. We recount episodes from our past, from the good years, none from the difficult years, though he says *our love was so profound, troubled but profound.* He keeps coming back to how much he has always loved me and still does, as if that was his soul, his bid to immortality: the love for me.

Pictures of me and my younger son are everywhere on the walls of his apartment, some of both my children, and of his other children, and many, many books in piles everywhere. The books he wrote, the ones he read, the books I wrote, the ones we had gifted each other with loving dedications, French poetry, the one that had brought us together twenty-five years earlier in our messy, delinquent, impossible love that now seems to shine one last time, a setting magenta sun drowning in the silvery plates of an ocean.

Children and books: he once told me early on at the very start of our relationship, "I have written books and made children my whole life, I am like a biblical character." And I thought then, *the arrogant bastard, of course you did, because you had the women to care for the children and to give you the time to write the books.* But now, some of the children and all the books are around him as he is dying.

A fierce sunset that sends one last magenta gasp of brilliance before disappearing in the sea! We both loved sunsets by the sea or anywhere else. I had no idea that in the face of the death of a dear person, past grudges melt, and the love sparkles desperately one more time as if then only it can prove its full truthfulness. There is beauty to his gaunt face too, the one I had always admired, aristocratic, delicate yet strong, and his eyes have the fixity and roundness of a bird, smaller but fiercer than ever.

So many of the American clichés about death and dying sound now as just that: vacuous clichés. "He has lived a full life", "he is surrounded by his loved ones" as if that is suddenly supposed to make that passage into nothingness an easy no big deal operation like taking the train somewhere. I had never heard of any of those clichés growing up about the people dying around me, only the priest mumbling something about a better place with a lot of sun and green grass. At least there was some color to that formula.

The nights are exhausting, eviscerating, filled with the insomnia of the dying. Why would someone so close to the final and eternal sleep even want to sleep at all? On the contrary, there is our desperate need for sleep, my son and I take turns comforting him with water, a wet cloth on his lips or sweaty forehead. The clammy heat on the hard sofas in the apartment is tangible and oppressive. The dying cling to you like drowning people with one last fierce bout of strength and energy as if trying to pull you downward with them.

Some of the nights are hallucinatory with too many people taking care of one person. Even a student of his is spending some nights there, and everybody seems to be camping out in this Chicago apartment. It's crowded in a comforting way though despite the discomforts: the solidarity of the living in front of the dying.

These nights are redefining my own journey. Despite the exhaustion, life feels fuller and sharper in the sound of the agonizing whispers, moans, requests of the dying man. You can feel a quiver, a breath fluttering around that is neither the breeze from the lake when the windows are open, nor is it the air from the inefficient air conditioning unit.

Maybe it's the flutter of the soul that neither of us believed in. The last couple of nights are muddy, sticky and they seem endless. The days are worse because we carry the tiredness of the nights. Between wakefulness and troubled sleep, the night sounds, the heat and the smells merge into one gooey substance that wants to drown us.

Decades ago, I had arrived in this city, first on a sweltering afternoon and the following year on a frigid night and the foreignness was so deep that it felt comforting. Now it feels familiar; a home where I conceived my children, and mourned the first dead. People get shot everyday only a few blocks from this here majestic Flamingo building, while the jazz music plays at Louie's bar downstairs every night. Maybe that's why the hot air at night feels sticky and sour, the blood of murders seeps through the heated earth and rises into the air.

If you live a few blocks from here and don't have insurance, there is no home hospice with Philippine caretakers, and you die alone in a project building with morphine gotten on the street. Not even the Philippine caretakers can afford the hospice services they give to others. So much depends on so little, like the block you happen to be born on. Some moments I have no idea why I find myself in an apartment in the Flamingo building crouched on a sofa smelling of urine, with a dying man a few feet away in a city with daily murders. My son whose blonde hair shines in the Chicago night reminds me why and then I know why I love this city despite its daily murders and despite my own self.

Some of us who ended up here instead of other countries, European Western countries for instance, love and hate these United States in equal measures. I have American sons and that roots me here more than anywhere else in the world. The dead and the dying I buried or will bury root me here. The books I have written root me here, a tiny entry in an enormously dizzying log of American writers, but an entry, nevertheless.

My son's pain for the impending loss of his father glows in the dark. Memories and episodes from the past get reorganized in my mind like an animated feature. The shapes of days merge and grow into one another: the long conversations between father and son over Thai lunches and dinners on fifty-third street or at Country Cooking in our Virginia small town, the slow walks, the drives along the Blue Ridge Parkway or on Lake Shore drive, oblique memories that don't even belong to me but to my son, brief yet regular encounters whose importance over the years I fully understand only now as I watch him moving gracefully and with infinite care around his dying father.

My sons and I take breaks by swimming in the lake off the rocks at a place called the Point where we all used to swim in the summer. The lake cleanses us of the smell of death, it is clear greenish, and it refreshes us. We make belief it's clean though we know that tons of sewage go into it every day but apparently, they neutralize that with chemicals. Who cares about sewage and chemicals? We swim in it thirstily trying to forget.

Yet the more I try to forget, the more I remember. How we had swum in so many of the worlds' seas, lakes, pools, frantic for swimmable waters, the Adriatic, the Mediterranean, the Atlantic, the Pacific in Hawaii at his son's wedding, even in the cold gray Northern Sea. We both loved the cold waters of the world and thirstily swam in them to cool off our burning bodies and hearts.

The penultimate night, it's only my younger son and I, taking turns sleeping and administering water, solace, medication, raspberries, soup, the only things he can still eat at the very edge of consciousness until everything locks up and words come out in an unstoppable chant to either the oncoming unknown or the departing life. My gratefulness for the life of my sons is infinite on this agonizing night while I am equally awed at the phenomenon of dying.

It is a formidable phenomenon indeed, like birth, only now I get it, the nakedness, the almost sexual abandon and throbbing of this passage into something else while still clinging to this here life. There is a point where one wishes for the final breath of the dying person just so that one can sleep.

My son says *let's give him the morphine that the doctor left us.* The doctor who had visited the previous day indeed left a vial of morphine that he had put in a box with a lock and a code which for some reason he only gave to my son. We laugh about that, in a kind of sinister complicity. "We could sell it at a high price in the street," my son says, laughing.

There is no reason to not have humor in the face of the finality of death. The last intelligible words he pronounces to me in the night are *I love you more than anything in the world*, before the final delirium of incomprehensible words and sounds before the morphine brings him to merciful sleep.

It has been a heavy burdensome love for twenty-five years in a myriad of different stages, demanding and atrocious, at times like a curse. We hear sirens in the night, voices, brawls, we open the windows—better the outside air hot as it may be, with the smells of the lake and the heated concrete. Life always goes on outside the windows. I think of all the people that I know who have died, like a badge of honor, like a proof I have lived fully and am fully alive. Also, fearful that one of us may catch it, that one of us might pick up the contagion of death.

Again, I think of my older son's good friend who had died alone in the streets of New Orleans during Mardi Gras of a drug overdose. I am seized by fury again at the American society that abandons its youth and its old people; it swallows its most vulnerable in callous indifference, highways, greasy foods, guns, religious fervor, malls and political demagoguery. My dying ex-husband had rooted me in his America, in the poetic, solitary, wild, sensuously irreverent America of Walt Whitman, Wallace Stevens and Emily Dickinson and is leaving me in this world with such a formidable declaration. And really, for all practical reasons this America is my only home, though it still feels so foreign. I guess foreignness is a way of belonging on this vast continent.

When it's all over, we sit in the front room quietly with the corpse in the adjoining room facing the lake. His older son had arrived only at the end, for the last night, too late to catch him while still conscious. He is my age. I could have been married to him instead of the father. This thought crosses my mind, but the old soul that I am was only attracted to the old man, and from that came this sunshine of a son crying over his father's corpse in the mercilessly bright Chicago morning.

There is grotesque comedy overlapping the sadness too. The youngest daughter arrives and asks if she can take pictures on her iPhone of her dead father. We stare at each other and roll our eyes and say *yes sure, go ahead*; we laugh through the tears.

Then the height of grotesque happens when the people from the morgue arrive with their mortuary plastic bag and ask us to provide clothes for the deceased before they take him to the cremation place. Everybody looks at me, and I understand that as the most recent ex-wife, I am expected to make that final decision and pick out of his closet the clothes he will wear before he is pushed into the cremation oven.

I pick the black pants, the brown blazer and the red shirt he wore at my book launch, which was also the last time I saw him in a place other than this hospital hospice bed. I pick out the clothes and hand them to the morgue people; they take them nonchalantly together with the heavy bag carrying the deceased.

We are left with the abundance of groceries spilling over the table in the Chicago apartment and are staring at the lake: the two sons, the Indian student, and me. The daughter has left but she has the iPhone pics. The light fills the room to excess.

My thoughts were snagged on the clothes episode with the morgue people, as I'm trying to wrap my mind around what just happened. A huge episode of my life has closed and there are pictures, books and letters everywhere around reminding me of various stages of the twenty-five years in which our destinies converged.

One thought persists and knocks inside my head like a woodpecker knocking on a tree trunk. I learned the denomination of pileated woodpecker from him, as he was also obsessed with ornithology and trees, Indo-European trees, birches, beech trees, sycamores, families and origins of trees. I promised him I am going to write our story. It has to be in the third person.

I said to him: I said, "I will write our story, I promise."

"It's a good story," he said, "very profound."

I wondered then how someone on their death bed uses such academic words as 'profound'; how someone on their death bed talks about the three main dialects of the Philippine language to their caretakers, knowledge they had no idea of themselves even though they must have been speaking one of those very dialects.

The French writer I used to love and wrote my doctoral dissertation on said that the manner of one's death is what ultimately defines one's life. I don't know, I'm not sure what defines our lives and what remains. I can only be sure of this moment filled with a palpable absence, with my son's cries, with the shameless blueness of Lake Michigan and the wrenching ache in my gut.

I can't get over the episode with the morgue people asking me to choose his clothes for the cremation and the colossal weirdness of it keeps me baffled in the gooey heat of the apartment. He will be dressed up in the blazer he wore at my book reading when the coffin with his body in it slides into the sinister crematorium and is engulfed in greenish flames. He melts to ashes, but then a simulacrum image of him like a hologram rises from the flames, asking me to dance with him to one of our favorite tunes. I can't fully settle on which tune.

All I know is that it must be a heartbreak sentimental melody, we dance to it floating across the seas and oceans we had swum in. No sea or ocean can extinguish the blazing fire that consumes him to a pound of ashes. It's a Mexican song about love and death, for sure, the soul, the desert, a last dance, and the heart again, *el corazón*. The soundtrack to this hologram theater can only be about love and death.

We are whizzing on Lake Shore drive during one of my visits of our good messy years. I start speaking fluent Spanish after we have seen *Como agua para chocolate/Like Water for Chocolate*, though I only took half a year of Spanish in college. Chicago is raw and brilliant like an unlikely postcard; it smells of burnt earth, of lake waters, of derailed passions. I can say all this in Mexican Spanish. I can speak all the languages if I only set my mind to.

I have a universal heart that cracks open to Mexican heartbreak tunes and melts in this love come too late, too messy, too wretched. Yet the hologram image of him is untouched and untouchable; he dances elegantly in his brown blazer that I picked for him to wear at his own final burning.

Loose Ends

I used to have a recurrent dream during the first ten years of my American life: I am back in Bucharest during the gray years. I am walking on side streets on my way home, to our apartment near the railway station but cannot find the street, and I get entangled in a labyrinth of streets. The more desperately I try to find the right street, *Bulevardul garii numarul* 5, Train Station Boulevard, number 5, the farther away I get from it.

I know I need to get back to the airport and back to Chicago in America where my home is now, but somebody is following me. I am going to be seized, arrested, and will never get out of here. I know this was the biggest mistake of my life, returning to my country just because I couldn't stand the yearning. As I get more entangled in the gray labyrinth of my native Bucharest, I have fleeting memories of my life in Chicago, particularly sitting in a classroom during an world literature class in the summer.

A breeze flutters through the open windows carrying with it the smells of the lake. The notes of a sad saxophone trail into the classroom, but stupid me I am back in Bucharest, and I can never leave again, an army of secret police are after me. I turn to dust. The most excruciating part of the dream from which I always woke up shaking and sobbing was the point in my chaotic rambling through streets that looked both familiar and unrecognizable.

As I am rambling on those Bucharest streets, I have a flashback to the moment in my American classroom with the summer breeze carrying the saxophone notes, and I am thinking *lucky me, sitting here in this classroom studying existentialist philosophy in Chicago, no more secret police, no more gray streets with secret police in them, just me and Lake Michigan and Albert Camus.*

I am wondering in my dream whether that happy memory wasn't itself a dream, a scene I had imagined from my desire to leave the country and from stories told by Zoila Valdivieso about Chicago.

Such a sense of disorientation seeped through every molecule of my being for the rest of my day in Chicago that I sometimes went rambling downtown for hours just to assure myself that I was not in the dream of the foolish return. One day on such a disoriented rambling on a side street off the famous Magnificent Mile walk, I walked into a familiar smell, a summer Bucharest smell. The street was lined up with linden trees which I hadn't encountered since my departure from Bucharest, in my last hot summer in that city of my birth.

It was June of 1989, the day before my birthday. I now had a three-month-old son, and in a couple of days I was going to be naturalized as an American citizen. Communism hadn't fallen just yet, and I was seized by an intolerable longing for that same bloody city that I was having nightmares about.

In a fairy tale that Romanians claim to be unique among all other fairy tales in the world, the prince protagonist goes in search of the kingdom of youth without old age and life without death. After many obstacles he reaches the magic realm, marries of course the most beautiful of the three sister princesses of the realm of youth and life everlasting, but is given the warning to never walk into a valley called the Valley of Tears. Woe is him if he does.

But of course, he does step into the forbidden valley one day as he is chasing after a rabbit. And indeed woe is him because from that moment on, he is seized by unbearable and unquenchable longing, the fierce *dor*, the longing without a name that is so ferocious it tears you to pieces as you are longing for Home, for something you lost forever and you can't recapture.

dor

Despite his wife's pleas not to return, the prince goes back on his valiant steed and woe is him all over again because centuries had passed while he was happily basking in the glow of youth everlasting. His old village is now just a big pile of dust and decay, his family long gone, and he turns to dust himself in a blink, touched by the angel of death that sat hidden in a chest in the old palace cellar, having been waiting for him for a couple of centuries.

Had I just stepped into the Valley of Tears? Was the America with glittery ads for cosmetics, detergents, antidepressants, glamorous cars, ultra-efficient menstrual tampons, the illusion of the realm of life and youth everlasting, a huge meadow with plastic flowers like the ones on the tombstones that my father mocked for their falseness, with perfect smiles whitened by magic toothpaste frozen in an eternity of niceness and plastic happiness?

The symbolism seemed to match perfectly but what I was experiencing on that summer Chicago day walking in a daze trying to find my bearings after my return to Romania nightmare, the wrenching ache in my gut was not a symbol, it was raw, and it hurt like hell. I continued my walk trying to shake off all the ballast of nostalgia. What good was it anyways?

I walked back towards the lake and onto one of the downtown beaches. American couples, families, groups of friends were splashing in the water, picnicking on multicolored ethnic quilts spread out on the sand with assortments of mayonnaise filled foods, playing ball or reading under a parasol. I felt removed from the entire scene as if I were looking at a picture in a museum.

Here is the little girl with a polka dot sun hat who is building a castle on the shore; there in a corner is the couple sunbathing on a Hawaiian beach towel; and over there almost in the center a group of kids throwing a beach ball right at the line where the waves break. They are laughing and shouting but all the sounds seem to come to me from afar.

And right in front of me under a big sun umbrella with multicolored stripes is a mother feeding her baby from a Gerber jar of baby food and going ga goo at the baby. I am outside the picture, looking at it.

The picture shifts, the colors start to melt, and another picture replaces it: a little blonde girl is squatting in front of a sandcastle and putting the last decorations made of tiny white shells and green curly algae all over the castle. Her mother comes near her and places a white cotton hat on her head and her father comes near her too and tells her *what a beautiful castle, and you have built it all by yourself.*

He lights a cigarette and stares into the distance at the intensely blue sea, because now it is the sea and not the lake that forms the background of this picture. And they are speaking in a different language that is not English, and she understands it perfectly. A Gypsy girl passes by with a basket filled with corn on the cob, and the little blonde girl asks her mother to buy her one, and the mother does.

It was a large beach ball landing on my head that broke the spell I had fallen under and brought me back to the sand of a beach by Lake Michigan in Illinois, the United States, with its strident cacophony of sounds and voices. My face was wet. I wasn't sure whether from the waves splashing in the lake or my own tears. I remembered I also had a child, born in the spring; he was waiting for me at my apartment on the south side of Chicago with my father, while my husband was at work. My breasts felt engorged and were leaking. That was my picture at that point in time, and I was inside it.

My aunt Nina visited us that year in late fall around Thanksgiving. She is someone who keeps returning in my novels, my dreams, my conscience times and again like a fairy godmother, with sweetness, wisdom, and the fragrances of apples, tarragon in delicious soups, and elderberry juice. She was happier than ever since she had retired from her engineer's job, but the heartbreak caused by our departure had not healed. A stubborn wound that would never heal.

We made a Thanksgiving dinner with foods that Romanians hadn't seen in stores in years, as the population was borderline starving while the megalithic House of the People was seeing the final stages of its construction. She only shyly, almost reluctantly, acknowledged the misery back home as if worried some secret police agent might be listening to her, or maybe just because she wanted to suggest we could have stayed, that we didn't need to break our family in two for the mega supermarkets in America, in which all the foods wrapped in plastic weren't that tasty anyway.

She showed little admiration for all things we had acquired: my mother's tiny Toyota Tercel that she got for a few hundred dollars from one of my graduate student friends, my husband's black Mercury Marquis that my parents-in-law had gifted us, the furniture we had acquired from garage sales or as gifts from rich friends of Zoila's and which filled our spacious Hyde Park apartment or my parents' apartment in Evanston.

She was only impressed by my baby son's plump blond beauty and sweetness. That was a real accomplishment indeed, she decided. Through her presence I mediated my longing for a country that seemed so far away that it had lost its sense of reality for me. The fierce *dor* hit me only in dreams or when triggered by a smell, a taste, a sliver of color. However, with the presence of the dearest member of my extended family that carried with her the aromas of my childhood and youth, that wicked *dor* both raised its fierce head during my waking hours and became its own medicine.

She returned to Romania the day before the revolution started and it was obvious, she was happy to go back, while I embarked on our bi-annual visit to my in-laws in Portland Maine, with our nine-month-old son. From the large TV screen in my in-laws' living room, I watched the most mind-boggling scenes happening in my native city while holding or nursing my baby son. Streets and roads, I had walked on thousands of times in my native city were now battle fields covered by tanks, soldiers, civilians with guns, people running for cover, shooting or getting shot at.

CNN showed sickening images of dead babies killed in the fighting which later were said to have been made up, as they removed recently deceased babies from hospitals and morgues laying them at various battle sites. However, right then before that Christmas of 1989, those sights of violence, murders, student revolt, chaotic street shootings, and dead babies laying on top of rubble in the capital where I grew up, gave me a ferocious desire to go back, pick up a gun, and start shooting at secret police gone rogue myself.

It wasn't clear to me who the so-called 'terrorists' were and it remained a mystery forever. Instead of being happy that I found myself in the safety of my in-laws' luxurious home, grateful for peace and capitalist well-being, I was dying to be where my people were dying in the streets. I fidgeted and paced on the fluffy carpeting like a caged beast, sobbing, sighing, swearing, calling my aunt who was describing what was going on in the streets and in their neighborhood, where there was also shooting and street fighting.

I wondered what the man I had once been so fiercely in love with was doing those days. Was he also out in the streets with a gun, or did he stay barricaded in his apartment safe from all the aimed and stray bullets flying around that city of my best childhood and teenage days? I was not going to find all that out until our encounter fifteen years later on a summer day at the beginning of the new millennium.

The sight of the execution of the Ceausescus on CNN in my in-laws' living room made me vomit. Despite all the hatred I and my people had harbored for this man whose dumb fake smile hung in every classroom, in every office, and on top of every official building in its larger than life version all throughout my life in Romania, and despite all the misery he had caused us, despite the irreparable pain I had caused myself by running away from the country in which he ruled, I couldn't help being washed over by an overpowering wave of pity and disgust.

He and his wife Elena looked so haggard, in coats that hung loose on them. He was wearing a typical lambskin hat that sat sideways on his head and looked utterly silly, and she had a babushka scarf on her head, like an old peasant woman. Depicted like this, they were the ultimate pathetic picture of the vanity of their dreams of glory and eternal power, reduced to only their shivering skin and bones.

The people who were holding them, pushing them around, interrogating them in the sham trial they were pretending to carry out at some sinister margin of my native city, seemed more wicked and sickening than the image of the old couple begging for their lives. I sobbed with hiccups holding my baby son, to the utter amazement of my husband and in laws. I had surges of disgust for the entire nation of people I had come from.

That Christmas was a colossal mess. The biggest political event of my life had taken place, the one I had waited for my entire life and I didn't know whether to get on a plane back to Bucharest, mourn the Christmas execution of a psychopathic tyrant, or simply enjoy the Hanukkah and Christmas combined celebration in the beautiful house of my in laws in Portland, Maine and as the cliché went, count all my blessings.

As the young mother barely turned naturalized citizen of United States partly dependent on my husband's income, with a graduate degree in the works and two struggling parents who had transplanted the totality of their lives to be with me, I chose the blessings counting option as the most viable one. The mourning part was going to become pathetic pretty fast, and there was no question of actually returning to Romania even for a brief visit. The fear of the secret police that raged in my recurrent nightmares was not going to leave me for another decade.

Soon after the images of heroic students and citizens falling in the university square from what was called on the news 'terrorist' bullets, and the gruesome execution of the Ceausescus, my country opened up its dark insides to the world: scabrous images of emaciated orphans with blank looks and dirty faces, locked in cages, tied to their beds, and crowded in squalid dormitories were filling the world's TVs like the rotting dark underbelly of Eastern Europe.

No other of the countries that had shed their communist shackles had anything as sinister as that to show the world. I longed for the times when Romania was shrouded in mystery and known largely for Nadia Comaneci and Dracula. And yet I missed it more than ever; in fact, that was precisely when I allowed all the *dor* collected inside my molecules to burst from the ventricle of my heart where I had kept it tucked in for the six years necessary to acquire my citizenship, and seep through all my veins and arteries like a slow thick irresistible, yet bitter sweet poison. It contaminated my thoughts and actions, my relationship to my own past and to the future, the way I thought of my son, my marriage, my world.

Was it worth it? Couldn't I have waited another six years? But the golden baby nursing at my breast annulled those retroactive doubts and made it all matter and be worth it. Still, the thought that my baby was born an American and was thus separated by an entire continent from my ancestry gave me the vertigo. A chasm of geographies, history, language, and culture spread open between us. The cliché that he is born in America, so he could become anything he wants, even the President of the United States, meant nothing to me and that was not in the least on my mind when I chose to throw myself into the abyss of countrylessness, that I would birth an American child who could be president one day.

It was as if we were foreign countries to each other. I relished in his greedy nursing thinking that through all that milk going from my body into his I could pour into him some of the substance of the land that had formed me and that flowed through my veins, the luminous parts that transcended regimes and history, that still flickered in my conscience, and under my skin with the fierce violet blues of the Black Sea, the heavy greens of the brooding Carpathians, the melancholy sunsets over Bucharest roofs and church steeples, the sweet lull of the diphthongs and triphthongs in our language, the irreverence with which we laughed at everything, including death.

It was going to be another ten years before I was going to take that first son born in the year of the fall of communism and his brother born four years later, back to my country of origins on that first momentous trip when I bought my colonial house over my cousins' clunky cell phone at ten thousand feet elevation on majestic alpine pastures with rabid cows and their manure all around me. It would be another fifteen years in all since that utterly confusing revolution, before I would sit face to face with the man who had influenced my entire love destiny in irrevocable ways.

I was returning for the third or fourth time to Romania, and by then each one of my returns felt like a necessary and sweet agony that my body couldn't get enough of. We were now in the new millennium, my father had died, I was a full professor, I had two teenage children, and the world had changed radically from my first return at the end of the previous century.

First, I called his cell phone from mine, which felt like a huge anachronism since our story was in a world of tapped dial phones and defective pay phones in booths or at street corners. His voice was faltering and soft. Sweet as always with haunting echoes of a deep past that arched over our common history, revolution, regime changes, post-revolutionary capitalist chaos, and the ripening of our personal lives into a well-established maturity with spouses, children, and hopeless longings.

He was suffering from a degenerative muscular disease that partly incapacitated his mobility, most likely muscular sclerosis. I had no idea. He invited me to his apartment not far away from the old neighborhood where he had lived when we were young and pathetically in love. He told me to just walk in, that he would leave the door ajar, so he wouldn't have to get up to open up for me since he didn't walk very well.

I must have changed my outfit ten times and ended up putting on a most extravagant and inappropriate multicolored silk party dress. What was I thinking? He made sure to schedule our encounter when his wife was at work, at the clinic where she was a doctor. I was thrilled by the possibility of adultery, seasoned as I was in that domain by then, wicked temptress, shameless me.

I have heard it said that the first love will set you up for the entire rest of your life, how you are going to love, be loved, what you want and expect or not from your subsequent love partners. I could blame it all on him that he had made me so voracious for love and erotic passion. My thoughts were an incomprehensible fuzz by the time I reached his door left ajar. I wanted to run away, or better yet, melt into the cement floor of the building until I reached the burning center of the earth. I wanted to be 17 all over again in the torrential rain on a mountain path in communist Romania with the twenty years old version of the man I was about to see.

He was sitting in a burgundy armchair and smiling. I sat down on the sofa facing him, and we both remained in silence, staring at one another for what seemed like interminable minutes. Then a separation between my body and my spirit happened, and I watched in silence as the woman dressed in the yellow, orange, and fuchsia party dress got up from the sofa, took off that dress and every single item of clothing she was wearing and lay on the floor in the middle of the living room like a corpse, for an indeterminate amount of time while he stared at her smoking his fragrant pipe.

Then she got up from the floor, put back all her clothes and sat in the arms of the man in the burgundy chair. She touched his face and kissed it with the tenderness of a lifetime of love. "You smell the same. You look the same."

She wasn't sure whether she had said those words out loud or just thought them, and it didn't matter. "You are just as beautiful. You smell like water, just as you did then," he said in the same low, slightly hoarse, and unmistakable voice. That was when it all broke down into a flood. She cried like she used to, she cried all the tears she hadn't cried for twenty-five years, she cried for the phone break-up in the frigid communist kitchen on a ruthlessly gray February communist day.

The paralysis that was slowly taking hold of his body, limb by precious limb, was irrelevant to her, as she found him to be the same as before, the feel of his skin, the feel of his scratchy beard on her face, the flutter of his eyelashes on her cheeks, the taste of his lips, his voice, the feel of his hands on her arms and the nape of her neck. The years had not changed any of that, on the contrary, they froze it at the exact moment of their last encounter, and it was now all thawing.

After a while, which to her could have well been a full month or two minutes, he gently pushed her away. He was being faithful to his wife. His wife loved him, he said. She was taking care of him. She was the mother of his child. The woman sitting in his lap didn't care a bit for any part of that story about his wife. Her skin was glued to his, and it stung like hell to move away, so she lay down again on the imitation Persian rug, this time dressed in her orange, yellow, and fuchsia silk dress, watching him smoke his pipe, much better smelling than the unfiltered cigarettes he used to smoke in their youth.

There were sour cherries hanging in heavy clusters in the tree next to the balcony of his apartment, kitschy still lives and paintings of mountain landscapes with orange sunsets on the walls, and the movie of her life was unfolding in rapid images before her eyes in between those still and moving images. She had two children, two ex-husbands, a majestic house with two acres of land in a small town in Virginia at the other corner of the blessed world, and for the length of the time she lay there in the smell of his pipe and the sound of his voice recounting to her the years after their breakup and her definitive departure, she saw herself as a foreigner to her own story, suspended and dangling above past, present, and immense expansions of continents.

He had taken a job deep in the Romanian countryside, teaching math to school children. He had spent many nights watching the wicked country moon, thinking of her and pining for their love, reliving every moment of it in his mind on frigid snowy nights in the communist countryside or on fragrant summer nights in that same countryside. He had been followed and interrogated by various secret police agents who wanted to know if he had helped her escape, if he was planning to leave the country himself.

He would have never left, of course, as he had never left the borders of his country even after the revolution. He blew off the secret police agents, moved back to the city, met his wife at some party where he had gotten drunk one night, had a son, got a PhD in mathematics, read all the Russian literature.

The woman lying on the floor in her multicolored party dress already knew some of that story from the long surprise email letter she had received from him and read sitting and crying in her corner office at the university where she worked in the Virginia small town, the previous year. But it still sounded new because she was hearing it now in his own voice.

She calculated the years and tried to remember what she was doing during those same years of his story: she was running the streets of Chicago in deadly winter cold or sweltering summer heat, surviving, having love affairs, almost getting married to an American poet in her first torrid summer in Chicago, teaching English to Cambodian refugees, getting her doctorate, getting married for real in a pink dress in a theater hall at her university and partying afterwards in a Cuban restaurant that belonged to Zoila's brother in the Hispanic neighborhood of Chicago where Mia and her mother's best friend from Colorado physically fought and slapped each other over the fact that Mia wanted to drive home in a state of complete inebriation.

Then the first child, the first divorce, the second child conceived with the only other man whom she loved with an equal, but different kind of love, and who had been married before and had several other children from his cornucopia of previous marriages.

Everything about her life was a bloody strident mess of overlapping infidelities which now, as she was watching the dark red sour cherries sway on their branches outside his balcony, seemed so far away and so immaterial that she almost couldn't believe they were part of her life. He had a big shaggy dog that came next to her and started licking her face.

She remembered her dog Moe that had bit an old lady on their street in the Virginia town and that had to be taken away like a huge failure by the kennel lady after being fed a Tylenol PM pill hidden in a spoonful of cottage cheese. Lying on the fake Persian rug in his apartment staring at the clusters of sour cherries outside and listening to the slightly syncopated soft melody of his voice telling the story of his life since their separation, she understood for the first time that he had been right to break up with her and leave her on the gray February day in Communist Bucharest.

He must have known it would have been impossible for them to be together. Love would have turned to drudgery and bickering, and she would have left anyways. He knew it himself. He knew her better than she knew herself then. By breaking up, they never fell out of love with each other. Some love stories need to be broken in order to keep their light and fullness. They laughingly made a vow that they were going to make love one more time right before they were going to die.

"Let me know when you feel the end coming, and I'll run to you," she said laughingly. She kissed him goodbye and ran down the cement flight of stairs in this old communist apartment building. She was glad she wasn't living there.

Between the very beginning of the millennium and that first mythic encounter in the mid two thousand, while I was laboring over my first novel, there were love affairs that took me from southern France to Paris to Normandy, to San Diego, London, Corsica, randomly across expanses of oceans and countries, a desperate merry-go-round in search of a place to rest. I stole bits and pieces of landscape and passion in between courses I taught, conferences I attended, and the children I raised.

It was as much about love as it was about traveling and being free. In fact, it was more about traveling and freedom than about love. The small town suffocated me and exacerbated my foreignness like a huge scar that everybody stared at while still smiling politely. Time was a compact mass in which days and years coagulated and suddenly one son was as tall as me, while the other a head taller and in college, a neighbor's hair had turned completely white, a child that I knew as a toddler was now a teenager, and someone I would run into at the local pool was no longer alive.

The monotony and predictability of life in a small town made one year indistinguishable from another, marked only by extraordinary events such as the drowning of a teenage boy or the burning of a church. For a refugee like the restless kind I have always been, that was a different kind of prison.

Everywhere I turned someone knew me, someone else knew bits of my life story, yet another person knew bigger parts of my life story. I felt watched and judged from every angle you looked at me. Was that why I had uprooted my parents and myself and broken my family in two? I often wondered. In order to be watched and judged by the nice smiling people of an old southern provincial town, who were often also racist and sexist despite their Christian faith and all?

In Paris, I felt more at home than on my own street, glamorous and erotic. I moved languorously amid crowds of busy Parisians. The French words in my mouth had just the right size and taste as I sat in a sultry café in Montmartre with a Tunisian lover, I had met at a conference on the French writer I wrote about in my doctoral dissertation.

My research was multicultural in more ways than one. Mixing in with the thousands of foreigners of all colors, with the thousands of happy or unhappy lovers pouring into the Parisian streets, in and out of the metros, holding hands with another French-speaking foreigner from a country on a 'watchlist' gave me more of a sense of belonging than the small town of my residence.

One hot summer, I pushed all the limits, to see how far I could go in my curiosity for multicultural loves and landscapes. It was the summer after the Iraq war had started, the world was boiling, and there was news that Americans in Europe weren't particularly liked. That was a good summer to be Romanian in Europe. I gloated as I prepared for my two months in southern France with a group of students, my children, and my mother. I had a feeling sunny Provence would welcome me and give me its all.

The Delights of Provence

The day in June when my younger son then ten years of age and I were preparing to leave Dulles airport on our Paris flight was raining furiously like a doomsday with blasting thunder after blasting thunder and huge bubbling puddles forming by the minute in the streets. The local Kmart was closing for good, and my son and I were both nostalgic as we ran to it for last minute errands.

The little merry-go-round in front of our Kmart with the doctor Zhivago melody playing and turning for two quarters brought back memories of many lazy summers, with he and his brother going for the fifth and sixth time on the *"Somewhere My Love"* song round and round, everything a delicious incongruity—a song from a mega Hollywood success about a Russian tragic love at the time of the Bolshevik Revolution, as local people with deep American southern drawl walked by with twelve packs of Pepsi and Root Beer on sale. We put the two quarters in the slot one more time, and though too big for it now, my son relished in one last ride as I did in the sentimental melody.

When we arrived dizzy with exhaustion after the almost twenty hours of traveling, Avignon was bursting with light and sound and felt familiar as I remembered it from the summer several years earlier when I had come in full family formation, with both sons and second husband, on my big return to Romania. There were now cracks in that marriage too, something wasn't sticking.

I didn't seem to hold the magic glue for marital happiness and solidity and though it would have been easy to blame it all on the chaotic family habits of my husband with his several past wives and many children, on the long distance relationship, the little to nonexistent help I received in my parental life and struggles, doing it all by myself, work, children, household, one truth that was shining more brightly than ever was how little I actually enjoyed marriage and how exhilarating I found the non-marital freedom and single motherhood with all its hardships. I hungrily descended into the Provence brilliance and colors of the city of the Popes our first morning. I felt unattached and wild. Free to the point of rawness.

I was going to spend a full summer teaching theater and producing a show for the Avignon theater festival with students from across the world, while gorging on the colors, tastes and delicious cacophonies that filled every corner and moment of that city. I knew I was not going to stay married forever; I knew I was going to pay for it too and I didn't care.

The first morning in the lavender and marzipan smells and tastes of Provence, I had a carnal realization of my freedom, of the thrills and pains that came with it and was ready for it all. I had earned it in the dreary boredom of the small southern town where I had been working for a decade under the petty scrutiny of mediocre colleagues. I had earned it in the provincial local courts of law of my divorce proceedings, on the playing fields of my sons' sports games under the hostile looks of local soccer moms and lacrosse moms and cookie baking Christian moms.

Mostly, I had earned that delicious tasting freedom in my long late hours of correcting French exams and in the early morning hours of writing scholarly articles and books, before and after taking the children to and from school, cooking my concocted stews and casseroles, and doing everything else that needed to be done in my old colonial house. I had earned my southern France summer glory with my American toils.

A writer I admired had once said, "...exile is the dream of a glorious return." Maybe that was one of my glorious returns, roundabout, oblique and perversely sinuous, not on native soil, but on make believe French 'native' soil, in a delicious pretense of native culture where nobody asked me about my accent. On the contrary, they asked me what part of France I came from. I had my vindication, and it tasted like marzipan and lavender in the fierce Provence light occasionally sliced by chilly slivers of Mistral gusts.

My son found myriads of distractions and entertainments in the melodious lull of Provence. He used all his French words and sentences with street vendors and neighbors in our apartment building, while I dove furiously in all the crooks and crannies of French language, pastries, and street spectacles. For my birthday, I put on my best party poufy bright burgundy taffeta dress.

My North African friend flew in from across the Mediterranean and three other scholar friends came by train from Paris to celebrate. Everything glowed and was golden, even sin, especially sin, because in the sunny freedom of the Provence air, what was considered sin in my puritanical America, was simply considered life. Luscious, no nonsense lived to its rawest core, life.

From then on, everything becomes a fast-winding carousel in the sounds of French music, in the inescapable southern sun, in the blazing blues, violets and oranges of houses, sea, sky, lavender fields like one thick three-dimensional whirl of a Van Gogh painting. Everything is here in a multicolored present throbbing with life and unleashed desires. We party late for my birthday going from bar to bar in a rowdy group, my 'four musketeers' as they call themselves and my son, four men, one African, one Jewish, two French and a Romanian American woman.

They had all gifted me a huge bottle of Chanel 5 perfume. I carry my perfume bottle like a trophy, and I become more perfumed as we all become more inebriated. Everywhere we stop there is a Romanian accordionist or violinist playing table to table for money and everybody finds it hugely amusing that I immediately recognize them, start speaking Romanian and ask them to play such and such a song from back home.

It's the Romanian me that they are all fascinated with, my French musketeers, not the American, not the wannabe French, no matter how perfect my French is. What I try to shed is what sticks the most and what gives the most spice. Fast paced spicy accordion music from a corner of the Balkans, played by a street Romanian musician gets everybody riled up in the Provence night. I watch my delicately angelic son watch me and all my dealings with French, African, Romanian Gypsy men, as I laugh and joke in three languages and drink more cassis, with curiosity and glee, a tiny trace of melancholy because he is also thinking of his father back in Chicago.

He forgives his mother everything and understands everything about her. They are in a deep complicity for life, with no conditions and no boundaries, and share an equal hedonistic voraciousness for life, fresh fruit, and adventure.

Working, living, loving in southern France agrees with me more than any place had ever agreed with me in the past. I am growing into my own forbidden fruit, sassy, exoticized, hard to get and light for the picking all at once. Fleeting thoughts that I was born in the wrong country cross my mind throughout the day when I am having my fluffy croissant and *café au lait* at a corner bakery in the morning before going to my classes.

At times, I want to steal everything French and be French, renege my Romanian origins, and renounce my American citizenship, speak with a Provençal accent, and adopt all the French mannerisms, like go "bah, bof…je n'sais pas, c'est pas évident", with a blasé hand gesture and swift shake of my head. But something always gives me away, and I realize deep down, in my gut, that I don't want to be French and that it's more interesting to be Romanian American speaking French with a perfect French accent.

I can be more things than any of the local born French people around me, solid and confident in their Provence roots and origins. I can be anything I damn want to be, the refugee con artist that I am. It was decided long ago on a September morning when me and my suitcase got on a one-way flight to Rome. I can be a theater director, a French teacher, a Romanian mother, an American tourist, an international writer, a world traveler, the lover of a Tunisian scholar, or of a French teacher and motorcycle rider.

Every once in a while, during the days of his visit to Avignon, after my rowdy fragrant and entertaining birthday party, my North African lover mentions the war in Iraq, America being at war again, as if I was America waging the war with Iraq. I vehemently react with French swear words. I'm always proud that I can fight and swear in four languages. He laughs and kisses my French swearing lips, as the Romanian accordionist smirks knowingly.

He passes by, looking for tourists that would drop euros in his tin box, but we are buddies by now and he doesn't beg from me anymore. He plays for me for free. We are sitting in a café next to the *Palais des papes*, the palace of the popes, those wicked popes burning in Dante's inferno, with more sins on one of their catholic fingers than I could gather in ten lifetimes. They are watching over me and my friends from the centuries-old Gothic magnificence of their past abode.

It is the hottest summer in decades, scorching across French cities, mountains, and lavender fields, with hundreds of people dying from the heat. The streets of Avignon are boiling hot and swarming with the rainbow mirages of performers, players of medieval farces or vaudeville sketches. The days are as hallucinatory as the nights. I move through the crowds with self-assurance and purpose in my gauzy pastel summer dresses gotten from African street vendors.

Once my mother and older son join us, it feels like we've lived here in the city of the Popes for centuries. During the day, I teach my classes and direct my show in a seven-century old building, a former Franciscan monastery turned school for American students, in boiling hot rooms with no air conditioning. At night I juggle love and friendship and marriage because my soon to be ex-husband decides to also visit us in the torrid Provence of this year at the beginning of the Iraq war when I seem to be at the height of my multicultural, artistic, and erotic thriving self and when the world is boiling with new conflicts and dangers.

I refuse to be American this summer though. I teach my American students in the sweltering classroom like I was from here, from the general area of European earth, because I am. I've never felt a stronger tie to this earth of the old world than I do this summer of my many loves.

The Maghrébin lover is jealous and lies to me about his wife or some lover back home, and the more he lies, the more jealous he gets of my husband and my past lovers. The absurdity of it makes me laugh to tears, but he kisses my tears and tickles my face with his thick mustache. I don't care about his primitive jealousy because he feels and looks magnificent, and I am still the one in charge in the tiny room of a coquettish hotel in a five-hundred-year-old building.

Everything here is centuries old, thick white stone that keeps cool, the small windows filled with blood red geraniums, white petunias, bright pink azaleas. Love is easy, smooth, and effortless like you are meant to dive in all its glory and rawness, just like in the smooth wickedly blue Mediterranean where we go for the weekend.

I am in my early forties, and I live to the fullest the brilliance of this transitory Provence moment, guilt free, conscious it will be over soon and that it all hangs in the thread of my small southern provincial American town status and hard-won university job. I am aware that it was only the life I built there that is allowing me the torrid glory of this summer. I drown the melancholy of that knowledge in more love and jealous lovers' quarrels like I care.

The French scholar and teacher friend courts me by riding his motorcycle from Paris all the way to southern France at one hundred kilometers an hour through the hot winds of the French highways only to visit with me for one weekend. How can I resist that? His blue eyes shine with desire as sweat is pouring down his face from the long bike trip.

We meet in Nice one weekend, and it smells of jasmine everywhere. The turquoise blue of the Mediterranean makes one insane with joy and all the desires of the world. The concierge of the little hotel smiles as she hands my friend the key to an attic room the size of a closet. He is carrying his motorcycle helmet and gear in one hand. A line from a French poet floats through the tiny room that is only bed and sky. The blue of Provence pours into it through the tiny roof window in irrepressible waves. The love is liquid blue. I make love like I was made for it, deliberately and with abandon at once. I am perfecting it like an art in fragrant jasmine breezes.

Somewhere along the way in this Provençal summer bursting with azaleas, jasmine, the demented blues of sky and water, theater and irresistible courtships my body grows into something new and mystical, my impertinent senses and greed for life finally find their voice and take over. I let it happen because I know it's short-lived and I know women and mothers aren't supposed to experience this totality of carnal and romantic thrill. They make for unlikable neighbors and unacceptable novel characters.

I know by the end of the summer, I will be in a small southern American town sitting in a stupid faculty meeting where balding white men sing their own praises or arguing with one of my sons' schoolteachers over an unfair grade. But I have now, and I am riding this magnificent wave as I am riding in the back of a motorcycle with my blue-eyed friend along the French riviera.

At the height of the heat waves when French people are dying all across the country from the dangerous temperatures and the lack of adequate cooling, images and scenes from this summer multiply at a faster pace and appear in delirious simultaneity, overlapping chaotically like the layers of a fantastical wedding cake, like overcrowded scrambled letters on a page in an old book of fairy tales. The July fourteenth celebration with my mother and children on the half bridge in Avignon about which I used to sing the famous children's song *"sur le pont d'Avignon, on y danse tout en rond",* under the tricolor fireworks, is one prominent page of this book of fairy tales, though overcrowded to excess.

We celebrate like we are French, like Romanian Americans wanting to be French, like it's our Marseillaise too, and our hearts swell in French patriotic pride until we are squished in the passage through a tunnel that goes from the Rhone river to the city inside the old walls. I start screaming in Romanian after my children to make sure they are next to me and are not getting lost and are not being crushed in the mindless crowd as crowds always are, whether French,

American, Chinese or from anywhere on the globe. Romanian remains my language of visceral maternal worries and cries.

An excursion to a place called Les Saintes Maries de la Mer shines with both brilliance and haziness, a slightly faded page in the magical book of multi-ethnic fairy tales. There are many charming side streets with colorful restaurants and always the view of the sea flowing in every which way you turn.

My North African friend, who is back in the picture, is sweet to my children and mother. It's a family trip of sorts, as if this were some new family of mine that moves smoothly through the maze of pastels of this Mediterranean town with its multilingual French Romanian English with touches of Arabic conversations and almond, sesame, and honey-soaked pastries.

Apparently, there are many towns called after Virgin Mary, but this one is a pearl of its kind. I remember my middle name is Mary, and I once fell in love with a Romanian boy on my very name day of the Saint Mary of the Ascension. I am attached to all the small and large towns we visit and imagine myself living in them. I have developed a chameleonic ability to feel at home in each little southern French town we cross.

I don't want to be a tourist. I pretend to be a local taking my espresso or café au lait every morning right here at this corner café in a bright yellow stone house with a patch of brilliant Mediterranean at the end of it, gossiping about the local news and the Tour de France.

The next page in this expedition is a cruise into the Rhone region of the wetlands through a hazy sun across silvery and milky delta waters where the freshwater and the salty waves merge, where the wild white horses of Camargue roam freely, flying in the distance like in a deep sweltering dream. We ask the guide to take a picture of all of us, mother, children, Tunisian lover as the boat slices through the swirling waters and am thinking that it's a useless picture.

Who and where can I show this picture to? I am still a married woman, soon to be divorced again, and in the small southern town where I actually live a planet away from this here boat ride in the land of the wild horses in the Mediterranean wetlands, my sons' friends' mothers look at me suspiciously from their eight-seater vans. I am the dangerous tricky foreigner full-time working single mother, thank god for the popularity of my children, or these good mothers might just run me over with their spacious minivans.

As the hallucinatory images of the mythic stocky wild horses pass by our speeding boat, I remember I too am from a country with a delta, the Danube Delta where the river flows into the capricious darker waters of the Black Sea. I remember that my parents and I spent a summer vacation there in a different century, staying with local fisherman peasants and eating sturgeon soup for breakfast despite the communist shortages.

I bathed naked on the very cusp between sea and river, at the foamy line where the Black Sea waves crush and merge with the flow of the Danube in some sort of cosmic copulation, as huge white pelicans and cormorants almost the size of these Camargue horses here were profiled against a magenta Romanian sunset. The picture of us on the boat is hazy and awkward, like a runaway make-believe family of sorts, with the Tunisian man slightly lopsided in between me and my mother appearing like an incongruous addition to the group because of a huge briefcase bag of sorts he is carrying on his shoulder, and the white suit he is wearing, like he is going to an academic meeting and not on a cruise in the Rhône Delta.

He seems to be the one on the run next to us all in summer sleeveless attires, gauzy skirts and shorts, and newly purchased French T-shirts. Somewhere in the space of that afternoon we also go to a nearby beach, with kilometers of humid shiny sands, these are French sands in the Mediterranean near the wetlands of the Rhône delta and not in the Black Sea and the Danube Delta.

This picture feels remote and faraway. I seem to be watching it from a ship in the distance, at the horizon line and not from the shore, a horizon line separating east and west, the prosperous occidental world across from the messy Balkan world. It separates my past from my many layered present that stretches out across the Atlantic and reaches all the way in the remote valleys of the Appalachians.

As I run into the waves of the Mediterranean with my children and I see the man in the white suit with a briefcase hanging on his shoulder standing on the beach and completely not belonging, even though he is more Mediterranean than I will ever be, I think, *why is it that I am always on my own with my children and my mother? And why are all these men-fathers always on their own while their children are somewhere else with a mother, while they write their books, go on delta cruises with their lovers and their lover's children, ride their motorcycles across the French highways to be with their lover and their lover's children?*

It's not a rhetorical question addressed to the universe and the entirety of society but to my own self as I delight in the coolness of the Mediterranean next to my golden sons swimming next to me, with the strokes I taught them, speaking in the languages I taught them. I can multitask at any time of my life, swim and care for my children, and ask my big existential questions in preparation for my big opus all at once.

In this blue Mediterranean moment, it's very clear to me for the umpteenth time that I have made my choices and I fiercely embrace them. Stroke, stroke, splash, a taste of the salty water, I feel at home in it. I love having my children next to me in the waves, on earth, in the streets of world cities, in our various homes. The men are secondary; they made their choices and I made mine. I have the work and the children, while they have the work and occasionally, they have me.

No wonder they are either jealous of the children or they pretend to be in love with them too. I am the one that has it all: children, work, love. They have bits and pieces and their great confidence in their utmost omnipotence. Let them think that and have less for me to worry about. The man standing on the beach in a white linen suit waving at me from afar looks funny, a stranger, an actor on a stage who has forgotten his role. *I'd rather be me than any of these men,* I think and plunge into the delicious Mediterranean waves.

Somewhere in the fast-moving kaleidoscope of this summer, my husband visits us as well. He brings his big American confidence and nonchalance into our Avignon apartment knocking down ornamental objects carefully placed on tables and walls as he clumsily moves around with his huge backpack, and as our hostess who happens to stop by at that same time of his arrival, stares at him with unflinching horror and disdain. It's best he stays at a hotel I say, more room, a better place to sleep. "There is a nice one right around the corner."

He does do just that and now the concierge at the corner hotel with geraniums and azaleas hanging from every window and balcony smiles at me knowingly, impertinently as he recognizes me from the last time, I accompanied my Maghrebin friend a few weeks earlier. I get a quick sharp feeling of nausea as I know what he is thinking. I know the box he put me in immediately from his lascivious smile. He even winks at me and I stare at him fiercely right in his shameless judgmental eyes.

I wonder how many women he has cheated with on his wife, and how much time he spends with his children every day. The shameless self-assuredness of men of all colors never ceases to puzzle me almost like a funny spectacle if it wasn't also exasperating. I give my husband a kiss goodbye in front of the damn concierge with his unctuous 'bonjour madame', 'bonsoir madame', and say, 'I'll see you later for dinner', and 'do you want to take an excursion to Arles tomorrow?' He is happy about the proposal and smiles for the first time since his arrival.

For an unfathomable reason, my husband became suspicious when he found out I was teaching a course on surrealist poetry and theater at the Avignon center. He loved realism, *Anna Karenina* and *The Brothers Karamazov*, the tormented Russian authors of suicidal heroines, of the heroines who die and kill themselves for the love of a man. It's what men love.

I loved the modernists and the surrealists, the anarchic and the rebellious, theater of cruelty and of derision, all in crushed strident colors, sexy, edgy, and messy. I was done with the Anna Kareninas and the Emma Bovarys of world literature and history once and for all.

"What's with this sudden love of surrealism?" He asked an hour into our encounter in the glowing light of the Avignon twilight. *That's why I don't want to stay married to anyone ever, see, this and a hundred other reasons*, I answer in my mind as we walk down the wide boulevard under the lush canopy of century old sycamore trees. I answer I've always loved surrealism and finally was able to teach and direct its theater that summer, he just never noticed.

I decide right then and there on that majestic promenade in the city of the Popes that I've had it with male whims, jealousies, and moroseness. I decide I will only take what I like and what agrees with me from the male substance of the world, from the comportment of these strange creatures that run the world and of which I have mothered two beautiful samples. *They will be different, a new generation, less full of themselves. They've seen their mother struggle between work and the meticulous care of them*, I tell myself looking at my ten years old son who follows our intellectual argument with interest and some level of irritation.

At least this argument is not about why his father forgot to pick him or his brother up from school or from the after-school piano lesson on one of his monthly trips to Virginia, but about surrealism versus realism. But it really is about his father's hold to the old-world order, the realist order depicting the women subjugated by the love of one unreachable man, the women whose entire lives rotate only around the men in their lives.

And it's about the freedom of a potentially new world of stridency and colorful messiness, of women making their own choices and not dying for the love of one unattainable man, and not living in endless frustration with the tired love of one clingy husband either, but living on their own terms, without even needing so much the enduring love of any man because they are content with their own lives, despite the difficulties of single motherhood and possibly precisely because of those assumed difficulties.

I see my son is getting bored by our argument, he is hungry and wants us to go into one of the many brasseries lined up along the famous avenue with its famous vault of sycamores. I say, "No, let's go to the one near the Palace; that one is better." And my son knows exactly which one I'm talking about because we celebrated my birthday there only a few weeks earlier, surrounded by the four adoring musketeers, French, Tunisian, Jewish French, scholars and academics who had traveled from Paris and from North Africa, on trains, planes, and motorcycles just to be with me on my forty-second birthday and celebrate my summer job in Avignon.

I had opened the gift package with the biggest bottle of Chanel 5 perfume and got tipsy on French wine and cassis and made everyone laugh with my Romanian humor and my American nonchalance and asked the Romanian accordionist player to play a sentimental song from the old Balkan world we both came from.

My husband agrees to go to the restaurant in front of the Palace of the Popes. There, we order a fish soup, which reminds us of the seafood velouté he and I had some five years earlier on our first French trip together, the dinner by the Loire river overlooking the magnificent Chambord castle, while this beautiful son we made in the depth of despair of our messy lives was staying with my parents in my first little house in the Virginia town where I live. The layered cake of my past and of my many present lives keeps unfolding at every moment, slice by colorful juicy slice, in the dry golden heat of this Avignon twilight.

Our trip to Arles is captured in Van Gogh yellows and blues in a photograph taken at a restaurant called precisely restaurant Van Gogh because it is next to the house the painter had once lived in and will end up on the wall in my husband's Chicago apartment. It will be there until his death, and I will stare at it as I will be holding his hand and listen to his final love declaration uttered with his last remaining breaths.

My son and I are next to each other at a restaurant table against a petulant yellow and turquoise background, and we are looking straight at the camera with wide equally blue eyes, our equally bright blonde hair shining out of the picture. Mother and son are captured in total synchronicity of thought, feeling, and color by the loving gaze of the man across the table.

My surrealist summer is still to bloom into more spectacular episodes dripping with clashing colors, irresistible tastes, and some dark spots too. As I am working on my theatrical production of surrealist and absurdist scenes with American students from all over the United States hungry for European experiences and thirsty for underage drinking, I befriend the Roma family of musicians and ask them to offer the musical segments and soundtrack for my show.

They are super happy about the offer, and they ask for a super high price for the gig. I withdraw the invitation because I don't know where to get the two thousand euros for a two-hour musical track for the show to be presented in the sweltering hall of the seven-century old building monastery turned language school, but they negotiate it down to a thousand and then to eight hundred and that's more feasible.

But the school director is unwilling to offer any support for the project, even though they are getting hundreds of thousands of euros from the students' tuition, and when she hears about who I am trying to hire, a Roma family of musicians, she mumbles puzzled excuses in her Parisian French transplanted to southern France and offers a categorical refusal. The French only like Gypsy music and art in East European movies and in artistic representations that hang in the Orsay museum of art, and not when they have to engage with the flesh and blood creators and producers of such music and art.

Never mind, I think, I'm resourceful enough. I end up using recordings of Cirque du Soleil music, and I try to avoid the Roma family as I go to work now. The Italian and Spanish songs of the Cirque du Soleil are sultry and poetic enough, heart-wrenching enough, torrid enough for this torrid summer. Their singers borrow Gypsy tonalities and make a lot more money than the actual Gypsies playing their own music in European streets.

In the oppressive heat of my working place, my psyche gets snagged onto the inequities suffered by the Gypsies worldwide and all the cultural appropriations inspired by their life and art. Something in me is wild and unleashed this summer.

I start correcting colleagues and students to use Roma instead of Gypsy and my blood starts boiling at the thought of the director's refusal to hire the street musicians for the show. My body and brain are delirious with the southern heat, as I talk to my North African friend on my French cell phone and listen to his long list of lies about why he must cancel his next trip to see me.

That's all right, I think, *there is always the blue-eyed Frenchman riding his motorcycle to see me*, and I hang up. Social inequities, personal betrayals, cultural appropriations, it all gets mixed up in the heat and incongruities of this summer and they swell inside my brain like mini volcanoes ready to erupt at any moment.

The day of my show premiere, I stop in the street on the way to work overwhelmed by the heat to the point of almost fainting. I stand dazed in front of the McDonald's restaurant, the only one place with air conditioning on the street, my heart pounding and my head burning and a dark feeling in my brain like it's all going to come to a halting stop, and all of me will melt or burn to death in the lava like air of this summer. Something is snapping inside my chest after which the street starts spinning around.

I resist going into McDonald's. My sons look at me worried and say something like *you need to sit down and drink some water, Mama*, but I'm not sure. All I care about is that my show opens tonight, and I have to be there in a couple of hours to get the students and the set ready, and that I don't want to go into the damn McDonald's. But my children push me inside where it's cool and it smells of hamburgers and something else that makes me queasy.

I get water and a salad that tastes rancid and sour, and a profound sense of devastation washes over me that in a couple of weeks I have to be back in the country that produced this lousy restaurant and that makes this rancid tasting food and exports it all over the world. I cool off a bit and leave the salad unfinished and try to put off the thought of my return which feels like a stinging separation from the sweetness of the blues and yellows and the wondrous cacophonies of this region on the planet.

When I go back to work that evening before the show wearing a long orange golden shimmy taffeta dress that matches the Provence colors, I find all the students practicing their lines in the extravagant surrealist costumes I chose for them, colorful feathers and sequins and flowing silks. The Cirque du Soleil singer fills the room with her heartbreak tango paced song about what else but heartbreak and the raw beauty of it regardless of the pain.

The big ventilators moving the hot air around swell my dress and my hair as if I had been riding a motorcycle. The heat has become irrelevant. I have overcome it somehow and am floating above it or with it. I'm becoming a bird of the Rhône Delta, or is it of the Danube Delta? I am large-winged and light.

The show is a smashing success in strident colors of incongruous combinations, funny and profoundly sad like only French poetry can be both simultaneously, though the center piece of the show is a play by a Romanian French absurdist playwright. My father once said the French stole from everybody and then called it their own. It's still the Balkans that drip their smoldering stridency, irreverence, and bitter sweetness into this French show with American students directed by a Romanian American French professor.

My motorcyclist blue-eyed friend is here accompanied by local friends, a French family with many children who lives in a gorgeous stone house in this city, all acquired from the commerce of *herbes de Provence*. You can get rich on just about anything in this Western world, even on tiny herbs and spices. My thoughts are jagged lines in all directions tonight.

My other 'musketeer' friends have come to see the show from Paris, minus the Maghrebin lover who had to cancel his visit at the last minute on account of a so-called 'emergency', which I know is a lie. His absence is a sting in my already stinging heart, and I realize a part of me is crying and is in love with his smoothness, his smoldering sexiness and delightful awkwardness, that my perceived Balkan 'exoticism' matches his perceived North African 'exoticism' and cancels out all damn exoticism. I miss the warmth and thrilling comfort of that match, but the show must go on as they say, and it's pointless to wait for him to give the starting signal. Lights off, lights on, go!

During the show, my blue-eyed friend squeezes my hand, and I know he is happy that his rival is not here, that he is thinking of the weekend in Nice we spent a few weeks ago in the utterly delicious blueness of the Mediterranean and the jasmine smells. *You can totally be in love with two people at the same time*, I think as I squeeze his hand right back, *even three*, I think as the actors on stage are acting out characters who become cats and chickens and are mewling in French in the Romanian playwright's absurdist play. *Yes, even three at the same time.*

I think of the trip to Arles of some weeks ago or maybe last week, with my septuagenarian husband photographing me and my son in the Provence twilight against Van Gogh yellows and blues. Time is melting in twisted unctuous red and vermilion rivers like in Dali's famous painting. *If only I could mix the intellectual soulfulness of my husband with the smoldering playful sweetness of my mustachioed North African lover and with the sexy adventure-seeking spirit of my blue-eyed French lover, then I would have one perfect mate,* I think as my student-actors are making animal sounds, uttering funny combinations of French sounds, and dancing the tango on stage, while the audience is laughing and clapping.

If I could only mix the open wide expanse of space and the gutsy freedom of America, with the sophisticated sweetness and artfulness of France, and with the raw sentimentality and spirit of derision of my Romanian roots, then I would have the perfect country, I am thinking in a messy combination of the three languages I am speaking to myself.

In the linguistic and cultural chaos of my brain that is melting like Dali's watches to the sounds of Eugene Ionesco's lines, I realize that this moment right here and this summer right here is a record moment and a record summer when I managed to create just that, the perfect mate and the perfect country, and that my heart will soon give, something will soon give from all this demented plenitude. But who the hell cares? The public is calling me to the stage for the final bow, success! From somewhere outside, through a side window comes the playful wailing of an accordion song, old and dusty, from far away, from long ago. My Roma friends are still contributing in a tiny measure to my show, from the outside, from the margins.

The day after the end of the summer semester at the American school housed in the former monastery, I embark with my children and mother on a ferry to Corsica, where my blue-eyed French friend is spending his vacation, and where he has invited us to spend the tail end of our trip with him. A deep tiredness washes over me as the ferry slashes through the intense blue of the Mediterranean, paradoxically accompanied by a profound clarity, like I am seeing all the way to the very essence of things.

I remember the theater director of the Attic theater in Bucharest where I spent all my waking hours when I was not in school, pushing us across the line of extreme tiredness in endless rehearsals, saying that was "when you get to the most authentic part of yourself, the raw core that is your truest self." We lived in grayness and fear, indeed we needed to break through all the layers of gray to get to the raw blues, to touch the unbreakable incandescent nucleus in us, hold it and embrace it before we moved back into the farcical conundrums of our everyday.

In the orgy of liquid and horizon blues all around us, lines from French poetry invade my overextended brain, *il faut tenter de vivre*, "we must attempt to live," *la chair est triste hélas, et j'ai lu tous les livres*, "the flesh is sad, alas and I read all the books." I hold the nucleus that is the rawest roundest shiniest bit of my own self, with no country and no allegiances except to the two children that I am pulling to my chest in a frenzy of maternal passion, as we stand on the side of the fast-moving ship, the wind whipping our sun-burnt faces.

One is tiny and shiny blonde, the other is strong and brooding blonde, while the blueness of our eyes seems to link us to the blueness around us. My mother is sitting on a bench watching the waters in a reverie, most likely thinking up a new poem. Mothers, sons, water, poetry, it's all in the mothering, a mystical secret of the flesh and of the mind and of nature that we hold. The goddesses, the sacred seas, my favorite Greek goddess Thetis of the silver feet. She often appeared in the Greek myths I read to my children in their earliest years at bedtime when I was also raw with tiredness. I think I always made the most of my tiredness, and thus my theater lessons served me well.

I get it, I finally get it on this fast-moving ship, and I should try to remember it when I am back, when I am back…Not yet though, because there is still time, and my French beau is waiting for us in a rented car and takes us to our lodging on the winding Corsican roads driving at one hundred fifty kilometers an hour while my head is bobbing back and forth in the front seat as I go in and out of sleep and don't care about the speed, about the winding roads.

Something in me snapped and opened in an infinity of blue, a reckless delirium in blues and in French melodies. I hear my children giggle at the looseness and bobbing of my dozing head, while dusk is falling over the Corsican winding roads between rock, forest and sea, the basics. I keep getting to the basics, so what more do I need? "Look at Mom, her head…"; "we are going to go scuba diving"; "no, snorkeling"; "maybe both"; "yea, both, pretty cool."

It's already dark on the road. "Are we there yet?" Children always want to know if we are there already, and then what! I hear echoes of other drives, on other roads, with another man, in another country, *the country doesn't matter*, somebody says in my dream, *the country doesn't matter*. We are there, *on est la*. It sounds better in French; everything sounds better in French. It's dark on the Corsican island where the great Napoleon was born and grew up in a family of ten children raised by a widowed mother. Always the single and the widowed mothers!

The family of Corsican peasants or fishermen where we are being lodged feed us abundant pasta and seafood freshly fished out of the Mediterranean Sea. The darkness and the moon shining through that darkness are like no other darkness and no other moon, sharp and thick. The sea is breathing gently, a constant whisper with an occasional quickening of her nightly moans like a throbbing lover, like a lover.

While my mother and children are sleeping in the spacious room fragrant with both pine and sea scents, I tiptoe on the gravel outside to my lover's room at the other end of the house. A wild youthfulness overcomes me. I used to tiptoe to my lover's house in the night long ago in a mountain city that was not in France and was not in Corsica, but in a small, ravaged country where I was born.

This French lover here is waiting for me like a timid teenager. He has quick caresses and restless kisses for me in this Corsican night lit only by a shameless full moon, in the quickening sighs of the sea, in its languid whispers.

The morning unveils a dazzling blue of the sea bursting from between wooded rocks and curvy beaches. We swim for hours in a cove that my friend knows. He apparently knows the island like the back of his French palms, as he has been coming here for twenty years. Time becomes irrelevant though. I could be thinking of what I was doing twenty years ago but I try not to. And then as we move dreamily through the clear turquoise waters hugged by the wooded rocks, children and mother and French lover like another family formation I have managed to create this summer of the gods and goddesses of the sea, the memory grabs me like a rabid animal, biting voraciously into my Corsican bliss. Because exactly twenty years ago, I was getting ready for my big escape.

It was the hot dusty Bucharest summer of 1983 when I was waiting feverishly for my passport, when I unexpectedly got my passport, I hastily got on a one-way flight to Rome Fiumicino airport, and I irreversibly tore my own heart out of my own chest saying goodbye parents, goodbye extended family, aunts, cousins, twice removed aunts and cousins, goodbye boyfriend, and goodbye all my life of loves and hates and studies and books and theater and vacations in the Carpathians and vacations on the Black Sea beaches, and goodbye me and my life.

All that became an irretrievable past the second I got on that plane with my pathetic suitcase and all the Romanian junk in it as my only possession. I hear children's laughter, and I realize it's my own two children because now I am a mother of two sons from two different husbands. Everything I do and have comes in pairs: two countries, two children, two marriages, two lovers on top of the two marriages.

I am always split in two like in a Frida Kahlo painting. Wild blues and greens all around and a big red throbbing heart divided in two parts right in the middle of its striated flesh. Because it has to all be beautiful and colorful, no matter the sting in the heart; it has to be artful; it's the promise I had made to myself then, and one of the few promises I have kept. And the Corsican gods only know it is artful and beautiful alright.

The Corsican days are equal to each other. There are never clouds, and the same dizzying sun rises over the same glistening turquoise waters over the same dark green wood spread over the same jagged rocks rising out of the waters. The city and the port are lulled in the same soft feathery breezes and light gusts, and the hilly narrow streets with white stone houses covered in brilliant ivy and flowers in all the shades of red, magenta red, scarlet red, ruby red, peachy red, are fixed in time like a postcard.

On one such day, my mother and the children go on a scuba diving trip on a Corsican boat that my friend arranges for them with a scuba instructor he knows. He and I roam the streets in the hot glaze of the Corsican sun, up and down labyrinthine streets and flights of stairs. We kiss against a white wall standing on the steps between such streets.

It's a hallucination in sparkling whites, magenta reds all trimmed with the mad, mad blue of the Mediterranean stretching down at the bottom of the steps. We are inside the moving postcard in this slowly moving moment in time, a slow, slow movie in shimmering reds and shiny whites, my back against the cool stone, his hands gliding on my thighs and breasts, the azure of the wide sky pouring on us, the quiet of the street enclosing us in a cocoon of sensuousness. I've never done this before.

There are so many things I haven't done before and am doing them all this summer as if making up for three lifetimes, for my torn apart youth in another universe, for my thirties with my mind and body exhausted to a raw pulp, for the years to come awaiting for me quietly in the nooks of an old house in a small town in the New World. Shards of thoughts and unprecedented sensations mingle in my body and mind simultaneously.

I understand the ancient sun worshipers, the body has a heart and the mind is carnal, there is no difference between the two. I'm experiencing this totality of being in this very Corsican moment against a cool ancient stone wall against which hundreds of other lovers might have shamelessly done exactly what I'm doing now.

We meet my mother and children later in the port. The scuba diving experience was thrilling and scary. Apparently, the instructor was too rushed with too many scuba diving thirsty tourists, and my younger son had a hard time with his oxygen mask which was too big for his small body. "It was scary," he says.

I fall back inside the contingency of time, terrified of what might have happened while I was making out on the steps of an old street. *There were so many-colored fish, Mama*, my kids say excitedly, and I want to go after the scuba diving instructor to grab him by his scuba suit and ask him why he allowed himself even a moment of inattention. *It's all right, Mama, nothing happened, it was fun, nothing could have happened, we are fine.*

They know how crazy I get about all the dangers that lurk around them at every step of the way, like the time I spanked my younger son when he was four and he crossed the street ahead of me. That was the summer my best Romanian friend's son was run over by a car and killed on a street in Brussels and when Princess Diana was smashed to death in a car accident in a London tunnel. So much hangs on so little.

Suddenly, the Corsican sun and sea don't look so friendly anymore, and the slow movie in colored frames breaks. I have been discreet in front of the children about my relations with my international male friends, and have included them in our outings only as 'friends'.

But now I worry that I may be breaking some cosmic balance that will affect them, not to mention a psychological one. They don't seem to care a bit though about any of my friends and keep recounting the scuba diving adventure and enumerating all the sea creatures they saw and even touched.

As for my mother, I know that once she gave up her dream of seeing me happily married with one dashing brilliant man of a reasonable age for life, and witnessed the parading of my marriages, divorces and love affairs, she no longer cares, particularly if my lovers speak French.

We have to leave the next day, back to Avignon to pick up all our luggage, back to Paris for one night between travels, and back to the United States. *And when can a mother relax, and not be on, and not be on the watch out for her children's lives*, I ask myself as we are eating our Mediterranean seafood at the charming restaurant overlooking the port.

Never, you can never fully relax, you always have to be on the watch out, I answer to my own self. *But then when is a mother, a woman who is a mother, supposed to have her own life, her own adventure? You've got to do it all if you want it all: children, work, adventure, be everywhere at the same time. You've got to do the impossible if you want the impossible. But then why can the men have it all, the children, the work, the adventure? They don't have it all, don't fool yourself, they live in half measures. You are the one that has it all, don't listen to the American clichés. Both the sexists and the American feminists have gotten something wrong. There is something else out there, other than this either-or reality, something in between, something that has yet to be invented. Like what? Like what you've got right here, this day in the Corsican sun and azure, your golden sons next to you after a scuba diving adventure. They are mortal just like you, and danger is always lurking around, scuba diving or no scuba diving, and your blue-eyed poet mother is watching over them too, she is the real co-parent, and your blue-eyed French lover is right here too, and you just had your teaching and theatrical success in the city of the popes; you've got it all, you fool, and you made it happen!*

A picture of me, my children, and my mother standing in front of the Corsican port against an orgy of blues, with our sun-burnt faces and matching blue eyes smiling at the camera is posted on my refrigerator even today. It was taken by my French friend who a year later broke up with me in an email. I felt relieved that I didn't have to do it myself, that I let him think he had the upper hand.

It's such a drag to always have the upper hand! And in that photograph in which we are all comfortably cuddled together against the azure of sea and sky, the ironic smile on my face seems to confirm that I was thinking again, *the men are secondary; the children matter most. The children and the work!*

Our journey back to Paris and back to the States is everything that our Corsican and the entire southern France sojourn were not: hard, laden with all our combined luggage that has grown in our summer French months, back breaking, with painfully early departures of trains and planes, filled with heavy silences, irritated exchanges, a real fall from paradise. Our 4 am risings are painful, though the children bear them with stoicism, going to bed in their clothes so at dawn they can just jump from bed half asleep and put on their backpacks.

I raised some real soldiers, I think through the fog of sleepiness as I see them standing in front of the door of our Avignon apartment of the last two months with their backpacks on and a glint of mischief on their faces, one tall, one small like a modern young blonde version of the old Stanley and Laurel pair.

I take in the apartment one more time and try to carve in my memory a compounded picture of our time there, the meals on the terrace with the view of the old city, tile roofs and luscious gardens hidden behind thick stones walls. I say a sorrowful goodbye in my mind. My children are going home to where they were born, while I am going some ten thousand miles away from this continent here where I was born. Dark sadness inundates me at dawn as I get ready for our long journeys back home, back to a place I have to call Home but will never fully be so. Just a refuge for the refugee that I will always be.

My mother calls a porter to help with our luggage in Gare Saint Lazare, and we look now even more like a family of runaway refugees taking their most precious belongings with them, next to the crowds of Moroccan, Senegalese, or Bosnian refugees filling the station.

We have one night in Paris, and we spend it in a fancy apartment in the sixth arrondissement where my Tunisian friend is staying for the rest of the summer. "Rich friends from my country own it, they work in the textile industry," he says, as he meets us in front of the building on our late arrival after our two days of travel from Corsica to Avignon to Paris and helps us with our voluminous luggage.

After the luminosity of Provence, Paris is harsh and gray, but even its grayness is elegant. My friend is tender with me, particularly affectionate with my mother and children like they were family. My sadness flows in waves, a dark river, bitter, heavy, and mixes with the Parisian melancholy. It drowns me. I realize it is him I care about, deeply, like a new kind of love that I haven't had before, that the blue-eyed French friend was a superficial flame lit by the Provence and Corsican sun and his biker adventurous sexiness.

I realize that between my Balkan sultry self and this man's Tunisian smoldering self, we have a deep tie of origins and flesh. I know he knows we will break up, that it's our last night in Paris or anywhere, because he lied to me all summer long with his excuses and delays, and I punished him back spending time with the French biker scholar. I know I would do it all over again, who am I kidding, because it wasn't just the punishment, but my own need for adventure and plenitude.

I know that I wouldn't trade the Corsican moment in the Mediterranean azure and the embrace on the steps against the white stone wall inside a frozen picture in time, in the blazing sun, like a myth. I wouldn't trade it for a long-term relationship with this man who would keep lying to me at each one of our encounters and on each one of our phone conversations. Superficial flames have their place in my life too, they add beauty to the work of art that I want my life to be. Not just to the making of art, but to the making of life into art, balanced between light and darkness, a stolen moment from the merciless rush of time.

My house in Virginia waits for us in its colonial stateliness from after the civil war, dusty white and quiet, estranged. It feels like we were gone for a lifetime. The vegetation around it looks bigger, stuffier. The house was supposed to be repainted in my absence, but the man I had hired to do it and who always called me 'babe' and 'sugar' is now in jail because, as it turns out, he was the leader of the biggest cocaine dealing ring in the area. Welcome to America! And who said our little sleepy town wasn't full of action and excitement!

The faded white of my house looks gray by comparison to the recollections of the impeccable whites of the houses in Corsica and Provence that flood my psyche. The big maple tree in the front of the house has been taken down because of a huge storm that apparently ravaged through the town in our absence and yanked many trees out of their comfortable earth.

Catastrophe after catastrophe seems to have visited my house and its surroundings. I remember how much I had wanted this house and how I closed the deal on it with my lawyer as I was talking on my cousin's cell phone from the top of the Carpathian Mountains surrounded by alpine pastures and cow manure. I have no car because I had sold it in the mad rain of the afternoon of my departure two months ago.

I'm a visitor in my own house and town. I walk on the empty streets and on the campus of my university in a daze, running errands and voraciously missing the lively swarming streets of Avignon, Nice, Les Saintes Maries de la Mer, Corsica, even the elegant grayness of Paris on our last night there.

Occasionally, I run into a colleague or local person who gives me the creeps. The department chair who had told me once that I destroyed the French program because I drew too many students to my classes, or that my articles published in French journals were like high school papers, the same man who asked if the stylized painted profile of the female nude on the cover of my first book was a picture of me and winked; the colleague whose wife testified in my divorce trial and who didn't address me for two years in the hallways of my work place; the student who also happened to be the son of the local judge who had told me in a divorce hearing that he was going to "take me out of the human race"; the colleague who together with his wife stood in my own living room and yelled threats and swear words at me because I had lost two screws from the crib he had lent us, while I was sitting with my own two scared sons on my own sofa in my own house!

A parade from hell of people from hell, all smiling and saying polite hellos how are you, some in flesh and blood, others in my singed memory. They are sinister ghosts waiting for me around a corner, on one of the pretty streets of the town where I've lived for more than a decade. I try to think in which circle of Dante's *Inferno* I would place them based on their different levels of nastiness; should it be the circle where sinners are gurgling and moving in and out of a river of shit, should it be the one where they have to run on burning sands, or should it be the one where their heads are twisted so that they look at their own asses for eternity?

They all sound good to me and the imagery gives me great satisfaction as I grimace a begrudging smile with my "hellos" and "how are yous". Hooray for Dante and his imagination of cruel punishments. He too must have had treacherous colleagues who bit and stabbed him from every which way and finally exiled him from his beloved art-filled Florence that he had himself filled with his immortal verses and hallucinatory images.

I decide to sequester myself in my majestic house for a few days and slowly unpack my suitcases that had traveled across the golden French Riviera, the majestic city of the Popes, the azure Corsican shores, the elegant streets of Paris and its picturesque train stations. It's a muggy hot Sunday at the end of August, and layers of white fogs are rising above the valleys as they tend to do at this time of the year, like the breaths of populations that must have roamed the surrounding wilderness hundreds and thousands of years ago in these ancient Appalachians, the oldest mountains on earth in this young New World.

My husband is visiting us from Chicago, spreading his mixture of chaos, wit, uneven affections, jealousies, and conversational skills throughout the house. It's hot and muggy as I take out from my suitcase the colored masks and feathered costumes from my Avignon surrealist show, the kind of hot and muggy that crawls on you and makes you itch. Patches of brilliant colors bring memories of a hot evening at the other end of the world with Cirque du Soleil music and hallucinatory images, me in a shiny orange taffeta dress bowing on front of a cheerful audience, mixed with other images in the Camargue wetlands, wild white horses flying against a creamy bluish horizon, in bluish fogs.

I'm having a splitting headache that feels like no other headache I've had before, sour and stinging my skull like a knife. As I rummage through my suitcase, I pull out a roll of drawing paper slightly crumpled, a caricature charcoal sketch of my four musketeer friends, myself and my son, which was done by a street artist the evening of my birthday party in the terrace restaurant across from the Palace of the Popes. On the back of it, written by different hands, is a lopsided haiku of sorts in French composed in a drunken collaborative effort that evening, "colloque de pénétration intellectuelle à Avignon où tous les vins sont acides le soir", or "symposium of intellectual penetration in Avignon where all the wines are acidic at night".

The poem is dated 17 June 2003, and signed by all six of us, as if it were a pact made for life over a moment of perfect harmony between body and mind, earth and sky, nature, urban, human, enveloped in Chanel 5 perfume. *We are already three years in the new millennium. I live in a country at war, on an old sheriff's estate.* My thoughts are throbbing daggers inside my temples. I think I should go to the emergency room at the hospital next door.

I live next to the hospital and the cemetery, both named after the great civil war hero, Stonewall Jackson. It's Stonewall country, where people carry confederate flags next to the hunted deer hanging in the back of their pick-up trucks. I tell my husband to watch the children while I go to the emergency room, and even as he is watching them, I still worry about them.

One time, they were playing soccer in the very middle of the street, one on one side and the other on the opposite side of the street, cars whizzing by and honking, while my husband was watching them and saying "No, it's good for them to play like that, like kids everywhere in the world."

I wanted to smack him and his anthropological perspective, *yeah, and kids all over the world get run over and killed every day like my friend's son was run over several years ago.* I tell him not to let the children play in the street. I tell him if something happens to them, I'll kill him, exactly like that, "I'll kill you if something happens to them, all right?"

He knows I'm not kidding, and I'm not entirely sure if this is playing out in my memory of another time when I made that threatening statement to him or if it is actually happening now in real time, when I am getting ready to get into my rental car to go to the emergency room. I think I'm having a stroke but I am still standing in my spacious kitchen staring at the big old tree in my back yard and worrying about my children playing in the street and getting hit by a car.

Once, my husband drove my older son to Chicago to see his grandmother, and I found out later that he was studying Chinese from a Chinese textbook while driving my precious cargo sitting next to him in the passenger seat. He got angry at my son for 'telling on him' and said that reading while driving helped him concentrate better on the driving.

Surges of anger flood me as I am still standing in the kitchen having a hard time moving and wondering why nobody is taking me to the hospital right now. A blur comes over my eyes, and I think I'm going to faint, but by an immense effort of will I take myself out of the kitchen and get myself inside the car and at the wheel, just like you would carry a child, only I am my own child, thank god I'm not too heavy.

I lost a lot of weight in the dry heat of Provence, and my Avignon gauzy blue dress like the Corsican Mediterranean is light as a feather. When this is all over, I'm going to divorce my husband. Who needs a husband anyways when I do it all by myself and he studies Chinese while driving one of my children? Why does one get PhDs and write dozens of books when one is not capable of caring for a child? I'm having all sorts of smart questions this morning or afternoon, who knows what time it is, and who cares!

By only a miracle of fate, I get myself to the emergency room and fall in the first chair I see at the front desk. They call it triage, which I think is a stupid word in this context and stolen from French. The woman taking my medical history is nice though, and she says she knows me from somewhere. It's a small town and everybody knows everybody like a goddamn family, only this town is not my family.

I have three friends, and they are all foreign, a French, a Spanish and a Russian friend, the United Nations of Small Town Virginia. One time the nice people of this town put a big scarlet letter on my chest and stared at me like I was the whore of Babylon, a fresco which my husband and I once saw on one of the walls of Westminster Abbey on our London trip several years before. Several bearded men were stoning to death the whore of Babylon in that faded fresco. Serves these townspeople right that their church burned down last year or several years ago, time is irrelevant.

I'm burning up like the burning church, and the woman at the front desk asks way too many questions. It's none of her business if I'm married or not. My emergency contact is my Russian friend, she understands me and my Romanian ways, and babysits for my children occasionally so I can rest or go to a conference. She speaks Russian to her children like I speak Romanian to mine, like my Spanish friend speaks Spanish to her children. We are the ones people always stare at.

I finally get taken to an emergency room where I am laid down on a hard bed. It feels heavenly to lay down in this white hospital bed, finally to rest with white walls all around and no associations of any kind. Blank. A woman doctor who is the mother of one of my younger son's school mates is on duty. I know all the doctors. I've brought my children here at all hours of the day and night with strep throat and chicken pox and heat rashes and stomach viruses and something called *evaso vago*, a kind of vertigo my younger son would get occasionally at the most unexpected times, and bleeding cuts that needed stitching, and even croup which sounded like a medieval illness and made my son's breathing sound like a braying donkey's.

I could get a degree in child medicine, plus five years ago my French friend brought me here with my wrists slashed in a moment of temporary insanity when I was too tired to even speak. I'm quite a regular at this provincial hospital.

It turns out my blood pressure is crazy high, a big number close to 200, and I was close to a heart attack or even a stroke. "My maternal grandmother died of a stroke in the middle of the street," I say, "and my paternal grandmother died of a heart attack and my father and his sister both died of heart attacks, and my great grandfather died in the bathtub in his own blood after he must have had a heart attack and pushed his arm through the window above the tub."

I don't think the doctor is interested in such a detailed report of my family's cardiovascular history, but I am proud of my heartbroken dying family members. We are headstrong people with weak hearts. The heart, the heart, always the heart. The doctor gives me a couple of pills, orders more heart tests, puts me on an IV because I'm also terribly dehydrated, and tells me to lie there for a while.

I finally feel an enormous sense of peace, and I think, *blessed be this hospital with its clean white emergency room where I can just lie with no chores, no worries, and all these kind nurses taking care of me and me not taking care of anyone. I just hope my husband remembers to feed the children, and if he doesn't, so what, they are smart boys who can feed themselves. Blessed be my congenital high blood pressure that finally kicked in this long hot summer of my Mediterranean travels and work and love and deadly heat. It must have all started in front of the McDonald's in Avignon where I almost fainted the day of my show premiere and I felt something snap in my heart and head and I still went on and on like an immortal energizer bunny.*

My headache is subsiding, and a pastel blue picture of the Rhône delta and the white wild horses roaming freely in the wetlands of the Provence floods my entire brain to excess. I have had a full summer that made my heart snap out of whack. I have an image of my heart roaming freely like a Camargue wild horse, white against white. I once taught a famous French poem about a white swan against a white frozen lake. It always comes back to French, only this is America, and I live here.

The nurse asks me, "Are you doing alright, honey?" and I burst into deep sobs. She holds me and says, "It's all right, sugar, you'll be alright." It's in that split second in the arms of the nurse of the emergency room that I have a feeling of being at home. This town here, and this hospital here that has the long history of my children's illnesses, and my house two blocks down the street is where my home is with my children in it, whether I like it or not.

My French teaching job, for whatever it's worth, is here, but it's worth quite a bit because it afforded me my luscious crazy French Riviera summer and theater show and the horses of Camargue. My three European women friends are only a few blocks away too, and this wonderful nurse is holding me with my IV stuck into my arm and doing her best to calm me down. I am supposed to be on something called beta blockers for the rest of my life, the woman doctor mother of Hannah from my children's school says. It sounds wonderful, I feel safe and relaxed, and "can I stay here for a while longer?" I ask.

She says, "Sure, take your time", and again, like I always do, I visualize the idiomatic expression of taking my time in a literal way of me carrying a package that is time in my arms. I try to hold this piece of time, but it keeps slipping away and out of my arms. It's a heavy package wrapped in one of my grandmother's dusty pink mousseline dresses and has a life of its own. I must have fallen asleep because another kind nurse touches my arm gently and says, "Are you feeling all right, honey, is anyone waiting for you outside to take you home?"

I mumble something about living two blocks away. I feel rested like I can start all over again now that my heart has the support of beta blockers.

Our Town

The fall after I return from Provence, I break up with my Tunisian friend via email, and I apply myself to writing one of the last versions of my first novel in my white colonial house while looking out at its long stretch of land with the old oak tree in the middle. By winter, my blue-eyed French friend breaks up with me by email too, shortly after an encounter we had in San Francisco for my annual modern language conference where we argued for hours about a potential Corsican vacation the following summer, my feminist research, and the time I spend with my children and he doesn't spend with his. Who needs a lover to argue with? Good riddance! All's fair in war and love, and one email break-up makes up for the other.

During the years of writing different versions of my novel and caring for my teenage children as they move from middle school to high school to college and go through all their growing pains, the local tragedies of teenagers dying in drowning or car accidents or committing suicide in our 'nice' 'safe' southern town, I develop a new kind of relationship with my ex-husband.

We start over on fresh terms, and I learn something valuable that helps me survive with less drama and less trauma. I learn to have no expectations of him as father and partner, but take what comes and make the most of what I do get: a family picnic together on a fall afternoon when the leaves are all ablaze, a ride on the blue ridge parkway in the winter, when the contours of the Appalachians are clear and dark blue, a meal at a local restaurant where some people who know me stare at me in surprise because they had thought I had gotten a divorce and others with fascination because maybe the idea of having a romantic dinner with your ex-husband sounds interesting and they had never thought of it on their own.

He is a visitor, a friend, a lover, an excellent storyteller and conversationalist, he is good at that, and a symbolic fatherly presence for the children, he is good at that too.

I see how so many women are clingy and needy and fuss over idiotic squabbles like who left the toilet seat up and why is the minivan parked in the driveway instead of in the garage. I think, these are middle class worries and squabbles of privileged white people. Most men I have known, including my now second ex-husband, my former Maghrébin lover, my former blue-eyed French biker lover, or just male friends in general, got married because their wives got pregnant first and they felt compelled to marry them, whether they liked it or not.

At one point or another, such a man is bound to feel trapped and want out. Then one day he gets a lover, the good wife finds out and throws a fit, most times she forgives him, once in a while she wants a divorce, and at other times he is the one who wants a divorce because he got sick of the nagging about the goddamn toilet seat and found a new kind of love with the girlfriend he met at work, while the wife, who had given up her career to be a stay-at-home mom, has become dowdy and uninteresting.

An eternal story of white middle-class America, I think as I make dinner for my growing boys, a vegetarian couscous recipe I learned from my Tunisian friend during the two years of our long-distance affair, plus grass fed bison burgers for my sons who are not vegetarian and need all the protein they can get for their growing bodies.

Again, I make fleeting friendships with female colleagues whose idea of fun at parties where all the adults get wasted just like the students they criticize, is to talk about university politics in self-important jargon and about the thrills and agonies of their vaginas and how they want to get away from their teenage children. They roll their eyes and have another drink. I feel remote from the whole scene, a planet away, on a Balkan mountain peak, on a Mediterranean beach, on a flight of steps in Corsica. I find my children more interesting than the vagina talk, and I leave the parties with a sour taste of not belonging anywhere, at least not among the university colleagues who all think they are God's given gift to the universe. I wait for my children until late at night when they are gone hiking in the neighboring woods or listen to the rowdy sounds in their rooms when they are having their friends for sleepovers, teenage boys bursting with hormonal abundance.

I remember the boys of my teenage years and Romanian youth: brooding, cunning, moody or sentimental, writing love letters on lined notebook pieces of paper, trading American music records acquired in the black market, Queen,

Pink Floyd. Their music is still in style among some of the retro throwback fads of the American teenagers of the two thousand, the millennial generation.

I get more settled and rooted in the Virginia town as my children grow. I find a groove in my writing voice and just then my ex-husband mellows out too, his jealousies subside, and his cantankerous moods soften. He stays at one of the motels on the side of one of the picturesque routes just outside of town writing his new book on Thoreau and the *Bhagavad-Gita* and waiting for me to show up for an afternoon visit.

We revert to our premarital, pre-child years, and it works just fine. I think we might just be one of a kind as they say, both made for a life of adventure and freedom, except I was also made for motherhood and household stability, the children's rock and hearth. But this is an arrangement I can live with. We each get what we want. Sometimes he takes the children out to dinner and a ride along the parkway scenic route on a 'boys' night out'.

People in town now recognize him as a regular at the Country Cooking restaurant, at the local grocery, or at the mechanic around the corner where he occasionally takes his Nissan Sentra for checkups after the thousands of miles he drives back and forth between Virginia and Chicago. How come we are more like a harmonious family now that we are divorced, and he stays at a side of the road motel than when we were married, and I insisted on regular mealtimes together?

Between the beta blockers, the groove I find in the town I have resisted for years, and the occasional trips abroad or to an American metropolis for conferences, my heart is re-calibrated to a regular beat and learns how to deal with the frenzies of our life, the highs and lows of our unusual family, without jumping out of its sockets like it almost did upon my return from my extravagant summer in southern France.

Maybe, just maybe, this is home, precisely because here is where I have dislikes and grudges and likes and passions and highs and lows and the streets are marked with the steps of my children going to the neighborhood schools. And there is the courthouse where I once nursed my younger son in front of the morose judge who threatened to "take me out of humanity" while I was wearing a scarlet red blouse just to take the impersonation of my literary heroine sister from New England to its utmost limit of literality. And there is the corner where my older son fell on his skateboard and made a big gash in his hand.

In this other corner, there have been three different convenience stores that didn't survive and now stands a lousy Greek restaurant that is always full. And there are the fields where I stood for hours in sun and rain cheering for my sons' soccer, baseball, lacrosse games, right behind our coveted house which is two blocks from the first house I owned, with an arbor vitae in the front in which the kids used to make a tree house and play for hours, from which my younger son fell one day all the way to the ground and his brother carried him in the house as if he were still a baby.

There is the house of my former department chair whose painful death I fantasized about many times, and there is the house of my French friend who took me to the emergency room with gashes in my left arm. I don't know where the house of my newest department chair is, and a good thing it is. He added insult to injury as the saying goes, pushed me to the brink of another breakdown with his pernicious double standards of course assignments and devious practices of saying one thing and doing its very opposite. He must have misunderstood the part about the honor thing that my university is so big on, actually meaning you have to match words to action and refrain from engaging in discriminatory practices. I will him out of mind and out of the landscape of this little town that is supposed to be my de facto home.

And ladies and gentlemen, this is the town where I always come back to after exotic trips to southern France, business trips to Los Angeles or Newyork, family trips to Chicago, one-day trips to Washington DC, or yearly trauma tourism trips to my own country of birth. And here is my favorite gas station where I fill the tank of my golden Mercedes or my newer Toyota minivan when I leave town or get back into town, and I get on the roads overlooking the layered bluish crests of the Appalachians.

Over there, past the county middle school is the field where a small private plane once crashed, killing the pilot and the passenger, and where their mangled body parts were strewn across the field and discovered the next day, right behind the municipal pool where my two children learned how to swim. At the other end of that same field, my children, my husband, and I almost pissed ourselves laughing one Christmas morning when the kite they had gotten from Santa and that we were trying to fly went too close to a bird that got all disoriented and made several crazy somersaults in the air before regaining its balance.

At this other corner—so much goes on in the street corners of a small town—is the bakery that replaced the Xerox shop whose owner's daughter used to babysit for my children and who was killed in a car accident with her boyfriend on their way back from the prom. And over there, right at the northern entry into town, is the pizza place where for years we had our midweek Wednesday night pizza and listened to Bruce Springsteen's *Hungry Heart* and Tom Petty's *Scar Tissue*.

And a little bit more outside of town, down one of the winding roads, is the bridge over the Maury river at the edge of which I once had sex with my second husband long ago, when my parents were visiting, and we didn't have any time or place for privacy. I was wearing a red polka dot dress I had gotten during our first trip to France, and I got poison ivy all over my body, including my bottom. That would have made a good vagina story at one of my colleagues' parties. You don't know a thing about the agonies of the vagina until you sat your ass on a pile of poison ivy for a quick tryst.

Love, death, sex, pain, loss, break ups, heartbreaks, reconciliations, accidents, violence, passions, and rock 'n roll, all the people you learned to hate, love, like, dislike, want to have sex with, or want to see dead, the people you feel sorry for or are scared of, the people you despise, the few you admire, the street corners with special stories attached to them, it's all here within a radius of two square miles. Who are you kidding; you'll never be able to leave this place!

Once after my first novel breakthrough occurred and I started to become more familiar with New York, the city where it seems that most of the successful stories about struggling refugees take place, I went with my friend Yasmine whom I had met at a conference in New Orleans the year after Katrina, to see a highly praised production of Thornton Wilder's *Our Town*. At the end of it, we sat in our seats holding hands and cried for a long time.

I felt immense love for my playwright friend and suddenly for the little provincial town where my immigrant journey had taken me and where I had spent by then more than fifteen years of my life, many of whom had been in resistance to and fighting the town. I felt like one of the ghosts in the last act of the play, one of the spirits of the characters from the first act, who, while gathered in the local cemetery for the funeral of one of the townspeople, reminisce with devastating yearning the lost moments of their lives, the moments they let pass without the awareness that they had it all in those moments, that they were alive and even happy without knowing it.

After seeing the play with my friend, I wanted to go back home and make it matter, treasure the corners and the scars of my town that often coincided with my own scars, the imprints of my life and of the lives of my children, ex-husbands, transatlantic lovers, Romanian family members, all who had visited me or had roomed with me in the three houses I had lived in. One at the top of a mountain, right outside of town when I moved from Chicago with my first husband, my then three-year-old son and another one in my womb.

One on a street that went down to the elementary school my children had attended, with the arbor vitae and the dogwood in the front yard, the house where I survived the three years of divorce proceedings, the pre-tenure years of departmental harassments and where my children were small, adorable munchkins to whom I read Greek myths and Grimm's fairy tales every night.

And the last one, the notorious sheriff's house that I managed to grab in one cunning move before any of its other potential buyers were able to, while I was hiking on a Romanian mountain top. I wanted to let go of the grudges, acknowledge the roots I had grown in that town almost despite myself. I wanted to start over, because when you are a refugee, you keep wanting to start over all the time, you keep remaking yourself until maybe one day you reach an image of yourself that might, just might match the image you created of your future self when you recklessly left for the wide world, long ago, with all your belongings in one small suitcase.

And surprisingly enough, with my first novel, my town embraced me and my success, bought my book until the local bookstores sold out of them over and over again, included it in the local book clubs, and attended my readings. People wanted to talk about it when meeting me in line for groceries or at my children's school events. One of my son's friends would say, "My mom read your book and loved it."

The owner of the local clothes store, where I had bought most of my work clothes over the years, came to my New York book launch, my hairdresser attended my locally organized book launches, and my mechanic listened to my book on tape and asked me, "When is the next one coming out?"

Everybody who had read the book now addressed me as the protagonist, sure that everything that had happened to her must have happened to me. I sometimes vehemently rejected the idea saying, "No, it's not my memoir", "no, it's not an autobiography", to no avail, until I let it be. Suddenly, it was ~~IRONIC~~ the story of the girl on the train leaving her love and her country forever that rooted me in the small southern town I had wanted to leave from the first day I arrived in it, one sweltering July day.

I was then married to one man, pregnant by another, with a three-year-old son and a doctoral dissertation I was still struggling to put the last touches on while fighting morning sickness and the even more colossal sickness of estrangement and loneliness that I was drenched in. I was then feeling like a newcomer from another planet, fumbling though the morning fogs and palpable humidity that crawled in from the surrounding valleys.

It was the story I had carried in my suitcase a quarter of a century earlier that connected me to the people of a remote southern town in the Virginian Appalachians. Becoming accepted and rooted in Chicago had been easy. Making friendships, even if superficial at times, being appreciated in school or at work, getting jobs, were no big deal in a city full of immigrants like myself. Had Zoila Valdivieso lived in New York and sponsored me to join her there, or in Los Angeles or Cleveland Ohio, most likely it would have been easier than my small-town Odyssey had been.

My ex-husband, now re-become partner of sorts and in his last years of life become benevolent co-parent, often told me, "You won! More people than you know like you here. There are more hidden riches in this town than you know it." There was a time when being liked by the locals wasn't even anywhere on my list of priorities.

On the contrary, I gloated in thinking I was being hated and hating right back. At some point hate felt empowering and refreshing, clean and sharp, until it got tiring. It's not like now I was suddenly overflowing with sisterly love for the entire seven thousand people that populated our town or that I had suddenly forgiven the colleagues who had made many of my working days a living hell, or the judges and lawyers who threatened and poisoned our lives for the three years of my gory divorce. It's not that I was no longer sickened by the sight of the confederate flags or by the cultish adoration of all the former slave owner generals whose names colonized most of the public spaces and buildings in town.

But I had found a groove of belonging and that brought with it a new kind of acceptance. I compared myself to a tree transplanted to a new earth which finds itself at the edge of drying out and dying in the alien soil, but in the end its will of survival is stronger than its alienation. At some point that tree starts growing crooked, twisted roots until it meets the roots of the other local trees underneath the humid clay. And at that point, that tree of the crooked roots starts feeling at home in that earth. I planted an orchard just to prove my point and match my metaphoric thinking with a literal reality.

I started looking at my town as if it were the town in Wilder's play: a stage where everybody had their role, some center stage, some on the sides, some way upstage in the distance, and what do you know: that perspective made me change my heart like never before. It took me deeper into its intricate workings, and I began to show interest in the town's many types, looks, psychologies, professions, squabbles, love affairs, hate affairs, secrets, couples swapping each other's partners overnight. I stopped looking at my town with the disdain of a marginalized European refugee and it felt freeing. It was partly the result of a play I had cried at in New York holding the hand of my friend, and partly that of my own story and of my heroine coming out into the world.

I sought out new friendships with some of the women artists in town. One day, a beautiful black-haired visual artist who painted blue swimmers sent me a call to join a small women's group and talk about art and death. No talking about men was the rule. I was in for that. It wasn't just New York or Chicago that had interesting edgy people with a tragic view of life. My painter friend's blue swimmer canvases ended up lighting a spark of inspiration in my imagination for my second novel for which I had a double deal contract with a big British press even before it was written.

That same novel about a Romanian painter growing up on the shores of the Black Sea ended up being the book my artist friend obsessed about, having read it breathlessly on a summer trip with her art students in no other part of the world but southern France. I had erotic dreams about my painter friend and wild desires to have my own nude painted in one of her blue canvases.

In our conversations, we often went back to our early years as divorced single mothers when we only knew each other by sight and stood in the rain at our sons' lacrosse games, watching our sons running their raging hormones to exhaustion, hitting each other with large sticks, and wearing heavy helmets. The loose threads in the tapestry of my life were starting to come together in spiraling and boldly colored figures, curving in turns and returns and tying delicate knots between a small town hidden in one of the crooks of the Appalachians and the rest of the wide world.

The dancer friend who joined the "art, death, and no men women's group" choreographed a dance and directed a theater number from a deleted piece from my first novel that described a dream about my female ancestors with me in the role of the woman dreamer of the dream. She had me recite the dream in Italian to give me the chance to get in touch with the language of my first immigrant experience in Rome, a language I sometimes missed so much that I dreamed in it.

Floods of Italian words would pour into my overextended psyche, and I would wake up whispering a mouthful of Italian words, choking on them like a child would choke on too much candy stuffing their mouth. I could say that the show literally made one of my dreams come true. A third woman of the group who could easily outrun a twenty-year-old man on a 10K run, and who was a freelance travel writer, hosted our meetings in her nineteenth century Victorian house in the country, overlooking the Blue Ridge mountains.

Our group meetings at times turned into dance parties and laughing parties, 'fuck men' and 'fuck death' hooray for female art parties as the mountains and valleys flickered with fireflies and filled with cicada songs and honeysuckle fragrance.

Where were these women when I was cursing every corner of the town and its psychotic judges and lawyers, and keeling over the kitchen sink with exhaustion and single motherhood rage and the rage of a woman with an accent, of a professor paid half of the salary of male colleagues who did half the amount of the work she did?

It turns out these women were also going through their own rages and divorces and single motherhood stories and disappointing love affairs and working themselves to death for lesser salaries than their male colleagues in their respective professions. These women were not clingy and needy, nor did they speak in worn out feminist slogans though they lived and acted every bit of feminism in some of its most colorful forms. They were the 'bad' American girls I had been waiting for.

They had raised sons and daughters by themselves, raced eight miles up our iconic House Mountain thus called because its lonely bluish contours against the Virginia horizons looked like a house from every which way you looked at it, won canoeing, bicycle, and running relays, were funny and sexy, and created art. That was ultimately where I always found my home and my people, either among the artists 'with an attitude', whatever that meant, among

315

the single working mothers in the margins, sassy and passionate, or among other immigrants and expats who knew what it was like to live with a big hole in the center of your heart, to have American liberal eyes rolled at you whenever you didn't subscribe to all their prescribed ideas, or be given condescending compliments about how good your English was by American conservatives with little knowledge of anything outside their white Christian world.

The Mexican family who took care of my house and at times, as a last resort in the earlier years, when I was at a loss for hands and legs to drive my kids around to their myriad after school activities, picked my children up from school or cooked a hot meal of cactus leaves nopals and zucchini for us—these were my people. The hairdresser who had survived an abusive husband, raising three children by herself, was a flaming democrat feminist who did art projects on the side and did wonders with my hair. She had babysat my younger son one frigid snowy morning when I married his father at one of the scenic lookouts in the area, and she was my people too.

The beautiful poet writing about witches' brews and the startling bits of her youth married to a psychopathic husband, she, too was my people.

I felt a solidarity with the women 'sinners' of our town, the working mothers and the artist women with turbulent pasts, and finally I was starting to feel part of a community.

I did not advocate adultery as a productive life style. Besides its great potential for hurt and grief on all sides, it was exhausting and finally unsustainable. But I could never wrap my mind around the perverse oddity that for millennia men of all ages, races, and social classes had shamelessly flaunted precisely that lifestyle, from factory workers, to professors, to presidents of state, while women were still lambasted for it in courts of law, in work places, in the street, on playgrounds, by men as well as by other women. Maybe even more by other women, blessed be their faithful hearts.

My world was unfolding and opening up in layers after layers of discoveries and new friendships and the town I had once hated so passionately that I even wanted to start a 'hate-our-town support group', was now acquiring depth, becoming humanized, and was no longer a flat painting like the three-hundred-piece puzzle of a small American town my older son and I had once put together, glued with scotch tape and posted on the wall in his room. It was becoming a three-dimensional stage of intricate destinies, flaming passions, and artistic epiphanies.

My ex-husband was right. I had won in more ways than one, not just because I reached my academic goals despite the blocks set up in my way, bigotry, sexism, scarlet letters posted on my chest, grudges and spiteful happenings and words thrown in my face, or just because I had a well published novel which was now traveling the world, but also because I had gotten to the heart of the town with its darkness and light. I was bursting the flat puzzle into a moving set with multiple facets.

It struck me one day that in a town that size, there was one of each, actors on a stage playing their parts, and when the actor died or left town, so did the part go with them. The idea came to me when I was walking along Main Street on a lazy fall afternoon and noticed the absence of the semi homeless man with the boom box. He used to stand at different corners holding his boom box like a baby and listening to his radio, reminding me of the character with the boom box in Spike Lee's film *Do the Right Thing*. There was no one to replace him, and that spot on the stage remained empty.

We had pretty much all the categories and types that you found in a big city by the thousands, only here we had one sample of each, and that made them unique. There was the woman who swam at the municipal pool regularly whose son had died in one of the Twin Towers on September 11 and who always greeted you kindly.

There was the beautiful artist who painted blue swimmers and human amphibians, once a New Yorker herself. There was the red-haired dance studio owner and dance teacher who had staged my dream in Italian. There was the good and honest balding lawyer who had brought the madness that was once my first divorce to a peaceful closure. And there was the bad woman lawyer who had asked me if adultery was so common in my country and sued me for not paying her last shameless bill of several unmerited thousand dollars but whom I cunningly tricked by filing for bankruptcy on the very day of the court hearing. There was the jazz band player and art teacher with a shrill voice and encouraging attitude.

And there was the eccentric Romanian French professor, novelist, playwright, who always dressed up and even gardened with her pearls on. Her first novel glowed in its bluish cover in the windows of the two local bookstores for a long time. And here stage right was the orthopedic doctor who

317

fixed both my kids' broken wrists, after which I walked into the local jewelry store and had a second set of ear piercings done to alleviate the anxiety about my sons' broken bones. This was done by the same jeweler who had polished some precious star diamonds and rubies jewels that my mother had once worn on the train ride to Austria when she left Romania for good, and that she had gifted me after my father's death.

Delicate entangled threads connected us to one another over time. Over there sitting at a table in our new sushi restaurant is our world-famous painter whose postmodern works are hung in the Louvre and the Hermitage. Here in this corner is the studio of the newest piano teacher also yoga instructor who taught my younger son Fur Elise and the Moonlight Sonata and had the saintly patience to teach me simplified versions of sonatas and waltzes by classic composers and a few jazzy songs. She lives in a yurt in the depth of our county forests and irradiates an ineffable goodness and joy, no matter what comes.

Once in a while, wearing a backpack, a baseball hat and a lost look that could be a smile but is most likely an attempt to hold back tears, the mother of the boy who died of a drug overdose in the streets of New Orleans and who had spent many summer afternoons playing music with my older son in our shed, crosses the stage. Every year new actors move onto the stage with new parts, while some of the old ones are forgotten or slowly fade out of sight when the lights go dimmer in some corners of the stage.

Throughout all the shifts of the actors off and on the stage that is my little town in the Appalachians, my exquisite Spanish friend has remained steady, dancing her way through all the different spaces of this stage and always returning to the center. She has been a sparkling lighthouse in calm and tumultuous weather alike, just as I had predicted the morning when I brought the quivering bundle of life that was my newborn son, and when she placed him with feathery gentleness in the lacey bassinet she had prepared for him a spring morning, almost three decades ago.

Some places on the set hold unbearable emotional intensity that I try to avoid or on the contrary keep returning to. On this side street next to the wine store, there is the studio of my painter friend who let me use her artistic space for two years when I was working on my novel about the two girls who had survived the Balkan genocides of the nineties while I was trying to survive the dark depression that had finally taken full hold of me.

This was after my last son left home for college and my single motherhood years were over, and when my older son had fallen into his own pit of sadness trying to figure out his life in the wilderness of the Rockies and the deserts of the Wild West, as he worked on archaeological sites on Indian reservations and drove to work at dawn on hairpin roads above twelve thousand feet chasms.

I was throwing myself into stories of genocide for my own survival like I had thrown myself into the lives of my English as a second language students who had survived Pol Pot's genocide and Thai pirate raids three and half decades earlier.

I sat on a folding chair in the middle of my friend's studio and wrote for hours surrounded by all the shades of blue and green of her large swimmer canvases. Cobalt blue, turquoise, Persian blue, French blue, cerulean blue, sapphire blue, and here and there a drop of magenta red to make the blues even bluer. This was my blue period, and I embraced it like one embraces a grieving crying child. It was one of the things I had learned with the passing of time as a refugee in a small town too: to embrace my grieving soul like you embrace a grieving misbehaved child and love it all the same.

While I was writing in my friend's studio, I would look over the red tile rooftops overlapping each other in a sweet asymmetry that looked disturbingly like the rows of tile roofs arranged in curving rows against my native Carpathians in Brasov, where my childhood and youth were ghosts roaming around among the symmetrical rows of fir trees. There, in the center of my friend's studio, I swam inside the blues of her canvases, missing my children to the point of a raw gaping wound, missing all the portions of my past that had gone too fast and hurting from all the portions that hadn't gone fast enough, trying to save my two Balkan heroines from their post genocidal war free fall into post traumatic sadness much deeper than mine, so deep that I couldn't find any appropriate color for it.

I was tying the knots and connecting the dots of my many lives spread across the world and the imaginary lives of my heroines, from the snowy tips of the Carpathians to the mellow dusty chains of the Mediterranean Alps, to the sulky borderline exotic Dinaric Alps, to the hazy deep blues of the old Appalachians and the top of House Mountain that loomed in its full square bluntness to the right of the main road.

The Romanian Reunion

It has always been in moments where my belonging to America has been challenged that I most cling to the right of that belonging. Whenever faced with suggestions of expulsion, of being unwelcome and foreign wrapped in the poisonous foil of condescending 'niceness', that's when I claim this harsh merciless American earth as my home. Or when I travel outside its frontiers and I hear others who never even stepped on American soil, spew vitriolic generalizations about the entire American nation in one nasty bulk of insults.

Just like no matter how harsh you might be criticizing or ranting against your own family, you can't stand it to hear strangers malign it. Such a formidable occasion was my ludicrous high-school reunion in Bucharest in 2009. A few of my former classmates had found me on Facebook following the publication of my first novel in Romanian translation and were suddenly possessed by an ardent desire for a high-school reunion, and for me to be part of that reunion.

I fell for the sentimental virtual exchanges of high school memories and scanned copies of old photos from our years of studying in the historic building of our high school which at one time in history was named after queen Mary of Romania and later, under communist rule, after a female combatant from the Bolshevik Revolution.

We had our main reunion party on the outdoor terrace of the restaurant in the park where my mother used to take me for long walks and Ferris wheel rides as a child. I sat at one end of the table, while our colleague who was now one of Romania's leading actresses and had acted in the role of Virgin Mary in Mel Gibson's film about the life of Jesus Christ, sat at the other end.

On my eighteenth birthday, she and I had jumped fully dressed into the lake that lay a few hundred feet away only to be apprehended and severely admonished by the communist police as we were emerging dripping wet with lake algae hanging from our hair and clothes. We wanted to be Ophelias and float on the greenish waters pretending to be dead, while our dresses ballooned up in the murky waters.

I suppose we were now the only ones with a modicum of international name recognition, and our classmates who organized the party figured it was appropriate to be seated this way. My few favorite teachers who had encouraged my writing talents in my rebellious school years had died and the only one alive and present, or barely so, was the mean spirited fourth grade teacher whom I suspected having been an informer and who had given me a grade of four when I whispered the answer to a math problem to one of my classmates.

Except for a couple of the women, I recognized no one and had little in common with the crowd lined up along the long restaurant table. We were now part of entirely different worlds and the fact we had all shared the same school building and teachers three decades earlier was not enough of a glue to bring us together.

The reunion dinner was bearable, but what came after turned into a nasty fight which ended with my violent and loud departure, that included me hurling the obscenest Romanian swear words at the whole lot of my former high school classmates and pushing the beautifully set and abundant dinner off the expensive glass top table in one dramatic gesture.

The day after the restaurant reunion, my former best friend classmate invited a select group of our colleagues to her house, where I was also staying with my younger son, to celebrate her birthday. I had wanted to stay at a hotel as I always did in Bucharest, having no longer any family or friends I cared about in my native city. But she insisted I stay with her in hers and her partner's newly renovated villa with a persistence that in the end broke my resistance.

Somewhere between the barbecued sausages and the grilled trout, the United States became the subject of conversations triggered possibly by my refusal to eat the much-praised sausages because I didn't eat any meat. First, I was ridiculed for my pescatarian diet, next I was told that recycling was a form of dictatorship in 'that America of yours', which led to the war in Iraq, which turned out I was also responsible for.

The husbands present at the birthday dinner were onto me, yelling in my face about all the American evils in the second person: "You started the war in Iraq, you bring drugs, prostitution, and violence all over the world, here in Romania too."

The American government was "shit", "your president was only elected because he is Black", "America has no history, no culture, is run by Jews and is full of stinking Blacks." A deafening choir of hate!

I yelled back using the best of my below the diaphragm voice from my acting days to cover the anti-American voices, damming Romanians' racism, antisemitism, "You exterminated four hundred thousand Jews and had Jewish pogroms; you held the Gypsies in slavery for hundreds of years and killed them in pogroms too; look at your stinking streets out there with potholes left from the communist era."

It got crazier and louder by the minute, the full-size trout on the table being the only silent creature with the dead stare in one of its bulging eyes. Some of the women joined in to support their husbands, others intervened to calm them down and to meekly defend me by saying, "You are just envious she left and that she didn't have to eat soy salami and drink soy coffee during communism. Leave the woman alone. She was smart to leave."

I caught a millisecond to intervene with a defense of "the American democracy", but what I received back was "What democracy? No democracy! You can't say anything against the Blacks and the Jews, that's no democracy."

I tried to explain "the separation of powers, the constitution", but they yelled back, "What constitution? You have no history!"

"Look at your own fucking corrupt government," I said.

"Oh, and your government is not corrupt, starting wars, and telling everybody in the world how they should run their country?" they retorted.

"You deserved communism, country of informers scum and racist pigs that you are…" I added.

Then the *piece de resistance* came when the man who looked and dressed like a mafia boss and was married to one of my friends from eighth and ninth grades, whose last name was Purcel, or Piglet, and who lived in a strikingly luxurious villa the size of which put to shame my historic house with its piece of land and a big oak tree, said with great panache, like a victory scream, "The only good thing that America ever did is the movie *Mamma Mia*! And maybe a couple more films!"

I had to burst out laughing at the enormity of the statement. It was so out of whack that for a second, I couldn't come up with anything to top that. Then my precious son in his admirable poise said, "There are no perfect governments", after which he gave a super condensed and eloquent mini lecture on the American founding fathers and the constitution which demanded everybody's attention for a minute, so precious was he and the most rational of the entire crowd.

After which, my hostess's husband said, "You could be a really nice kid, if only you were European."

The ferocious mama bear in me or the tigress in me or whatever wild mama beast lived in me, roared and scowled, broke china, pushed things off the outdoor glass table in a dramatic move she must have seen in some Hollywood movie that was not *Mamma Mia*! She amassed the richest combinations of insults that flooded her mind and threw them like burning coals at the Romanian gathering and their Romanian sausages, trout, and tomatoes, "Don't you dare as much as pronounce this child's name, you racist bunch of motherfuckers. Stick your fucking party up your sticking Romanian asses and your mafia villas made from shady money."

Then my son intervened and tried to calm me down, as he always did, "Mama, there are racists everywhere, there are no perfect governments."

The Romanian Jewish actress who had once been my partner in mischief thirty years ago got up to leave. She had a rehearsal to go to. "You people have fun with this," she said.

Michael Jackson had just died that day and his song *Beat it* was playing on the hosts' CD player. "Why are you listening to Michael Jackson if you hate America and Blacks so much?" I heard myself say and thought that was the first fully rational and cuss-free sentence that I had uttered in that angry avalanche.

No one said anything. The only sound was the sonorous slam of the glass door slicing into the Michael Jackson song. "Let's get the hell out of here," I told my son. I slammed and pushed off the table everything I could get my hands off, then turned around and slammed the glass door with all my might, regretting that I hadn't slammed it hard enough to break it to smithereens, and left the premises, going from the garden inside the house. Since we were staying at her house, I hid in our room until the next morning when we left without as much as a goodbye.

It so happened it was the Fourth of July, and I had the idea of taking my son to the Romanian village museum to see the poetic, idealized version of my country, in the form of miniature villages from all the regions of the country. Stone houses from Transylvania, wooden houses from Moldavia, buried mud houses from the plains of Walachia, white stucco houses from the Danube and the Black Sea regions, the museum offered a rural paradise of an utopian country.

I needed to walk inside each one of the homes and breathe in their old wooden fragrances, stare at the colored hand-woven rugs and tapestries hung inside, touch the warm wooden door sills, like a cleansing, telling myself that everything and everyone in that country of my birth was not rotten and racist scum as I had pronounced them a day earlier.

That July day was burning hot and dry as we walked from village house to village house, traversing the virtual map of a country that had known every historical violence, invasion, and occupation under the sun. Turkish invasions and impaling sprees by the all too famous Vlad the Impaler, the corrupt rules of Greek Phanariotes, the harsh and ineffective rule of Austro-Hungarian kings, the Nazi occupation and exterminations of Jews and Gypsies, the Stalinist occupation and brutal political prisons, every shade of communist dictatorships, bloody revolution, post-revolutionary chaos, orphans in cages, the emergence of savage capitalism—that was my country that landed all in shreds and rags in the lap of the European Union!

I had never processed the anger and pain that had driven me out of it twenty-five years earlier. I had processed somewhat the yearnings, the nostalgias for all that had been beautiful and worthy, the uprooting from my land and people, but not the ugliness, oppression, crass provincialism, and fear that had made me get on the one-way plane to Rome.

I needed that spark and the gathering of some of the country's dumbest specimens at one reunion party in a garden, was what ignited the disgust and grief and my desire to burn them to ashes. We walked through the simulacra villages among the gardens of roses and houses of all colors that had been brought from all the regions of the country trying to absorb the luminous essences out of the darkness of history.

It seemed that groups of benevolent peasants were alluring me to their abodes, *come live in this white house with brilliant blue doors by the Black Sea, you always liked the sea; no, come here to northern Moldavia into this house here with a wooden ornate veranda where your father grew up; no, no, come here little girl, to the rock-solid houses of Transylvania where your mother grew up and where you had your first feverish love.*

The entire country was auctioning for bits of my heart and soul while three blocks away in the same luxurious area of the city with large boulevards lined up with old linden and chestnut trees, was the Fourth of July celebration at the American Embassy. Not just one but two countries were auctioning for my soul, and for the first time I missed the winding roads and wide highways cutting through the ridges of the Appalachians where my house with bay windows and a nice plot of land was waiting for me, guarded by the big oak tree in the back yard.

I was caught in a fever of claiming and reclaiming of homes, the best and the worst of both worlds, and fantasized about a fault line that tied these precious vestiges of Romanian rural life from the Carpathians to the Black Sea, to the mellow countryside of the Appalachians and the wide expanses of land that opened up in all directions, the bustling streets of Chicago, the fierce rawness of the Wild West and all its frontiers. I was expanding myself into something of a formidable yet beautiful anomaly of lands, cultures, mountains, cities, seas with a gigantic but sorely broken heart in the middle, like the emblem of a different kind of hybrid country.

It was the first time since I had started the cycle of my returns a decade earlier that I was happy to leave, and staring at the yellow and green squares of native land that got smaller and smaller as our plane was taking off, I told myself the colossal lie that I would never return again. I perversely wanted to relive the original departure of a quarter of a century earlier and punish myself for it with the same medicine. It only worked for three years, and once the medicine wore off, I did return. And I keep returning in an unstoppable merry-go-round. Here is Home, and here is Home, too. Aren't you lucky, you've got two of everything!

Entangled Roots, New Suitcase

"The town with very nice people", as I call it sometimes, keeps changing while also remaining the same. It has entered my bloodstream and has mixed up with my native Romanian roots, my borrowed French and Italian roots, forming a true multicultural stew. I have entered and absorbed its cycles. I pay more attention to the discernible and less discernible transformations, the movement of seasons and people.

In the spring, the dogwoods and the red-buds in my back yard and in the valley burst in their painfully transient glory of reds, magenta and pastel pinks, the first hyacinths and daffodils, the first lilies, peonies, fill the front lawns and gardens, the valleys acquire a fairy tale haziness of pastels pierced with blotches of strong greens and reds. The orange red lilies and the blue irises come and go, as the heavy greens fill in all the gaps and become one thick blanket across the ridges, valleys, and the peaks of the surrounding mountains. The summer nights are cooler and sparkle with fireflies and unlike anywhere in the cities, you can discern the shapes and places of the constellations.

I am sure I stand on a fault line that starts here and stretches all the way to my childhood city in the Carpathians. It's a crooked line that cuts through the entire chain of the Appalachians, the plains and the cornfields of the Midwestern states, the indomitable Rockies, traverses the bed of the Atlantic, the European Alps, the French Riviera, and the Maritime Alps where I once had a delirious summer of compounded heartaches and forbidden delights, and reaches the country of my birth after thousands of kilometers, but nevertheless the same uninterrupted line.

It reaches all the way to my favorite place in a Transylvanian city at the foot of the Carpathian, with narrow hilly streets and stone houses painted in multicolored pastels. The blankets of russet golden and magenta leaves glow across the valleys in the fall and when they are all gone and the trees remain bare, only the coniferous assert their dark greens. Then the view is wider, cleaner, starker, across hundreds of miles of mountain ranges that were once inhabited by many Indigenous tribes wiped out by the much-idealized European pilgrims and settlers.

It's not that I am no longer a foreigner, it's not that I am now brimming with endless love for the small town where I have spent more time living than in any other part of the world, or that I no longer yearn for the continent and country whose earth holds my original roots somewhere in its chaos of histories, revolutions and regime changes. The foreignness is still there, the yearning even stronger at times, as if over the years it has grown too. It has ripened and evolved into a creature in its own right.

It has occurred to me recently that in that last scene of Thornton Wilder's *Our Town*, when all the spirits of the town's characters sit and talk in the cemetery at the occasion of a new burial, none of the spirits of the Polish immigrants mentioned in the beginning of the play are present at that gathering.

It's maybe the only fault of the play, that the immigrants are only mentioned in the beginning, when the stage manager-character-storyteller speaks about the Polish woman in town who had just given birth to twins. Immigrants multiply and have babies and then are forgotten. It's only the Americans at the end, in life and in death, the American-born that rule and are worth of a theatrical ending. I wonder where I would be in this play about our town, in that last scene of the dead looking back at their lives.

Most likely, I wouldn't be invited to this after-death chat. I would have to make my own 'our town' after death, and it would be a gathering of the Spanish, the Russian, the French, the Mexican, the Honduran, the El Salvadoran, the Indian families, looking back on our lives in the small southern town from the margins, definitely not in the central cemetery named after a famous civil war hero, not that any of us would even want that. Even though recently the name of the confederate hero was dropped from that of the cemetery, we still wouldn't want to be buried there in the vicinity of the confederate heroes still adored by many of our townspeople.

Maybe I should suggest the creation of a multicultural cemetery, an immigrants' cemetery in one of the rustic groves just a bit outside of town. Or maybe I should write a different ending to that play, one with the immigrants' ghosts in it, reminiscing on their lives as foreigners and as people with accents, regretting not having known better to appreciate that they were alive when they were alive in a foreign land, but instead crying over their lost roots, striving like mad to grow new roots.

Or maybe not, who cares; they are all down there with the worms anyways, all one good southern earth mixed in with dogwoods roots and iris bulbs, the native species mixed in with the imported ones. My father was adamant he did not want to die and be buried in America, but in his native land, and he never got his wish: he died in Chicago and was buried in Michigan in the Romanian cemetery, at least in the company of his diasporic compatriots.

My ex-husband was adamant he did not want to die in confederate land but in Chicago and be buried with his family in the Sleepy Hollow cemetery in Concord, Massachusetts. And he got exactly what he wanted. I guess he would be part of that lyrical spirited conversation of the ghosts at the end of *Our Town*. There you have it: the difference between being a native and a transplant is that you get to choose where to die and where to be buried, and chances are that the natives are going to have their wish fulfilled.

With the passing of time, the burning hole lined with all the yearnings and *dor* of my native earth isn't getting any smaller. The burning isn't getting any lighter, and the hole in my heart remains a crater with the perpetually smoldering lava of longing. Suffices a breeze carrying a certain smell, a lilac tree in bloom, the smell of snow on a dark moonless night, the taste of a piece of fruit, or the feel of the sun on my skin, the sounds of children playing outside, an old American song, the sound of thunder on a summer day, the smell of mothballs on an old coat, the slant of a sun ray filtered through the gauzy material of a curtain.

The tiniest thing can prick the bubble of memories filled to excess and let the contents of it flow out with a vengeance, a true volcanic eruption. The difference is that now you own your little impetuous volcano of longing and remembrance like the little prince living on the tiny planet somewhere in the galaxy from the book your mother used to read to you and in turn you used to read to your own children. You clean it out, you care for it, you watch it fill up again and wait patiently for its new irruptions. You travel around the world, you keep returning to that initial crater where you were born and grew up.

Irony of all ironies, while you are there in the mushy squishy sweetness of your mother country, eating some pastry you remember from your childhood, you now start missing the corner of the world in the small town where you spent your thirties, forties, and are racing through your fifties and most likely are going to spend all the days of your life minus the intervals of traveling abroad and to larger cities in your adoptive country.

You realize it's not just the children you miss, but the places, the sounds, the expanses of land that you like driving across, your little piece of land with the very imperfect orchard you planted, and you realize you are screwed either way. You are one flying burning body with flames at both ends like a double comet. You take refuge in the knowledge that you are part of a large group of such double comet people, that whether you left your country of birth by plane, by boat, by crawling under barbed wire, by walking through the desert, by swimming across a dangerous river or expanse of sea, you are part of that growing fraternity of the uprooted, walking around with your little volcano of memories good and bad, yearnings and gashes and you are among the lucky ones.

Unlike your father or your ex-husband, you don't give a damn about where you'll die and where you'll be buried. Maybe right there in your backyard, under your majestic oak tree. Because as the manager character in *Our Town* points out, you are under the same stars, part of the same galaxy, and the same universe, a tiny traveler on a tiny planet.

One luminous June morning of the year 2011, in the miniature town of this tiny planet, when I came out of the local outdoor pool after my habitual swim, with raccoon circles around my eyes from the goggles and my wet hair stuck to my forehead, a tall slender man came towards me and said, "Your stroke is all wrong."

I thought it was funny, and I answered back, unflinching, "Show me the right stroke."

In a complete non sequitur, he then proceeded to tell me he was going through a divorce, and then to congratulate me on my recent teaching award, a report of which had been published in the local paper. We exchanged a few more sentences, and in turn, I told him I had been through two divorces. He wondered why I would have wanted to marry a second time and shared with me his desire to never marry again.

While attempting to push my hair into shape and off my face, I made some quick calculations in my mind about the sexy stranger who had criticized my swim stroke and praised my recent professional achievements while also announcing to me his availability, as well as his distaste for marriage, all in the span of one minute. I thought he used a non-flattering, clumsy line as a pickup line, which was endearing and original. But he also valued me for my work or pretended to, was available and wanted me to know it, and he wasn't interested in marriage.

In three days, I was leaving for London, Serbia, and Bosnia to talk to war survivors and learn first-hand about the history and lives of the heroines of my third novel. I was taking my younger son along as a gift for his high school graduation and beginning of college. Unlike what anybody rational might have thought, starting a romance on the cusp of a departure, appealed to me. Something relaxed and unassuming in his manner and way of carrying himself appealed to me.

An uncanny feeling of an ancestral familiarity appealed to me. I wasn't looking for anyone at that point in my life. I didn't want anyone in my life other than my children and my work, and I was sore in anticipation of my younger son's leaving home for college. I had embarked on a new creative journey and was consumed by the two heroines that were emerging from my dreams and taking shape every day out of the rubble of a war that had haunted me since it had started in the early nineties. I had no time and no breath for it then as I was barely surviving day to day in my sleep deprived agony of mega multitasking.

Now, with both children soon out of the house, I was looking for other jobs, and I was not looking for other men. But the bold swimmer approaching me on that brilliant June day as I was dripping wet, three days before another epic journey, caught my attention and made me reconsider all my previous promises to myself. Maybe this was something new, a place I had not been before, a shore that was beckoning to me and where I could drop down anchor. What if this was going to be my last shore!?

Maybe we refugees are supposed to do precisely that: shake up and reverse the order of things in the pre-established order of our adoptive countries. The man who appeared in my life from practically next door, at the swimming pool, has stood by me during my blue and black periods, and thanks to him, I had become a better swimmer and a more tolerant citizen of our town. Not to mention that I got to finally taste the mellow soothing happiness of a contented home life with a male partner.

Meeting him at the edge of the local pool on a June morning was the only thing that could not have happened if I had not moved there in the early nineties. I had already had my husbands, my children whether in or out of my womb, I would have written my books and most likely would have had a house or a condo apartment anywhere else on the North American continent; my lovers would have been from out of town or from out of the country, and my degrees all from Chicago.

I came to this small southern town with a full package and many of the major existential choices already made or in the making. Here I let them bake. In the infinitude and mysterious paths of our destinies, it finally made sense to have moved and lived in a southern version of *Our Town*, with all its messy stories, its samples of humanity of all kinds, its slowly growing communities of immigrants.

The town in the Appalachians gave me a different understanding of America, a different kind of struggle, a different kind of home, the environment for my sons' childhoods that they carry with them wherever life takes them like I carry my Carpathians and my Black Sea.

During the times of a global pandemic, it gave me the oasis of glorious nature, wide open spaces, and clean air when my favorite cities in the world went silent and turned off their blinding lights.

Most importantly, it gave me the beautiful mysterious swimmer for mysterious shores. For my forever shore. And that's another story for another suitcase.

CPSIA information can be obtained
at www.ICGtesting.com
Printed in the USA
BVHW042155220122
626944BV00011B/431